If They Don't Bring Their Women Here

The Asian American Experience

Series Editor
Roger Daniels, University of Cincinnati

A list of books in the series appears
at the end of this book.

If They Don't Bring Their Women Here

Chinese Female Immigration before Exclusion

George Anthony Peffer

Foreword by Roger Daniels

University of Illinois Press

Urbana and Chicago

Library of Congress Cataloging-in-Publication Data
Peffer, George Anthony.
If they don't bring their women here : Chinese female immigration
before exclusion / George Anthony Peffer ; foreword by Roger Daniels.
p.   cm. — (The Asian American experience)
Includes bibliographical references and index.
ISBN 0-252-02469-9
ISBN 0-252-06777-0 (pbk.)
1. Chinese American women—California—San Francisco—History—
19th century. 2. Chinese American women—Government policy—
California—San Francisco—History—19th century. 3. San Francisco
(Calif.)—Emigration and immigration—History—19th century.
4. Chinese American women—History—19th century. 5. Chinese
American women—Government policy—History—19th century.
6. United States—Emigration and immigration—History—19th century.
7. United States—Emigration and immigration—Government policy—
History—19th century. 8. China—Emigration and immigration—
History—19th century. 9. Women immigrants—History—19th century.
10. Chinese—Foreign countries—History—19th century. I. Title.
II. Series.
F869.S39C56   1999
305.48'8951073—DDC21   98-58013
CIP

Contents

Foreword

Roger Daniels

Until George Anthony Peffer published an important article about the Page Law of 1875 in the *Journal of American Ethnic History* in 1986, most historians who wrote about the anti-Chinese movement, myself included, paid little attention to it. In this we were following the pioneer historian of the anti-Chinese movement Elmer C. Sandmeyer, who made just two brief mentions of it in his monograph *The Anti-Chinese Movement in California* (1939). Peffer demonstrated clearly that the law, however ineffective, was an important step on the road to exclusion, which came seven years later. He expands on that work in this book and also sets himself the task of helping to restore pioneer Chinese American women to history, a task he has been pursuing since at least the beginning of the 1980s.

Peffer demonstrates that from early in the history of Chinese immigrants in California there was concern among the state's power elite, most of whom welcomed the needed labor of Chinese men, that these men would bring women with them and begin families whose American-born offspring would be, after the adoption of the Fourteenth Amendment in 1868, American citizens even though their parents remained "aliens ineligible to citizenship."

In addition, he shows that Chinese women played roles that were, to a greater degree than hitherto realized, "normal" for the wives of working immigrants in mid-nineteenth-century America. As late as 1980, Gunter Barth, a Harvard-trained historian on the faculty of the University of California at Berkeley, who had long maintained that Chinese Americans were not immigrants but sojourners, could still insist that Chinese were mere victims:

> In a world in which most people were strangers, the Chinese seemed the strangest, in appearance, speech and customs. Their age-old cultural heritage stressed loyalty to their families in distant China, so that, in order to earn money for the support of their extended families, many Chinese laborers were indentured to Chinese merchants who had pro-

vided their transportation across the Pacific. The resulting living and working conditions dispersed early exalted visions of citizens of the oldest and newest empires meeting in harmony in the American modern city as the expression of a new humanity. Crowded into a few city blocks by American hostility and Chinese clannishness, their teeming squalid quarters seemed to challenge American beliefs more than did other ghettos. Unable to fathom the exploitation that set Chinese against Chinese in the guise of benevolence, many Americans thought that a country dedicated to ending slavery should not allow the city to shelter men living voluntarily in bondage.[1]

Such was a prevalent view in 1980 as Peffer was beginning his graduate work. By now, as his account of the literature makes clear, such views have been cast on the rubbish heap. A number of scholars have demonstrated that some Chinese American men were, from the beginning of their American experience, not just victims but agents of their own destiny. A few works, of which Judy Yung's *Unbound Feet* (1995) is the most detailed, have even described the lives of Chinese American women. Peffer significantly adds to that literature by providing the first detailed account of Chinese American women's lives in the preexclusion era, primarily by teasing evidence out of largely impersonal government documents, documents created by government agents who were anxious that these women not become Americans. The faint voices that Peffer records are probably all that we will ever hear from the Chinese American women of that era. We must be grateful to him for making this possible.

Preface

The following chapters challenge an assumption long held by the interpreters of Chinese American history—that an analysis of cultural restraints is sufficient to explain why few women immigrated to the United States during the thirty years before passage of the country's first Chinese Exclusion Act in 1882, which comprehensively disqualified all members of China's laboring class. After an introductory presentation of the competing argument that American legislation, expressly designed to preserve gender imbalance, outweighed the importance of such restraints, this study's second chapter will compare Chinese female immigration to America with the patterns of their settlement in five other areas: Hawaii, Australia, and the Malay settlements of Singapore, Penang, and Malacca. Such a comparative study will demonstrate that the American pattern was not typical but rather indicated the influence of forces peculiar to its environment. Chapter 3 describes the central environmental factor in the American case: its legacy of gender-specific immigration restriction. Because the Page Law, a federal statute, excluded laboring women at a time when their husbands still could freely come and go, the chapter will focus on the political forces that created it. Recognizing that the 1875 law did not contain a clause prohibiting wives of workers from immigrating, chapters 4 and 5 explain how American officials did, in fact, pursue a course of action that prohibited the immigration of legally unrestricted women. Chapter 6 will assess the role that California's anti-Chinese press played in both shaping and reinforcing expanded applications of the Page Law's ban on the immigration of prostitutes. Chapter 7 examines the likely impact of anti-Chinese sentiment on the enumeration of San Francisco's Chinese population during the final two decades before exclusion. Finally, chapter 8 explores the ramifications of de facto female exclusion for Chinese American history and suggests some possible means of reclaiming at least part of the record of women's contributions to its evolution during the preexclusion era.

The effort to piece together this account has led to an array of sources. The comparative chapter relies upon the combination of census records and compilations of immigration law. The *Congressional Record,* along with official transcripts of treaty negotiations and law digests, also played a pivotal role. The recounting of American efforts to stop the emigration of women from Hong Kong depends on the dispatches of consular officials stationed there during the Page Law's lifespan. For my account of the ordeal awaiting female immigrants who braved the consular examinations, records of the U.S. Treasury Department, the federal courts in San Francisco, and articles from city newspapers have combined to present a rich supply of sources. The archives of selected papers as well as H. H. Bancroft's exhaustive collection of Chinese-related articles from newspapers across California have supplied the information for my critique of the treatment that female immigrants received from the press.

My examination of the role that anti-Chinese prejudice may have played in the compilation of the 1870 and 1880 San Francisco censuses has depended primarily on census schedules for Chinatown wards as well as from supplemental information contained in both governmental histories of the census and additional stories culled from local newspapers.

For each of these chapters, I also owe a great debt to the authors of numerous secondary sources whose work spans nearly the entire historiographic chronology of Chinese American studies.

Despite such rich sources, this study no doubt suffers from a limited ability to realize Takaki's inspired challenge of presenting the story through the "voices" of the women themselves.[1] Few Chinese laborers—female or male—wrote letters or kept diaries, and only scraps have survived from their scarce endeavors. Moreover, when confined to women living in the United States before exclusion, the supply of such firsthand accounts goes completely dry except for the transcripts of testimony from a series of 1882 habeas corpus trials that inspired my initial work on Chinese female immigration. On these pages, female immigrants and their families have attempted, before hostile audiences, to explain both their relationships to each other and their reasons for coming to the United States. Regrettably, however, federal judicial policy limited the number of witnesses whose words can still be read. Although minutes and motions from all the trials have survived, court archives only kept the complete transcripts from the first hearing of its kind. For the others, it is necessary to depend on occasional excerpts found in the minutes and in reporters' accounts published in San Francisco newspapers. Although I wish this story could be told primarily from the perspective of the women who lived it, the record does not permit such an approach.

Recognizing its shortcomings, this study seeks to accomplish three objectives. First, I intend to help correct Salyer's insightful complaint that "historians have not given adequate consideration to how [immigration] laws were actually enforced by the administrative agencies and the federal courts."[2] Second, I propose to create a more accurate division of Chinese American history before exclusion. Finally, I hope to establish clearer continuity between the stories of Chinese women who came to America after 1882 and those of their predecessors. Because government officials recklessly applied popular anti-Chinese stereotypes to exclude women whom the Page Law technically regarded as eligible, the record of its enforcement is much more critical than an analysis of its clauses. Consequently, the complexity of female immigration confounds efforts to analyze its history through the unrestricted period–exclusion period dichotomy first proposed by Mary Coolidge in 1909.[3]

As a result of her extensive work on gender-specific immigration restrictions, Sucheng Chan has proposed a more complex division for Chinese American history after exclusion but has presented a mixed interpretation of the period from 1849 to 1882. In her study of immigration restrictions targeting Chinese women, she followed Coolidge in designating the preexclusion era as "years of free immigration"[4] Paradoxically, in her comprehensive study of Asian Americans, published in the same year, she has both referred to the "three decades of unrestricted Chinese immigration" and alluded to 1890 as marking the fifteenth anniversary of female exclusion.[5] Perhaps the answer to this apparent ambiguity lies in her conclusion that the 1882 Exclusion Act, in contrast to the Page Law, restricted the immigration of women who were not prostitutes.[6] If such an interpretation does justice to her position, the 1875 legislation, when one focuses on enforcement rather than language, proved equally effective in excluding those who worked as prostitutes and those who did not.[7]

After accounting for the distorted implementation of gender-specific restrictions before 1882, the record of female immigration during this era should be divided in the following manner:

1852–68	The period of male sojourning
1869–74	The period of unrestricted family immigration
1875–82	The period of female exclusion
Post-1882	The period of general exclusion.[8]

Reflecting the absence of such a chronological revision, however, studies of Chinese women's history have tended to relegate the preexclusion period to a position of relative obscurity in the efforts to correct earlier, male-dominated narrations.

Yet a few works have made great strides in refocusing Chinese American history to include women. Tong, for example, has built upon Cheng's earlier work to more extensively examine the lives of prostitutes, and Chan has added new, gendered perspectives to the analysis of exclusion. Peggy Pascoe has described the interaction between female immigrants and the San Francisco missionary societies that attempted to rescue them from exploitation.[9] Still, Yung's *Unbound Feet* thus far represents the only attempt to produce a comprehensive social history of Chinese American women. For the postexclusion period, the book masterfully "fills the information void and restores Chinese women's rightful place in ethnic, women's, and American history, acknowledging their indomitable spirit and significant contributions."[10]

Although I cannot, to the same degree, amplify the voices of female immigrants who came before exclusion, experiences Yung has recounted reflect a continuation of, rather than a departure from, the earlier story. Therefore, my hope is to attach this work to the front end of Yung's work and in so doing help smooth the historical record of Chinese women in the United States.

Acknowledgments

When I entered San Francisco State University's history program as a graduate student in 1980, the Chinese American experience constituted a fairly small segment of my more broadly focused interest in cultural dynamics. Then I enrolled in "The Chinese in America," a course taught by George Woo. A major assignment was to tell the story of our families' immigration from China and settlement in the United States. Although that task offered both academic rewards and an opportunity to better connect the rest of the eighty or so students with their heritage, my ancestral background did not include China. So Woo allowed me to substitute a research paper on an undetermined Chinese American theme.

Struggling to find my topic, I stumbled upon newspaper accounts of an 1882 habeas corpus trial in which a group of Chinese women were seeking to overturn a deportation order identifying them as prostitutes. Port authorities in San Francisco had detained them under the authority of a federal statute that neither my professor nor my textbook had mentioned: the Page Law of 1875. As I followed the trial's progress to its completion, prosecutors presented no substantive evidence of their accusations. Yet both the presiding judge and the local press seemed convinced that all of these women had immigrated in violation of the law. Fortunately, the judge did not allow his obvious prejudice to alter evidenciary requirements but still chose to announce the release order with a preamble predicting that the "lewd" women standing before him would be plying their immoral trade in San Francisco's Chinatown before the end of that same day.

Saturated with mystery and pathos, the trial so captivated my attention that the task of telling its story ultimately evolved into a comprehensive study of Chinese female immigration before exclusion, first in the form of a master's thesis at San Francisco State University, later as a doctoral dissertation at Carnegie Mellon University, and finally as this volume. Through my struggle to complete such an extended project I have tallied a substantial debt of gratitude to those who have assisted me along the way.

From the beginning, hours of research were made more fruitful through the kind assistance of personnel at the San Francisco Public Library, as well as the libraries of San Francisco State University, the University of Pittsburgh, Carnegie Mellon University, the University of Wisconsin, and the U.S. District Court for the Northern District of California. Employees at the University of California's Bancroft Library and both the National Archives and its branch office in San Bruno, California, willingly searched for obscure and often uncataloged records. The San Francisco, California, and Wisconsin historical societies graciously opened their holdings for my inspection. Martha Perry of Bellarmine College and Chuck Romaine of Lakeland College provided valuable assistance with numerous interlibrary loan requests, and Lakeland's talented library staff offered both willing assistance and consistent encouragement. Without the help of these gracious people, many important documents would doubtless have escaped my notice.

A number of colleagues also deserve recognition. In addition to assigning the research paper that launched my journey, George Woo served effectively as a reader of the subsequent master's thesis. At Carnegie Mellon University, John Modell, Donald Sutton, and Joe Trotter endured many readings and offered valuable suggestions as members of my dissertation committee. Tammy Proctor of Wittenberg University added her considerable insight to both the revision process and development of the book's title. Before assuming her current position at the University of Minnesota, Erika Lee showed great kindness in retrieving documents housed at the Bancroft Library while at the same time preparing for her wedding and completing her doctoral dissertation. The University of Nevada's Sue Fawn Chung provided a thoughtful review of the draft manuscript and a heartening appraisal of its importance, and Judy Yung of the University of California at Santa Cruz offered wise advice and welcome friendship.

As I was struggling to comprehend the significance of the trial that sparked this project, San Francisco State University's Moses Rischin encouraged me to pursue a story that traditional studies had labeled as nonexistent. After serving as the chair of my thesis committee, he played a major role in securing the fellowship that enabled me to pursue doctoral studies. In the years since completion of my degree, his assistance has continued beyond academic endeavors to include professional—and sometimes fatherly—direction. A proper expression of gratitude for his contributions to both my career and life exceeds my vocabulary.

The final stage of this project owes much to the editorial staff at the University of Illinois Press. First, Veronica Scrol attended the Association for Asian American Studies panel at which I presented a draft of chapter 7 and initiated the contractual process. Roger Daniels, editor of The Asian American Experience series, helped me transform my rough prose and incomplete arguments into a more polished document. Karen Hewitt, executive editor, and Madeleine Marchaterre steered the book to completion with patience and perceptive suggestions. Mary Giles prepared the copyedited manuscript with meticulous attention, and members of the production and marketing team have ensured that the finished product lives up to its full potential. Given the aid of such advisors, whatever shortcomings from which the book still suffers are mine alone.

Finally, highest recognition belongs to my wife, Myra, and daughter, Charity. For more than two decades they have patiently and lovingly supported me through years of uprooting, schooling, and research. Their encouragement has permitted me to overcome frustration and resist the urge to quit. The pride now evident on their faces more than rewards my efforts.

If They Don't Bring Their Women Here

1

Invisible Women and Untold Stories

[My father and mother live in San Francisco], in a store. [My father's name is] Tin Yung. [He has been here] about five years. [My mother] came with my father. When I lived with my grandfather [in China], my father sent letter to me and called me to go back to California; that he was in a store. My grandfather had a ticket for [me]. [He paid] $35. [I came to California on the steamer *Anjer Head*], in the care of Ah Yeun.
—Loy How, age fourteen, March 1882

[I was married] in Canton three years ago. [My husband's name is] Ah Po. I came with him. [Loy How's] grandfather knows [my] husband, and when I go on the ship he told me, "You take care of her, go together." [My husband stayed] in the ship in between decks. Of course I see lots of females there—I live with the woman's part. [My husband is] also twenty-two years. [He is a] laborer, working. Sometimes [he] work on sailing steamer, or on ship, sometimes work in store. I came here try to earn some money sewing clothing. I don't know [who paid my passage money], my father-in-law or my husband. I don't know about that business. [My passage was] somewhere about $35.
—Wang Ah Yeun, age twenty-two, March 1882

[I am from] Hong Kong. [I have never been in California before.] [I was married in] Canton City two years ago. [I boarded] the steamer *Anjer Head* with my wife at Hong Kong Port. [The fare cost each of us] $35, [and I paid the fare]. [We occupied] separate [berths]. I never with my wife [on board the steamer]. I talked with my wife very seldom. Sometimes I have leisure. I talk to her. When she feels good I talk to her. I have been China, work on ship. I came here with intention to work, or go fishing, or anything else. I took my wife, come here. I try to go to business and wherever I go—If I go fish my wife go fish—Monterey or Santa Cruz. Lots of Chinamen down there fishing.
—Ah Po, age twenty-two, March 1882

[In China I worked] on a sewing machine on clothing. The grandfather of [Loy How] told [me] to bring her over to her mother. [Her mother and father live here in California.] Her grandfather gave [me] the passage and took her on the boat and told [me] to take care of [her]. Her grandfather had the ticket all ready and

took her down to the boat and told [me] how to take care of her. I know him over ten years. [I] got on board the steamer at Hong Kong and was examined by the American Consul there. [My] uncle took [me] to the consul.
—Wah Ah Chin, age unknown, March 1882

[I have been] altogether twenty years in California. [I was married] in China. [My husband] keeps store, Tung Ti and Company, on Sacramento Street—Chinese call Tung Ung Gee. [My husband's name is] Tin Yung. [We have] two boys and a girl. My daughter is fourteen years of age. [She was born] in China. I sent for her, and my grandfather sent to me. He is over seventy years of age. Seventeen years [ago] I was married. [I live] on Washington Street, right over here near the Plaza—near to Washington Street—one store from Washington Street. [I do] sewing. [A] tailor bring in pants and I sew it. I have been here twenty years in California altogether, but I have been home several years and then come back again. I got back in California five years now. My grandfather sent letter to me and I give it to my husband. My husband read to me, if there was any friends with them [our daughter] will come. Somebody in care with her—some friends she has come with her because she couldn't come alone.
—Ah Tchut, age thirty-nine, March 1882

[I was] married in China, somewhere over ten years [ago]. [My wife and I have] two girls, one boy, that make three. One [of the girls] is five years another ten. The boy is left home in China. [He is] twelve. [I came to California] twenty years ago, [and have been working in the] fishing business. I have been China once ten years ago. [I stayed in China] five years [then returned to San Francisco] five years ago. [The first time I came to California, my wife lived with me.] [My] wife came out here do sewing clothing—[and I am] going to work fishing, or something else. [My wife came back to California] to find [me]. [We live at] 924 Dupont Street. At present time, [I am in the] fishing business. [I fish] across the bay [and have been] about two or three years interested in it, [and before that I kept] kind of a small shop or store, sell small articles. [I never sent my wife money to come back here.] Probably she has money from her relatives, or relations, or friends. [I didn't know she was coming before the steamer arrived.] I went down steamer. I see her—she has arrived.
—Ah Sui (aka Tin Yung), age forty-six, March 1882

[I married] Wong Cum Chow in China about two years ago. [Before our marriage, my husband] had been a resident of California for about seven years. [He then] came back to California about the middle of June 1881. It was understood when he left China that [I] was to follow him as soon as the necessary and proper arrangements could be made. [I arrived] as a passenger on board the *Anjer Head* in company with Sin Far [and her husband], Ah Fook, who are relatives of [my husband].
—Chin Ah Fong, age nineteen, March 1882

[My husband], Ah Fook, [and I married] in China about one year ago. [We] were passengers [with] Chin Ah Fong on the steamship *Anjer Head* from Hong Kong to San Francisco. [We] arrived on the fifteenth day of March 1882.
—Sin Far, age seventeen, March 1882.

[I am] a married woman, and [my] husband Wong Tuck resides in San Francisco. [He has] resided there for [the past] five years and is a laborer by occupation. [I] made the journey from Hong Kong to San Francisco for the purpose of joining and living with him. . . .
—Chou See Ti You, age twenty-eight, May 1882

[I am] a niece of Chou See Ti You and accompanied her on [this] voyage. . . .
—Choy Chook, age nine, May 1882

[I am] a married woman, [and my] husband Quen Ti Pon resides in San Francisco. [He] is a trader by occupation and [I] came to San Francisco to join and live with [my] husband. . . .
—Chung See Ling Quy, age thirty-eight, May 1882

[I am] the daughter of Chung See Ling Quy and accompanied [my] mother on [this] journey to join [my] father.
—Chy Ping, age twelve, May 1882

[I am] married and [my] husband, Lee Sow, resides in San Francisco. [I made this] journey to join and live with him. . . .
—Wong See Ah Yook, age twenty-six, May 1882

[I am] the servant of Wong See Ah Yook. [I] accompanied her . . . on [this] journey.
—Sing Muy, age eleven, May 1882

They came for the same reasons that motivated immigrants from all parts of the world to transplant families in the United States: to celebrate prosperity, to create an economic team, and to end the loneliness of long separation. Indeed, perhaps the most striking characteristic of these personal accounts is their normalcy. Yet beyond the year in which they were recorded, each person shared the experience of enduring a habeas corpus trial before being allowed to enter the country. I have pieced their stories together from affidavits and testimony collected in two separate judicial proceedings in which the female petitioners were seeking to overturn deportation orders that accused them of prostitution. Legislation enacted by Congress in 1875 had prohibited the immigration of women for such purposes, and port officials in San Francisco had detained them onboard ship in an attempt to enforce this prohibition.

Refusing to accept their fate, the detainees' families—aided by local Chinese leaders—engaged the services of prominent attorneys who petitioned the courts for redress. The resulting judicial battles proved difficult ones to win. Despite the common sensibility of their stories, female immigrants faced judges who blatantly favored the prosecution. Although the government's cases, which depended solely upon stereotypical stories of Chinatown prostitutes, eventually collapsed under the burden of proof, the orders granting their freedom were announced with reluctance, lamenting the lack of evidence.

Such terrifying ordeals normally arouse the interest of historians looking for a good story. When I first discovered the records of these trials in 1981, however, none of the contemporary secondary sources included even the briefest discussion of the Page Law—the 1875 legislation that had authorized port surveyors to act on their unsubstantiated suspicions. Accounts of Chinatown's prostitution industry had so completely dominated the primary sources that the historiography of the early 1980s had rendered other classes of female immigrants invisible. Thus, both discovery and mystery captured my fascination, and I spent most of my master's program, as well as my doctoral studies at Carnegie Mellon University, attempting to understand the significance of this new-found history.

In addition to a graduate thesis and doctoral dissertation, my efforts produced two articles in the *Journal of American Ethnic History,* one published in 1986 and the other in 1992.[1] These monographs attempted to establish a place for women who were not prostitutes within the historiographic framework of Chinese American studies. Scholars such as Ronald Takaki, Sucheng Chan, Benson Tong, and Judy Yung have both expanded upon and challenged the results of my work in a way that has greatly increased our knowledge of gender differences in the history of Chinese Americans.[2] None of these studies, however, including my own, has adequately explained the dynamics of female immigration before passage of the first Exclusion Act in 1882.

As with many other immigrant groups in America, unattached males composed more than 90 percent of the initial current of Chinese arrivals. Attracted to the country by news of the forty-niner gold rush, workers from China joined in the hunt for quick riches (and a quick repatriation) in the California goldfields. Yet long after other gold-seekers had resigned themselves to failure and embraced the process of planting families in the rich California soil, the number of Chinese women who came to the United States remained so small that the nation's Chinatowns did not achieve an approximate balance of the sexes until the middle of the twentieth century.

Beginning with the publication of Mary Coolidge's pathbreaking study in 1909, scholars have made a significant contribution to the task of explaining this repressed community development through their explorations of what have become two well-documented forces: the joint-family structure and the sojourner men-tality.[3] The former analysis noted that parents dominated the Chinese concept of family, requiring married sons to "bring their wives home to the family" and con-sidering husband-wife responsibilities secondary to those of child to parent and younger to elder.[4] Therefore, a married woman's first obligation was to her par-ents-in-law, in whose home she assumed specific, prescribed responsibilities un-der the direction of her husband's mother.[5] To abandon these obligations in fa-vor of emigration would have brought disgrace upon both daughter-in-law and son. The latter analysis pointed out that because sons regarded themselves as so-journers—as pursuing a temporary journey from home for the purpose of mak-ing money—they may well have regarded a decision to travel without dependents as more in keeping with the objective of achieving economic success and return-ing home. This commitment to temporary emigration complimented family re-straints in a manner that effectively persuaded most wives to remain in their hus-bands' villages.

The joint family and sojourner mentality do explain why fewer females than males entered the Chinese American community in the years before exclusion, but they fail to account for the magnitude and duration of this gender disparity. Both Takaki and Sandy Lydon have noted that a number of European groups initially immigrated as sojourners but after perhaps ten to twenty years began shifting their focus to permanent settlement.[6] Thus, among the Chinese, one would expect the strength of family structure and the sojourner mentality to have varied between individuals and to have eroded over time. Moreover, sociological studies of Chi-nese villages have suggested that families did not place entirely inflexible restric-tions upon daughters-in-law but adjusted their control to accommodate changes in the local economy. In order to increase their income in times of economic hard-ship, for example, laboring families could expand the legitimate domain of women, allowing both husband and wife to freely leave the home of his parents in the at-tempt to earn a living.[7]

Families with multiple sons could adopt such a revision of the sojourner men-tality without compromising those cultural principles that called for married women to remain in the homes of their parents-in-law. Olga Lang has demon-strated this possibility by explaining that instead of sojourning daughters-in-law, it was the prospect of abandoned parents that Chinese families refused to allow.[8] Maurice Freedman has shed further light on this clarification of family obligations by noting that the inability of poor families to provide land for multiple claims of inheritance often forced younger brothers to postpone or even forego marriage.[9] The families of emigrant sons, however, usually felt compelled to reject such an option and arranged marriages before a sojourner's departure in order to cement his ties to the village.

Because scholars generally agree that the growth of a landless, or nearly land-less, peasantry contributed significantly to the great waves of Chinese emigration during the final half-century of Ch'ing rule, the policy of marrying off prospective emigrants must have produced an overabundance of wives in their parents' households.[10] Finding themselves with more daughters-in-law than their resources advised—with each one attempting to guard her husband's interests—the likelihood of an economically disastrous call for division of fraternal inheritances threatened the parents of emigrant males.[11] By allowing, or perhaps encouraging, the emigration of such unneeded women they could have reduced this danger. Significantly, Yung has noted that among those wives who did come to the United States before exclusion, most were married to laborers from economically oppressed villages in southern China.[12] Thus, the years before 1882 contained sufficient incentives for a number of Chinese families to have tolerated female emigration rather than prohibit it, suggesting that family restraints and sojourner mentality alone fall short of explaining thirty years of profound gender imbalance during the preexclusion era.

When seeking to examine the lives of those women who did come to the United States before exclusion, yet another unsolved mystery presents itself: the remarkable decline in the number of prostitutes in the Chinese female population of San Francisco from 1870 to 1880. Before 1882 the city served as the undisputed center of Chinese American society and as home to most female immigrants. Both censuses recorded nearly identical female populations, but the 1880 enumeration showed nearly 75 percent fewer prostitutes than its predecessor had reported.[13] Previous investigations of San Francisco's prostitution industry have depicted these plummeting numbers as merely signaling its decline and identified 1870 as the peak year.[14]

Although they are generally accurate, the record suggests a more complex answer than these analyses convey. Lucie Cheng Hirata has estimated that the average Chinese American prostitute served about seven clients per day and worked an average of six days each week.[15] The federal government's summary census reports list the total Chinese population of San Francisco at 12,022 in 1870 and 21,745 in 1880.[16] Although Hirata's estimate does not account for the likely prospect of repeat customers and is, therefore, somewhat suspect, thus far no one has offered a more reliable measurement. A combination of her approximation and my own previously cited calculations of the female population suggests that the number of Chinese prostitutes recorded by census enumerators in 1870 could have accommodated more than sixty thousand men every week.

Although a large number of transients did move through the city in a virtually constant stream and non-Chinese males also patronized Chinese houses of prostitution, only about ten thousand resident Chinese males lived in San Francisco when the census was taken. Considering the competition provided by nearly five hundred non-Chinese prostitutes, it is doubtful that even all three male constituencies (along with those who paid multiple visits) could have supplied enough customers to prevent Chinatown's commercial sex industry from suffering a serious oversupply. Indeed, even in the less robust environment of 1880, the 408 Chinese prostitutes discovered in my own survey of the census schedules could still have served a maximum clientele of more than seventeen thousand men per week while competing with approximately 265 non-Chinese counterparts—numbers that indicate that Chinese prostitution remained a profitable enterprise despite the apparent decline of its workforce.

Hirata and Yung have agreed that a prostitute regularly serving her full complement of clients could generate five times more annual revenue than could a male laborer.[17] Yet Hirata has also pointed out that the expense incurred through smuggling a single prostitute into the United might have been as high as $2,500, suggesting that the importation of more women than the market could fully exploit might have seriously jeopardized the profitability of such a capital-intensive enterprise.[18] Thus, if one assumes that those who controlled Chinatown's commercial sex industry were competent businessmen, the 1870 numbers engender skepticism about their reliability.

Mary Coolidge identified the likelihood of exaggerated prostitute numbers nearly a century ago: "with the general tendency to enhance anything adverse to the Chinese, it would be inevitable that the number of lewd women would be greatly exaggerated and the number of wives underestimated."[19] Cheng, on the other hand, argued that the desire of Chinese prostitutes to conceal their true occupations would have counterbalanced the enumerators' preconceptions, the result being that "they tend to neutralize each other."[20] Although that assertion might seem plausible, the census schedules bear no evidence of hidden prostitutes.[21] Consequently, a definitive explanation for the astounding disparity in recorded prostitute populations for the final two censuses before exclusion cannot be derived solely from economic and political fluctuations in San Francisco.

In light of the apparent failure of previous studies to develop a truly comprehensive explanation for either unusually extensive shortages of female immigrants or unlikely fluctuations in the number of prostitutes, I would contend that the reasons for these phenomena are linked. When large numbers of Chinese males began arriving in 1852 they quickly became a source of irritation for many Americans, especially white workingmen. Because of their reputation for accepting more oppressive working conditions and far lower wages than white workers, labor leaders on the Pacific Coast branded Chinese immigrants as the central reasons for white unemployment and called for their expulsion from the country. That angry rhetoric, in turn, sparked a movement in Congress that culminated in the Exclusion Act of 1882.

Although its unprecedented scope has brought justified scholarly attention to the Exclusion Act, a long history of restriction efforts on both the national and state levels predated the law. At the federal level, restriction of Chinese immigration to America began as early as the Burlingame Treaty of 1868, which prohibited contract laborers, criminals, and those likely to become wards of the state from coming to the United States but failed to establish a procedure for enforcing such restrictions.[22] Without the benefit of federal enforcement guidelines, local and state governments in the West enacted restrictive legislation of their own, such as California's 1874 law prohibiting the immigration of "coolies" and prostitutes from China.[23] Because they violated the provisions of the Burlingame Treaty, however, the Supreme Court declared these laws unconstitutional shortly after their enactment.[24]

Failure to develop a legal means of restricting Chinese immigration on the state and local level then led to the passage of America's first "solution" to the problem of Chinese immigration: the Page Law. Enacted in 1875 under the sponsorship of California Congressman Horace F. Page, this law contained many flaws, most notably its failure to establish a system for the restriction of Chinese laborers.[25] While recognition of such flaws ultimately produced the Exclusion Act in 1882, which went into effect in the latter half of the year, the Page Law served as America's central anti-Chinese legislation for seven years. During this tenure, the law did little to halt the immigration of men but focused its most severe articles on female immigrants. As reflected by the detention of those whose stories introduced this chapter, the act authorized American officials to prohibit the immigration of Chinese women whom they suspected of coming for "immoral" or other "lewd" purposes, establishing a penalty for this kind of illegal immigration that more than doubled the severity of its anti-coolie section.[26] Thus, before exclusion, the most effective legal barrier directed at Chinese immigrants focused on preventing women from coming to the United States.

Although entrusted with targeting prostitutes, the enforcers of this legislation expanded its scope—perhaps intentionally—to encompass those who were not prostitutes but whose true identities had been obscured by anti-Chinese prejudice. Lucie Cheng and Edna Bonacich have suggested a possible motive for the likelihood of such de facto expansion of the law in their general discussion of capitalist motives for restricting female immigration: "Immigration law can select for ablebodied young men while excluding all dependent populations, such as women, children, the elderly, the sick, and paupers. When they are not permitted to bring families, they can be housed in bunkhouses, compounds, or other substandard housing, while educational facilities need not be supplied, and so on."[27] America's nineteenth-century social mores would not have recognized the distinction between working wives and dependent female immigrants. Therefore, although white workingmen called for the exclusion of male laborers, those who exploited Chinese labor must have worried when female immigration increased substantially during the late 1860s.[28]

The addition of unemployed women and children would have forced male immigrants to press for higher wages, upsetting their employers' payroll structures. That perceived threat to profits encouraged American capitalists on the Pacific Coast, who vigorously opposed exclusion, to support the enactment of the Page Law. Long-established assessments of Chinese character added the endorsements of moral crusaders. Even though Congress would not enact a general exclusion bill until 1882, this coalition of exclusionists, capitalists, and moralists refused to recognize the existence of women who were not prostitutes and expected the Page Law to eliminate female immigration.

Charged with the task of implementing the new antiprostitution legislation, immigration officials relied on images of Chinese moral decadence identical to those which had secured the bill's passage, thereby converting it into what amounted to a female exclusion law. Indeed, the 1882 legislation did not completely replace its gender-specific counterpart. Chan, for example, has noted that the Page Law was still being used as a means of deporting immigrants throughout the 1880s.[29] In her discussion of the Exclusion Act's 1907 version, Vincente Tang has also described a process of harassment based squarely on the 1875 law: "Since immigration officers could rule on claims of United States citizenship, women coming as wives of United States citizens could be labeled prostitutes, denied entry and their citizenship ignored. Wives or daughters who had already entered or who had never set foot outside the United States were equally threatened and liable for arrest and deportation. This method was by far the most popularly used method to deny entry to women and deport those already legally admitted."[30] As further testimony to their longevity, Tang has observed that government officials were still using such stereotypes in the 1920s as a basis for intimidating Chinese women.[31]

Clearly, government officials who enforced anti-Chinese legislation both before and after exclusion demonstrated a consistent unwillingness, or inability, to recognize women who were not prostitutes among all but wealthy applicants for immigration. Such prejudice forced all the wives and daughters of laborers to join prostitutes in running and enduring a formidable gauntlet of interrogations and investigations designed to discourage women from attempting a journey to the United States. Beginning with consular officials in Hong Kong and continuing through an array of customs officers, law-enforcement agents, and (for those determined enough to resist formally) judges, the Page Law made female immigration a uniquely difficult and uncertain enterprise during the final seven years before general exclusion.

For those who survived the ordeal and became part of the Chinese American community, census enumerators, operating in a political and social environment that sensationalized Chinese prostitution often appear to have also ignored the existence of women who were not prostitutes. The apparent objectivity of their reports has, in turn, further obscured the presence of all but the prostitutes and reinforced stereotypical images of the Chinese women who immigrated to the United States before 1882. Thus, the mysteries surrounding Chinese female immigration share a common thread of "invisibility." At every step, governmental officials applied predetermined labels in identifying female immigrants and exhibited no genuine interest in ascertaining the true reasons for their residence in urban Chinatowns.

Since the late 1980s, when I first complained about the limitations of cultural impediments and the suspect nature of prostitute numbers, some notable exceptions to earlier patterns of overreliance on them have been produced. For example, Chan has argued that "from the 1870s onward, efforts by various levels of American government" played a more important role in limiting female immigration than either the sojourner mentality or joint-family influence.[32] In his discussion of Chinese struggles against exclusion, however, Charles McClain has still mistakenly characterized the 1882 law as "the first federal immigration statute to single out an ethnic group for invidious treatment."[33] Moreover, even in newer works that recognize the importance of U.S. efforts to impose legal restrictions on female immigration, none have explored the day-to-day enforcement of such legislation. Yet that history holds the key to understanding what June Mei has called the "pull factors" of Chinese immigration.[34]

I do not contend that gender-specific exclusion should supplant cultural restraints in the analyses of the social dynamics of Chinese female immigration before 1882. Family obligations and sojourner objectives clearly did impede female immigration, and prostitutes composed a large percentage of the women who came to America during this period. Yet one cannot hope to bring clarity to the role women played in the preexclusion story without accounting for the impact of the host society's reaction to their coming. Economic conditions in China no doubt encouraged the emigration of nuclear families at a higher level than previously believed, but governmental interference on the part of the United States appears to have provided the necessary counterbalance to this stimulus. Such an assertion does not imply that, without such external opposition, the Chinese American community would have reached gender parity before passage of the Exclusion Act. Instead, I would argue that it exacerbated the results of cultural restrictions by creating an effective barrier against female immigration.

Had one or two thousand more women been living in the United States at the time of exclusion's enactment, males would still have composed an overwhelming majority of the Chinese American population. Yet the presence of these women would have significantly changed the character of postexclusion society. Likewise, probable exaggeration in the censuses does not significantly change the story of prostitution in nineteenth-century Chinatowns. Even if census enumerators did allow their prejudices to inflate the number of prostitutes they recorded, the extensiveness of this industry is beyond question. Thus, whether the correct number of prostitutes in 1870 should be 1,585, as Tong has suggested, or even somewhat lower than a thousand—an approximation for which I would argue—this industry would still have employed at least 50 percent of San Francisco's Chinese female population.[35] If, however, enumerators failed to acknowledge perhaps four or five hundred wives, a correction of that oversight would elevate the role of nuclear families in building San Francisco's Chinese American community from the position of historical oddity to that of significant minority.

If one studies only the stereotypical women—prostitutes and the wives or concubines of merchant middlemen—the explanation for their chronically small numbers seems self-evident. Because they served a finite clientele, the need to preserve their economic efficiency would have limited the immigration of prostitutes. Saturating the market with constant new arrivals would have driven down prices and undercut the prostitution industry's profits. Men who occupied positions of material security, however, did not need their wives to produce revenue. Although some purchased concubines to accommodate their sexual appetites, they could support dependents more easily in China, where the cost of living was cheaper. They also possessed the capital required to make frequent return visits feasible. Indeed, Yung has argued that merchants were the only male immigrants who could have afforded to support wives in both China and the United States.[36]

In contrast to the merchants, economic incentives may have persuaded Chinese workingmen to bring their wives and daughters to the United States. Chan has rightly observed that the needs of unproductive dependents could have been met more cheaply in China, but female laborers could have aided both husbands and the joint family by pursuing economic opportunities abroad.[37] Thus, within the few hundred working families that lived in nineteenth-century San Francisco, Yung has recognized immigrant wives as "essential helpmates in the family's daily struggle for socioeconomic survival."[38] Because cultural restraints likely would not have prevented many of these women from coming, and male workers could not have afforded concubines or second wives, their failure to do so before 1882 leads one to question whether the American story mirrors or contradicts those of female immigration to Chinese communities in other parts of the world.

2

A Comparison of
Chinese Immigrant Communities

With its massive population and dependence upon a largely agricultural economy, the constant political upheavals and economic disasters that followed China's defeat in the Opium War swelled the number of emigrants leaving the shores of the empire to an unprecedented magnitude. Throughout the second half of the nineteenth century, displaced Chinese peasants traveled by the thousands to new settlements in Southeast Asia, Australia, the islands of the South Pacific, and the Pacific coasts of North and South America. Each emigrant made the journey to these settlements in search of economic gain and usually with the hope of making an impressive return to the ancestral village. Given the temporary nature of their emigration, the joint-family ideal appears to have encouraged wives to remain in the ancestral villages of their husbands. With the exception of Australia and the United States, however, the number of Chinese female immigrants in each area of settlement had increased significantly within twenty years.

Many Chinese men immigrated as contract laborers, bound to a term of employment in exchange for their passage to new settlements, whereas Chinese women often came under similar contracts as prostitutes.[1] The nature of their labor contracts forced most of these immigrants to work for low wages under miserable conditions, leading thousands to make the return trip to China at their earliest opportunity. Wives certainly would have preferred communities possessing large numbers of independent immigrants to such oppressive and unstable environments. Still, both male laborers and prostitutes sometimes emigrated from the same village under a group contract. Although such groups suffered the same hardships as those bound to individual labor contracts, the support of family, clan, and village ties may have encouraged both men and women to remain outside China at the end of their group's term of service. Wives also might have immigrated to settlements in which a majority of Chinese came under the contract system—perhaps as contract laborers themselves—when other conditions stimulated their coming.

The distance that separated a new community from the home villages of its residents along with the community's population also may have affected female immigration. Although women could travel more cheaply to and from closer communities, larger settlements could better insulate them from anti-Chinese hostility. Therefore, one would expect destinations requiring a relatively short trip to a well-populated area such as Singapore to have attracted more immigrant wives than the small and distant Chinatowns of Australia. Yet although San Francisco's Chinese community was far away, its population had reached more than twenty thousand by 1880.[2] Because steamship companies kept the fares for passage from China to California low, this large Chinatown should have attracted a significant number of wives despite its distance from home.[3]

Chinese emigrants were also drawn to areas that afforded excellent economic opportunities. Because the initial emigration of wives created both emotional and financial stress, male laborers no doubt hesitated to attempt joint sojourns in places where they could secure only temporary employment. If both husband and wife could find jobs that promised to last for several years, however, the potential advantages justified the trauma and expense of her immigration. In America, events such as California's depression in 1876 and 1877 escalated white unemployment and intensified the anti-Chinese movement, but lineage ties and Chinese workers' reputation as an especially cheap labor force enabled continued employment despite the economy.[4]

While such ties helped keep the Chinese in what Lucie Cheng and Edna Bonacich have characterized as a "superexploited position," the same ties would also have held middlemen responsible for the employment of female immigrants whose husbands belonged to their district or clan associations.[5] Thus, wives could have found jobs in San Francisco, whether in the laundry, cigar-wrapping, shoemaking, sewing, or other trades in which Chinese entrepreneurs engaged. These opportunities offered long hours at low pay, but their reliability made the trip's economic potential much less speculative.

Economic crises within China would have fostered female emigration by reducing the strength of joint-family restrictions. Thus, the displacements caused by events such as the Hakka-Punti War, which by its end in 1868 had devastated Kwangtung, likely would have increased the number of emigrant wives.[6] Indeed, given the intensifying poverty that Chinese families suffered throughout the latter half of the nineteenth century and the abundant opportunities available to laboring men and women in the United States, America's Chinatowns should have represented the most attractive of all distant destinations for female immigrants before exclusion.

Although one must not discount the importance of cultural traditions restricting women, such traditions exerted less influence over the families from which most prospective emigrants came. Maurice Freedman and Francis Hsu have observed that poorer husbands and wives within Chinese village society tended to establish stronger, more intimate unions than did their more economically advantaged counterparts.[7] Although noting that immigrants from Kwangtung—who composed the majority of America's Chinese community throughout the nineteenth century—possessed a greater commitment to the lineage-based family system than did the residents of other provinces in China, Olga Lang has further clarified this class distinction: "The myth that the joint family of several generations and branches is the 'normal' has arisen because conditions in the upper class have been taken as representative of the population as a whole."[8]

Even though most immigrant laborers came from Kwangtung, their likelihood of transplanting nuclear families to America would have been much greater than Chinese cultural ideals implied. Consequently, Gunther Barth long ago suggested that after a generation of Chinese settlement in the United States, the American-style family had begun to serve as a new model for immigrants.[9] More recently—and with the support of more empirical evidence—Yung has concluded that "unlike in China, where three generations often lived under the same roof, the typical family structure in San Francisco Chinatown was nuclear, including a married couple, the husband about nine years older than the wife, and one or two children."[10] Therefore, wherever external conditions proved favorable, as they did in the United States, female immigration should have been relatively substantial.

Yet the degree of social hostility that Chinese immigrants experienced could still have exerted a great deal of influence on whether they established nuclear families. If a host society did not limit job opportunities and protected them from abuse, men—and women—no doubt immigrated in greater numbers. Conversely, if, while coping with being confined to the most menial and dangerous jobs, male immigrants found their lives or livelihoods threatened by hostile natives, they undoubtedly would have been reluctant to bring wives into such an environment. Still, women continued to join their husbands in Hawaii, although they often found their reception less than hospitable, as long as economic opportunities remained favorable.[11] Their resiliency under such pressure points to a final restrictive factor that I regard as the most effective deterrent to Chinese female immigration: the erection of legal barriers such as the Page Law.

Formalization of social hostility through anti-Chinese laws would have seriously undermined the confidence of male immigrants in their ability to either earn a living or keep wives safe from harm. Chinese men may have trusted large Chinatowns to insulate wives from extralegal belligerence, but government-sponsored repression threatened to unravel that blanket of safety. Moreover, when legislation specifically restricted female immigration, as was the case with the Page Law, the incentives that normally attracted Chinese wives would have been substantially diminished. The prospects of economic gain and reunion with husbands may have convinced the women to brave hostility, but few would have made the journey knowing that they could be turned away as illegal immigrants.

The remainder of this study will focus on the governmental variable, but all the factors discussed in this chapter merit in-depth exploration. The absence of statistical data renders a comprehensive analysis impossible, however. For example, records relating to contract labor/independent labor and individual immigration/ group immigration do not exist in English and may be unobtainable, even in Chinese. A partial report from British colonial officials in the Southeast Asian settlement of Penang, identifying the number of contract laborers among Chinese arrivals from 1881 to 1915, represents the only known governmental attempt to divide the Chinese according to a specific method of immigration.[12] The report, indicating that more than 50 percent of Penang's Chinese arrivals had bound themselves to labor contracts, cannot be measured against reports of Chinese settlement in other areas.[13] Furthermore, not even the Penang record identifies the method of immigration used by more than 112,000 Chinese females who arrived there between 1881 and 1915.

The few records that do exist permit a brief sketch of immigrant characteristics during the preexclusion period. First, the majority of Chinese sojourners in all parts of the world used labor contracts to finance their journeys, and many immigrated in village or clan groups.[14] Although the extent of labor contracts and group immigration likely influenced the number of females traveling to new communities, the actual weight of these factors can only be imagined. Yet the variables of distance from home, size of community, social hostility, and legal barriers do permit comparative analysis. Records related to each factor, and covering the entire half-century from 1861 to 1911, exist for the following six areas in which Chinese immigrants settled: Singapore, Penang, Malacca, Hawaii, Australia, and the United States.[15] Immigration statistics for three of these communities—Singapore, the United States, and Penang—have also been tabulated.

Unattached men dominated the initial Chinese population for each of these destinations, and in every instance the female-to-male ratio remained unbalanced between 1861 and 1911. The degree of disparity varied substantially among communities, however, indicating that sojourners remained more central to the fabric of some settlements than to others. Chinese immigration followed three distinct patterns. First, the Chinese in Singapore, Penang, and Hawaii experienced a steadily but slowly eroding dominance of sojourners and a corresponding growth in the prevalence of nuclear families. Second, the role of gender in Malacca's Chinese immigration fluctuated, leaving the proportion of female immigrants between 1901 and 1911 at the lowest point of the entire period. Finally, both Australia and the United States contained Chinese communities characterized by an entirely different growth trend. The female-to-male ratio never reached a level of even a hundred to a thousand.

Both the Chinese immigrants who settled in Penang, located on the Malay Peninsula, and on the island of Singapore just off its coast demonstrated a consistent tendency toward sojourners-to-families immigration, with those coming to Singapore establishing a larger community. Within seven years of its founding in 1819 as a British trading post, colonial authorities placed both Penang and Malacca under the control of Singapore's government, thus recognizing it as a primary center for their Asian trade.[16] Natives from the peninsula joined the British and other European traders who dominated economically and politically. These newcomers settled in significant numbers, but Chinese immigration, which reached impressive levels in 1821, grew concurrently with the island's meteoric rise in importance. By 1860 the Chinese population had reached fifty thousand, making them the largest ethnic group on Singapore, and Chinese merchants and laborers had established themselves as indispensable elements in its economy.

Male laborers traveling without their families made up the vast majority of Singapore's early Chinese immigrants. The number of women grew significantly each decade, however, making them an increasingly influential part of immigrant society. Consequently, although Singapore's Chinese community contained only sixty-nine women per thousand men in 1860, that proportion grew substantially with each census. By 1911 there were 350 Chinese women for every thousand Chinese men (table 1). Although the 1911 ratio still reflects a great gender disparity, the presence of Chinese women on Singapore grew at this pace despite the fact that the British approved of intermarriage between Chinese men and local women of other races.[17]

Natural increase certainly accounted for much of Singapore's steadily growing female population, and native-born Chinese women were responsible for most of the family-building. Still, female immigration also contributed to this process. Immigration statistics for the period from 1861 to 1880 have not survived, but

Table 1. Chinese Female Population in Singapore, by Census Year

Year	Chinese Females per 1,000 Chinese Males	Year	Chinese Females per 1,000 Chinese Males
1860	69	1891	214
1871	159	1901	257
1881	196	1911	350

Source: Statistics taken from Victor Purcell, *The Chinese in Southeast Asia* (London, 1965), 234.

records for 1881 to 1911 reveal that the number of Chinese females arriving on the island increased almost yearly.[18] Moreover, while Chinese male immigration always dwarfed these numbers, the percentage of females among new Chinese arrivals rose every decade—from fewer than 5 percent in 1881 to more than 10 percent by 1915.[19] Thus, the island's Chinese community contained a steadily growing female population; immigration, although not the most important factor, contributed significantly to that growth.

Such consistent movement toward a sexually balanced community corresponded with the encouragement of Chinese immigration to Singapore by the island's British governors. For many years after they began to immigrate there, the Chinese on Singapore governed themselves in most areas of life and encountered little interference from the British.[20] No effort was made to limit their immigration, even when rioting between rival groups of Chinese led to stricter outside control of their affairs, and Chinese residents never lodged a formal complaint of ill-treatment by British immigration officers.[21] The Chinese enjoyed equal rights with all but British immigrants. Their interests were guarded by a protector of Chinese, an official who served as the government's formal representative to the Chinese community, controlled the accommodations of Chinese passengers on ships, and explained labor contracts to Chinese immigrants.[22] As a result of these actions the Chinese in Singapore, both male and female, found hospitality and governmental support of their presence.

Buoyed by an atmosphere of welcome, new immigration continued unabated, and, in keeping with the sojourning tradition, single males made up the overwhelming majority of new immigrants. Yet an increasing number of female immigrants joined their husbands on Singapore each year as their native-born counterparts married sojourning males and instituted the family-building process. The relative smallness of this immigrant constituency affirmed sojourners' importance, but their expanding presence also signaled that the nuclear family was becoming an increasingly significant part of Singapore's Chinese community.

Like Singapore, Penang owed its development to traders from Great Britain. When the British settled there in 1786, virtually no one lived in this section of the Malay Peninsula, which made establishing a British trading post simple and profitable. Until the founding of Singapore, Penang was the primary trade center for ships flying the Union Jack, and it remained second only to Singapore after that island gained prominence in Britain's Asian trade interests. Chinese males were among Penang's earliest immigrants, and these pioneers, like those who first settled on Singapore, came as sojourners. They intended to exploit the colony's booming economy and then return to their home villages as wealthy and respected men.

Having come to this trade center for the same initial reasons as their counterparts off the Malay coast, the Chinese who immigrated to Penang also followed the sojourners-to-families pattern of settlement. Reflecting its thirty-year headstart on Singapore, by 1860 Penang's Chinese community already contained 339 females per thousand males (table 2). Although that ratio dropped to 205 per thousand during the next decade, the succeeding four census enumerations recorded a steady movement toward sexual parity within the immigrant community. By 1911, the female-to-male ratio had reached 424 females per thousand men—a more balanced community than Singapore's Chinese population had managed to achieve.

Census data for Penang, as with all the Straits settlements, is limited. The 1881 census contained an age breakdown of Penang's Chinese immigrants, however, which may be cautiously regarded as typical of other such settlements. The report showed that nearly 53 percent of the community's Chinese females were between the ages of sixteen and thirty-five.[23] Thus, as in Singapore, natural increase no doubt accounted for most of the growth in Penang's Chinese female population. The percentage of females among new Chinese immigrants also followed the Singapore pattern, however, and increased steadily from 4 percent between 1881 and 1890 to 13 percent from 1911 to 1915.[24] Probably due to its economic superiority, Singapore possessed the larger Chinese community, whereas Penang, as the older of the two settlements, contained the larger proportion of Chinese women. Yet the growth patterns of both suggest that the sojourner's relative importance gradually decreased in large Chinese immigrant communities located relatively close to China.

Chinese immigrants to the islands of Hawaii also followed the sojourners-to-families settlement pattern. Unlike their counterparts in and around the Malay Peninsula, however, Chinese sojourners coming to Hawaii had not merely moved off the Chinese mainland but had crossed great expanses of ocean in search of success. Moreover, they did not find themselves participating in the establishment of trading centers on largely unsettled land. Instead, they entered a society dominated by a generations-old monarchy struggling to maintain independence amid European and American exploitation. It is not surprising, therefore, that Hawaii's Chinese immigrated at a much slower pace and began coming much later than did the Chinese residents of Singapore and Penang. The 1853 Hawaiian census

Table 2. Chinese Female Population in Penang, by Census Year

Year	Chinese Females per 1,000 Chinese Males	Year	Chinese Females per 1,000 Chinese Males
1860	339	1891	267
1871	205	1901	337
1881	228	1911	424

Source: Statistics taken from Victor Purcell, *The Chinese in Southeast Asia* (London, 1965), 232.

recorded only five hundred Chinese inhabitants, and by 1866 that number had grown to only 1,206.[25] The proportion of females among these early immigrants had reached fewer than sixty per thousand men in the first census and just 101 per thousand in the second (table 3).

Hawaii's Chinese population exploded after European and American plantation owners pressured the monarchy to allow the mass immigration of laborers for their sugar and rice fields. Beginning in 1872, several thousand Chinese workers came to the islands, and the 1878 census recorded 6,045 Chinese residents.[26] Although the female population increased by 167 percent between 1866 and 1878, the massive influx of male laborers still reduced the ratio of females per thousand males to fifty-one. Still, the flood of sojourning males proved merely an intermission in the movement toward a sexually balanced population of Chinese immigrants. By 1890 the proportion of Chinese females had recovered almost to the level it had reached before the immigration boom of the 1870s, with ninety-two females per thousand males, and then it increased steadily to 264 per thousand by 1910, a figure approaching Singapore's Chinese community. Neither female immigration statistics nor age divisions for the female population exist for Hawaii, but this growth must reflect more than the birth of Chinese girls on the islands. Hawaii's great distance from China may have limited the size of its Chinese communities, but its pattern of settlement remained consistent with corresponding settlements in Southeast Asia.

Chinese women who left the homes of their parents-in-law for Hawaii entered an environment that offered a real, although qualified, welcome. Edward Lydon has noted that European and American planters, in an effort to curb some of the undesirable activities reported in other immigrant Chinatowns, included married women in their recruitment of Chinese contract laborers.[27] Employers promised work for both husband and wife, further guaranteeing that labor assignments would not separate the couple.[28] Anti-Chinese rhetoric pouring out of the United States, however, intensified the Hawaiian government's concern over the magnitude of Chinese arrivals at its ports and eroded much of the planters' interest in Chinese labor.

In 1883, when a group of Chinese men infected with smallpox attempted to land on the islands, Hawaiian officials responded by declaring a temporary quarantine

Table 3. Chinese Female Population in Hawaii, by Census Year

Year	Chinese Females per 1,000 Chinese Males	Year	Chinese Females per 1,000 Chinese Males
1853	58	1890	92
1866	101	1900	156
1878	51	1910	264

Sources: Statistics for 1853 and 1866 taken from Edward Lydon, *The Anti-Chinese Movement in the Hawaii Kingdom, 1853-1890* (San Francisco, 1975), 43. 1900-1910 period: Eleanor C. Nordyke, *The People of Hawai'i*, 2d ed. (Honolulu, 1989), 186.

of all ships containing Chinese immigrants and asking authorities in Hong Kong and Canton to allow no more emigrant ships to leave those ports for Honolulu.[29] Still without an alternative labor supply, plantation owners pressured the government into lifting those restrictions, but new waves of Japanese workers in the late 1880s marked the end of planter support for Chinese immigration.[30] By the time the white planters gained control of the Hawaiian legislature in 1888 they were the chief sponsors of newly enacted anti-Chinese legislation.[31] The annexation of Hawaii to the United States in 1898 brought the Exclusion Act to the islands and thereafter made immigration from China a difficult ordeal.

Yet Chinese women could easily gain admission to the islands throughout the 1880s and were even granted special exemptions from laws restricting Chinese immigration.[32] Hawaiian officials, like the European and American plantation owners, saw the opium dens, brothels, and epidemics reported in other immigrant Chinatowns as products of an exclusively male immigration. Therefore, they welcomed the immigration of wives as positive moral additions to Hawaii's Chinese community. Clarence Glick has highlighted this atmosphere of hospitality by pointing out that Chinese women, at least as late as 1887, could easily obtain permits to immigrate, especially if they identified themselves as the wives of Chinese laborers living in Hawaii.[33] The government of Hawaii's immigration legislation focused on controlling the number of male laborers and preventing epidemics but never addressed the issue of female immigration.

In addition to the opportunities for entry available to female immigrants, the ability of Chinese leaders to participate in the political process—at least until the islands came under the jurisdiction of American law—also aided the establishment of nuclear families in Hawaii. When the United States enacted general exclusion in 1882, Hawaii's Chinese community responded by forming the United Chinese Society, which actively lobbied against all attempts by the Hawaiian government to restrict Chinese immigration.[34] Beginning in 1887, the organization also worked with officials in Honolulu in an effort to prevent the fraudulent immigration of Chinese laborers, and, in Glick's estimation, proved fairly effective.[35] As white planters wrested power from Hawaiian leaders during the late 1880s, the islands' Chinese residents participated in political resistance efforts and were accused of providing financial support for Hawaiian counterrevolutionaries.[36] Despite earlier movement toward limited restrictions by Hawaiian officials, they enjoyed the political freedom to influence the extent and longevity of this legislation and also the necessary political organization to help resist exclusion when the United States gained control of the islands. In these efforts they clearly deviated from the tendency toward passive behavior characteristic of the sojourner's classic image.[37]

Hawaii's Chinese population, in part because it was politically active, experienced a steady increase in the number of nuclear families it contained, despite limited immigration restrictions against male laborers and diseased persons. Moreover, whether or not men found an open door, female immigrants continued to come, and "generally, Chinese prostitutes were absent in Hawaii."[38] As long as the government did not move to restrict female immigration, anti-Chinese hostility, reduced job opportunities, and even general restrictive laws did not prevent Chinese women from leaving their husbands' villages and traveling far beyond Asian settlements such as Singapore and Penang. No doubt distance from home affected the rate at which they came, but Chinese family life in Hawaii continued to grow despite the journey's length, cultural prohibitions, and the Chinese sojourner tradition.

In contrast to the thriving Chinese communities in Singapore, Penang, and Hawaii, Chinese immigrants in Malacca witnessed a gradual decline in their female population from 1860 to 1911. By the nineteenth century Malacca, unlike Singapore and Penang, was an old settlement and had achieved the status of being a central city in the Malay kingdom and an important trade center when the Portuguese occupied it in 1511. A few Chinese immigrants migrated shortly after the Portuguese occupation, but in 1795, when the British replaced their European rivals, the city still contained only a small number of Chinese. Malacca's importance receded with the establishment of new British trade centers on Singapore and in Penang, and roughly an equal number of men and women made up its Chinese immigrant population.[39] When large groups of Chinese laborers began to arrive during the 1820s, however, sojourners without families dominated the new wave of immigration.[40]

By 1860 the number of Chinese males living in Malacca had more than doubled, dropping the proportion of females to 427 per thousand males (table 4). Although that ratio reflected greater parity between the sexes than in the other Chinese immigrant communities discussed in this chapter, it marked a severe decline from the near balance that had previously existed. Furthermore, the proportion of females fell to 365 per thousand in 1871 and 256 per thousand in 1881 as unattached men continued to pour into Malacca's Chinese sector. During the next two decades, a sharp drop in all Chinese immigration combined with natural increase

Table 4. Chinese Female Population in Malacca, by Census Year

Year	Chinese Females per 1,000 Chinese Males	Year	Chinese Females per 1,000 Chinese Males
1860	427	1891	277
1871	365	1901	293
1881	256	1911	204

Source: Statistics taken from Victor Purcell, *The Chinese in Southeast Asia* (London, 1965), 232.

produced a slight recovery in the proportionate female population of Malacca, and the per-thousand ratio was 293 by 1901. The absence of new immigration coincided with a widespread decline in Chinese immigrant communities' populations from Singapore to the United States, perhaps because of the beginning of exclusion in the West and the conscription of Chinese males for the British Empire's wars with France in the 1880s and Japan in the 1890s. The advent of the twentieth century brought an economic boom to Malacca, however, and created yet another explosion in the number of male immigrants. Even though the female population increased by 38 percent between 1901 and 1911, the new wave of male immigration dropped the female-to-male ratio within the city's Chinese sector to only 204 females per thousand males.

While strong economic growth produced steady and dramatic population increases among both the male and female Chinese of Singapore, Penang, and Hawaii, immigrant settlement in Malacca remained nearly stagnant unless stimulated by occasional economic booms. Then, many women joined the flow of new arrivals, but their numbers were dwarfed by the thousands of men, exacerbating the community's sexual disparity. Moreover, despite Malacca's relative closeness to China, its history of booms and busts clouded prospects for sustained employment. Given the insecure environment, one would expect fewer Chinese women to have endured the traumatic departure from their villages in order to join husbands who could lose their jobs at any time.

Because Malacca offered the same atmosphere of openness and welcome found in the other settlements in and around the Malay Peninsula, economic factors assume an even more likely importance in its peak-and-decline pattern of Chinese immigration. Notwithstanding the numerous brothels that thrived throughout its Chinatown, it was not until 1927 that the city's British governors attempted to create even "paper restrictions" on the immigration of Chinese prostitutes.[41] Moreover, even those laws did no more than prohibit the immigration of women whom the government had proven to have been imported as slave-prostitutes.[42] Chinese women could immigrate to Malacca without fear of deportation; only the power of their ancestral ties to the homeland and the need for a little traveling money hindered their coming. Their failure to do so after 1860 suggests that economic opportunities within the host society significantly influenced the rate of nuclear-family growth in immigrant Chinatowns.

Although uncertainty shaped the development of Malacca's Chinese community, the government of Australia frequently erected legal barriers to restrict Chinese immigration. Drawn by the promise of quick riches in Australia's newly discovered goldfields, thousands upon thousands of Chinese men began to immigrate in 1854, and within a year several Australian colonies had already enacted laws restricting the men's ability to enter the country.[43] Then, when the Chinese population shrank to acceptable levels, Australian authorities would repeal the restrictive legislation only to reinstate it with greater intensity at the first sign of an appreciable increase in new immigration.[44] This hostile setting, combined with the goldfields' undesirability as a place to bring a family, helped limit Australia's Chinese female population to minuscule numbers.

In 1861, seven years after Chinese miners began pouring into the goldfields, Australia contained 38,247 Chinese males, most of them miners, and only eleven Chinese females. Although immigration restrictions had reduced the male population by almost ten thousand ten years later, the ratio of two females per one thousand males remained far below any recorded in Hawaii or the Malay settlements (table 5). Relaxed immigration laws characterized the 1880s, and, despite continuing social hostility, the increased openness resulted in the number of Chinese males returning to almost precisely the 1861 level. At the same time the female population grew to 259, or seven females per one thousand males.

This glacial increase continued throughout the next thirty years, reaching a perthousand ratio of only forty-one by 1911. Such small gains likely reflected nothing more than the births of Chinese girls and the departure of male laborers looking to escape the growing severity of anti-Chinese legislation. The male population experienced a net increase in only one decade between 1861 and 1911 and in 1911 fell to 21,156—its lowest level since 1854.[45] Given the cultural barriers that discouraged them, Chinese women could not possibly have been attracted to a place whose male population had experienced more emigration than immigration for years.

In addition to policies that led men to repatriate, Australian attempts to impede the growth of its Chinese communities included a direct attack against the immigration of women. The first significant increase of female immigrants in 1903 prompted the repeal of clauses in the 1901 Commonwealth Immigration Restriction Act, which had permitted the immigration of the wives and dependent children of nonrestricted Chinese men.[46] To justify its action, the government complained that too many women had taken advantage of overly lenient laws. Australia's Chinese female population increased by 366 between 1901 and 1911 and, aside from the growth created by births, most of the increase must have taken place

Table 5. Chinese Female Population in Australia, by Census Year

Year	Chinese Females per 1,000 Chinese Males	Year	Chinese Females per 1,000 Chinese Males
1861	0.28	1891	8
1871	2	1901	16
1881	7	1911	41

Source: Statistics taken from C. Y. Choi, *Chinese Migration and Settlement in Australia* (Sydney, 1975), 22.

between 1901 and 1903, thereby forcing the enactment of what amounted to female exclusion.[47] The government vigorously enforced its new prohibition: "The restriction of female entry was strictly carried out. After 1905, only wives of well established merchants were admitted and for short periods only, usually six months. Subsequent petitions for the re-incorporation of clause 3m [the clause which had permitted the immigration of wives and children] were met with firm rejections from the government."[48] In adding this final layer of restriction, Australia seemed determined not to prevent the immigration of Chinese prostitutes but to control the Chinese population by forbidding women to establish permanent residence.[49]

As in Australia, Chinese laborers suffered ill-treatment by the host society from the early years of immigrating to the United States. Still, the country's extensive economic attractions continued to lure thousands of workers; responding to the news of gold discoveries in California, more than twenty thousand arrived in 1852 alone.[50] Then, beginning in the late 1850s, many immigrant workers moved from the mining frontier to the urban centers of the Pacific Coast, particularly San Francisco. This extensive urban migration, focused on a single city, encouraged the immigration of Chinese women, whose numbers had grown to 4,566 at the time of the 1870 census and created a female-to-male ratio of seventy-eight per thousand (table 6). Although both men and women suffered occupational discrimination and threats of physical harm from white laborers, the vast and expanding regions of the American West provided such an array of job opportunities that Chinese immigrants, pushed out of one industry through such instruments as the foreign miners' tax, could easily find another way to earn a living. Given such appealing prospects for financial gain, more and more Chinese came to the United States.

Admittedly, the number of Chinese females in America remained quite low in 1870, yet Australia had not managed to reach a sex ratio of even fifty per thousand as late as 1911. Nevertheless, the anti-Chinese movement in the United States gained tremendous momentum during the 1870s, and the enactment of the Page Law in 1875 brought the country's Chinese female population growth to a near-standstill.[51] At the same time, the continued promise of wealth offered by states on the West

Table 6. Chinese Female Population in the United States, by Census Year

Year	Chinese Females per 1,000 Chinese Males	Year	Chinese Females per 1,000 Chinese Males
1860	54	1890	37
1870	78	1900	53
1880	47	1910	70

Source: Statistics taken from U.S. Department of Commerce, Special Report, *Chinese and Japanese in the United States, 1910,* Bulletin 127 (Washington, D.C., 1914), 8.

Coast, reminiscent of Malacca's boom periods, combined with the threat of general exclusion in the future to draw Chinese men at an astonishing rate. As a result, the proportion of females in America's Chinese population declined to only forty-seven per thousand in 1880.

The Exclusion Act of 1882 limited the immigration of both men and women. As in Australia, this more comprehensive approach halted male population growth and caused a general Chinese exodus. Initially, women left more quickly than men, and in spite of the growth that might have been expected through natural increase the proportion of females fell again in 1890, to thirty-seven per thousand. The number of males then plummeted in the following two decades, standing at only 66,856 at the time of the 1910 census—a little more than eight thousand above the 1870 figure and nearly thirty-seven thousand below the number recorded in 1890.[52] The decline combined with a return of the female population to nearly its level in 1870—the result of births and a trickle of new female immigrants—to create a female-to-male ratio of fifty-three per thousand in 1900 and seventy per thousand in 1910. Still, America's Chinese community did not begin to approach sexual parity until after the Exclusion Act was repealed in 1943.

In both Australia and the United States, restriction of female immigration appears to have exerted a strong negative influence on the development of Chinese society. Governmental hostility produced common elements in the patterns of Chinese immigration to both countries. Both immigrant communities began with virtually nonexistent female populations that started to grow after the first few years of settlement. In each instance, the enactment of discriminatory legislation also inhibited Chinese population growth, ultimately leading to a slowly balancing sex ratio produced not by significant female immigration but by a decline in the number of male immigrants.

Notwithstanding their similarities, however, American and Australian trends also exhibited important differences between 1860 and 1890. First, almost no women participated in the early movement of immigrants to Australia, so its Chinese female population could do little but increase. More than 1,700 Chinese women had migrated to the United States by 1860, however, giving its Chinese community a female population large enough to make significant decline possible.[53] Second, the remarkably early adoption of Australian immigration restrictions, which focused on limiting the number of laborers, caused that nation's male growth rate to drop much earlier than in the United States, where Chinese male immigration remained free until 1882.[54] Finally, American legislators achieved their first success in the effort to control the country's Chinese population by focusing on restricting female immigration, whereas female immigrants to Australia did not face restrictions until 1903.

Although the Page Law established the American practice of gender-specific exclusion, it still tends to be overshadowed in scholarly works by the more infamous Exclusion Act of 1882, which accomplished the same general prohibition of all Chinese immigration enforced at various periods in Australia by closing American ports to all Chinese laborers as well as to the wives and dependent children of laborers living in the United States.[55] No longer able to bring other family members to America, and prohibited from making periodic trips home, many Chinese men and women responded to exclusion by leaving the United States, thus creating a steady reduction in the country's Chinese population and retarding the likely contribution of immigration toward sexual parity in U.S. Chinatowns for the next sixty-one years.

Exclusion unquestionably damaged the development of Chinese American society while at the same time dramatically reversing U.S. immigration policy to focus exclusively on the race and class of prospective immigrants. That dual importance gives a deserved position to the act of 1882 and makes it the most studied and discussed piece of American anti-Chinese legislation, yet the Page Law also merits careful examination. Through the abuse of clauses prohibiting the immigration of Chinese prostitutes, this legislation exploited the anti-Chinese prejudices then flourishing in America to stop the flow of female immigrants at the precise point when the approach of exclusion was creating the biggest boom period in the history of Chinese immigration to the United States.[56] Consequently, in a period much like those that reduced the proportion of females in Malacca's Chinese community, the Page Law intensified gender disparity in America by preventing Chinese women from adding their numbers to the country's exploding Chinese population.

Comparative analysis of growth patterns among the six Chinese immigrant communities discussed in this chapter indicates that the sojourner mentality should not be discounted as a primary factor in their relatively slow movement toward sexual equilibrium. Even in places like Singapore and Penang, which encouraged female immigration and required a relatively short trip from the Chinese mainland, many decades passed before the female population began to approach the same numbers as their male counterparts and natural increase appears to have played a more important role in this gender balancing than did female immigration. Yet existing immigration records indicate that, in addition to gains from natural increase, the proportion of females among new immigrants grew, wherever possible, with each passing decade—suggesting that the sojourner's dominance underwent a process of erosion. Although distance from home appears to have affected the size of Chinese immigrant communities, with larger communities attracting more female immigrants, distance and size variables did little to alter the general trend of immigration. The limited data on Hawaii, Malacca, and Australia indicate that Chinese women overcame the barrier of distance when conditions favored their immigration and passed by closer settlements when social hostility and economic discrimination limited opportunities for success. Furthermore, recognizing the impact of events inside China on the emigration of its people (as evidenced by phenomena such as the worldwide drop in immigrant populations during the 1880s and 1890s), Chinese internal affairs seem to have created only generic changes in the number of emigrants. Such changes produced little or no difference between patterns of settlement in the various emigrant destinations.

This presentation of the ways in which different Chinese immigrant communities developed contains some inadequacies in addition to possible problems associated with focusing on the nuclear family. Future studies should both develop a detailed analysis of economic conditions in China and examine additional communities, such as those in Peru, Canada, the Philippines, and Cuba. Moreover, they should also make an exhaustive attempt to locate the data needed to create a more complete list of the factors that affected Chinese immigration. The purpose of this chapter, however, is not to establish a hierarchy of factors that influenced Chinese immigration tendencies, but to make a case for the importance of gender-specific restrictions like the Page Law.

The history of Chinese immigration to places such as Singapore, Penang, and Hawaii indicates that it is shortsighted to focus on the sojourner mentality of Chinese immigrants while treating exclusion as the final seal on a pattern of settlement established by the Chinese themselves. The United States offered a tremendous array of job opportunities for Chinese laborers and, in spite of its distance from China, contained an even larger Chinese population than Singapore in 1870.[57] Given the sojourners-to-families pattern of immigration found in these other immigrant communities, which also possessed large Chinese populations and appealing economic climates, one would expect America's Chinese female population to have increased slowly but steadily right up to the time of exclusion. Instead, their numbers remained virtually unchanged after the 1870 census, a phenomenon shared only by the Chinese in Australia—who began to suffer national immigration restrictions as early as 1854. The joint legacy of an abnormally low Chinese female population shared by these two countries suggests that the Page Law, more than the sojourner mentality and cultural restrictions, impeded the immigration of Chinese women between 1875 and 1882.[58] Because both sociologists and historians point to the absence of women as central to the abnormal development of Chinese American society, the 1875 act may well represent the most important event of the preexclusion period.

3

A Stop on the
Road to Exclusion

Although the Page Law represented America's first attempt to restrict Chinese immigration on a national basis, a number of antecedents, enacted by the California legislature, determined its form. This large body of anti-Chinese legislation provides a context for understanding both the source of the law's effectiveness and the shortness of its tenure. Two decades of frustration in their efforts to regulate Chinese immigration to California made state leaders intensely determined to ensure the law's enforcement. From Hong Kong to San Francisco they monitored its implementation, not allowing federal officials to treat it as less important than other duties. The Page Law, however, still fell far short of the ultimate goal of these lawmakers: general Chinese exclusion.

Reducing the number of female immigrants could potentially inhibit the establishment of Chinese American families on the Pacific Coast but offered no solution to the problem of sojourning males. When these threats to white labor continued to arrive in San Francisco, Californians lobbied Congress for additional anti-Chinese legislation. Thus, the Page Law marked a stop on the road to exclusion—an important step in the transformation of Chinese immigration from a western to a national issue. The Page Law also represented a reapplication of state laws that had been ruled unconstitutional by federal courts, and its passage emboldened legislators to take additional steps that anticipated federal adoption of the Exclusion Act. Therefore, in order to comprehend the magnitude of its importance, one must place the law within this transitional context—between the California legislation that shaped it and the laws that it spawned on the way to exclusion.

California's anti-Chinese legislation originated with the first significant movement of Chinese into the state in 1852, when more than twenty thousand immigrants arrived in San Francisco.[1] Fewer than four thousand Chinese had entered the country since 1820, so government officials could not help but notice this mass immigration.[2] Already hard-pressed to accommodate the flood of would-be millionaires who had saturated the goldfields since 1849, they were alarmed by the exploding Chinese population. A limited supply of cheap Chinese labor helped accelerate economic growth in the state, but such a huge volume of new arrivals threatened to glut the job market and thereby discourage the migration of Americans and immigrants who could attain citizenship. These citizen-laborers, and not the Chinese, held the keys to California's social and economic status and to its national political future.

In April of 1852 Gov. John Bigler responded to the unwanted flood of workers by delivering a special message to the California legislature, warning of the need to control Chinese immigration.[3] That call to arms was quickly converted into the state's first restrictive legislation, which it enacted before the year's end. The law required ship owners to submit a report on the character and health of all immigrants debarking in California. In order to ensure the accuracy of such reports, immigration officials were authorized to collect an indemnity bond of $500 to $1,000 from shipping companies for every alien passenger as a means of protecting the government "against expense incurred for charitable aid within two years."[4] McClain has noted that, in practice, port authorities transferred this company obligation to the immigrants themselves, charging each Chinese passenger an additional $5 to help defray the costs of possible future assistance.[5] Thus the law served primarily to notify companies that the business of transporting Chinese immigrants could instantly lose its profitability if their response to concerns about excessive immigration displeased those charged with its enforcement.

Nearly all Chinese traveling to America in the 1850s entered through the port of San Francisco. Because only four thousand arrived there in 1853, state leaders had reason to believe that the new law would limit Chinese population growth to an acceptable level.[6] Yet despite the enactment of additional legislation designed to provide for more effective administration of the 1852 law, their optimism faded when San Francisco port authorities reported 16,084 Chinese arrivals in 1854.[7] Apparently, immigrants found the extra $5 fee to be an acceptable inconvenience, provided it would guarantee their ability to land. At any rate, given the importance of maritime shipping to the city's economy, officials would no doubt have been reluctant to alienate the companies by actually collecting the threatened penalties. Moreover, the law was likely unenforceable. The government would have found it difficult to prove the identity of specific immigrants who became wards of the state, and therefore it would have been impossible to hold a ship owner liable for their support. The initial decline associated with the restrictions should no doubt be attributed to coincidence—as part of the frequent ebb and flow of Chinese emigration around the world.

Acknowledging the ineffectiveness of indemnity bonds, legislators took the bold step in 1855 of imposing a more direct penalty on the transporters of Chinese immigrants: "The master, owner, or consignee of any vessel arriving in any of the ports of this State from any foreign State, country, or territory, having on board any persons who are incompetent by the laws and constitution of California or the United States to become citizens thereof are hereby required to pay a tax, for each such person, of fifty dollars."[8] Two aspects of this law make it significant. First, by levying a direct tax, rather than requiring a bond, the state could penalize vessels carrying Chinese immigrants without resorting to the lengthy and expensive process of litigation. Second, and more important, taxing only those who were constitutionally prohibited from gaining citizenship permitted direct targeting of the Chinese without inciting protests from other immigrant groups.

Although declared unconstitutional by the California supreme court in 1857, the legislation's enactment coincided with a sustained reduction in the number of Chinese immigrants coming to San Francisco.[9] Yet most Californians still regarded the number of annual arrivals, which would remain below nine thousand for the next thirteen years, to be unacceptably high.[10] Therefore, in 1858 legislators attempted to prohibit all future Chinese immigration to their state.

> On and after the 1st day of October, A.D. 1858, any person or persons of the Chinese or Mongolian races, shall not be permitted to enter this State, . . . and it shall be unlawful for any . . . person . . . to knowingly allow or permit any Chinese or Mongolian on and after such time to enter any of the ports of the State, . . . and any person or persons violating any of the provisions of this act shall be held and deemed guilty of a misdemeanor, and upon conviction thereof shall be subject to a fine in any sum not less than four hundred dollars, nor more than six hundred, for each and every offense, or imprisonment in the county jail . . . for a period of not less than three months nor more than one year, or by both such fine and imprisonment.[11]

That law, too, was struck down by the state's supreme court in 1859, but its passage indicates that by the late 1850s state leaders had come to consider exclusion the only acceptable remedy for unwanted Chinese immigration.

Within a year, judicial nullification of their first attempt at this ultimate solution had prompted the legislature to resurrect a modified version of the 1852 statute that resorted to the more legally acceptable indemnity bonds, created a superintendent of immigration, doubled his commission from the collection of bonds, and gave him the power to interrogate shipmasters who submitted inadequate reports.[12] Legislation in 1863 replaced the superintendent with a commissioner of immigration, who possessed the same powers as his predecessor but received double the commission for his attempts to collect bond revenue.[13] Although proof of liability remained difficult, the added monetary incentive created energetic commissioners, and over the next three years the volume of Chinese immigrants reached its lowest level since 1851.[14] Still, the immigration commissioner's impact on that decline remains unclear, and the number of Chinese arriving in California began to increase again in 1867.[15]

Frustrated by judicial roadblocks against general exclusion, state officials had already begun to redirect their efforts toward limiting one of the more visible by-products of Chinese immigration. With the first waves of gold-seekers, males had made up an unusually high majority of California's residents—a pattern that continued to cause concern long after the development of a more complex economy.[16] Consequently, a thriving, multiracial prostitution industry blossomed in San Francisco. Women from all over Europe and Latin America joined European Americans from the East in selling their sexual services to thousands of resident and transient men.[17] Moreover, because Chinese males suffered the city's most profound gender imbalance, their sexual frustrations created an especially lucrative economic opportunity for everyone involved in importing prostitutes from China.

A minority of women entered voluntarily into prostitution, and, whether their initial involvement resulted from personal choice or coercion, some succeeded in earning enough money to establish their own brothels. Among this group, the most well-known was Ah Toy, who achieved the status of a sexual icon in San Francisco in the 1850s and therefore could demand extravagant fees for her services.[18] Because prostitution was legal in the city, she regularly used the local court system to collect the unpaid bills of patrons.[19] Although others did not reach the same level of notoriety, they also obtained a degree of economic independence. For example, Ty Moin, only thirty-one, employed five prostitutes at her Sixth Ward establishment and declared a personal estate of $750 at the time of the 1870 census.[20] Seventeen other women in the same ward, most of whom were considerably older, also operated houses of prostitution and claimed capital resources varying from $100 to $700.[21]

Notwithstanding such examples of economic prosperity, the vast majority of Chinese prostitutes were brought into the country by competing tongs (secret criminal societies) that had taken control of the industry by 1860.[22] First, traders procured women through outright purchase, deception, or kidnapping.[23] They then sold them at great profit to a third party in San Francisco.[24] Those who controlled the local industry then distributed the newcomers to various locations throughout Chinatown and, according to Hirata's calculations, reaped no less than $2,500 a year from the labor of each prostitute.[25] In turn, although their rate of pay is unknown, both female and male managers earned their livelihoods by overseeing the operation of individual sites. Because non-Chinese property owners held title to virtually all the real estate in Chinatown, they could demand rents far in excess of market value for housing the businesses.[26] Finally, law enforcement officials supplemented their incomes at unrecorded levels through collecting bribes in exchange for agreeing not to interfere with the trade.

Government leaders, attempting to protect San Francisco's position as chief economic and cultural center of an increasingly important state, had long agonized over the moral embarrassment created by its diverse prostitute population. Thus, Chan has noted that the first local ordinance designed to eliminate this perceived problem had been enacted as early as 1854 and was directed at the entire industry.[27] Twelve years later, members of the state legislature belatedly attempted to assist the cause while narrowing their focus to what appeared to be the less politically volatile problem of Chinese prostitution. The resulting statute, however, assessed penalties against both brothel owners and their landlords, prompting the latter's wealth and influence to eventually force a compromise that allowed the industry to continue but only in designated sections of Chinatown.[28] As a result, Chinese prostitution continued to flourish alongside its immigrant and native counterparts while a new element had been added to the legislative mix.

The shift from general exclusion to targeting women was further encouraged by congressional ratification of the Burlingame Treaty in 1868. Whereas previous treaty relations between the United States and China had only protected the right of American citizens to settle and conduct business in China, the new treaty established reciprocal privileges for Chinese and American citizens abroad. As part of the agreement, the United States recognized the right of Chinese subjects to immigrate to America, providing their immigration was voluntary: "The United States and the Emperor of China cordially recognize the inherent and inalienable right of man to change his home and allegiance and also the mutual advantage of the free migration and emigration of their citizens and subjects, respectively, from the one country to the other, for the purpose of curiosity or trade or as permanent residents. The high contracting parties therefore join in reprobating any other than a voluntary emigration for these purposes."[29] Through such language, the Burlingame Treaty summarily voided California's collection of immigration taxes and indemnity bonds. Encouraged by their new freedom, which came at a time when the Hakka-Punti War was causing severe hardship in South China, the number of immigrants traveling to San Francisco exceeded ten thousand in 1868, 1869, and 1870.[30]

After recovering from the shock of America's new reciprocal treaty with China, the California legislature responded to such unwanted increases by expanding its new genre of immigration legislation. Two separate bills, enacted in 1870, prohibited shipping companies from allowing either male or female Chinese passengers to disembark until the state commissioner of immigration was satisfied that they had come as voluntary immigrants of good character.[31] Furthermore, anyone judged guilty of attempting to land illegal immigrants could be sentenced to a fine ranging from $1,000 to $5,000, a jail term of two to twelve months, or both.[32] Although the record of its enforcement is a sketchy one at best, port authorities appear to have successfully used the law to deny the landing of twenty-nine female passengers aboard the Pacific Mail Steamship Company's *Great Republic* on June 14, 1870.[33]

Although state lawmakers were thus enjoying some success in halting the immigration of Chinese prostitutes, two separate challenges confronted them at the federal level. First, Sen. William Stewart of Nevada introduced a bill in January that guaranteed equal protection of the law and due process to all residents of the United States, without regard to race.[34] Before the beginning of summer, Stewart's legislation had been incorporated into the Civil Rights Act of 1870 and had, at least in principle, voided all of California's anti-Chinese laws while affirming as well the admissibility of Chinese testimony in all legal proceedings.[35] Then, in the same congressional session, Sen. Charles Sumner pressed for a vote on his proposal to remove racial references from the naturalization clause of the 1790 Immigration Act.[36] If passed, his amendment would have enabled Chinese immigrants to apply for citizenship and, as citizens, to develop into an influential political force on the Pacific Coast. California's congressional representatives managed to stave off that threat by leading a defeat of the Sumner amendment.[37]

Despite managing to balance defeat with victory, the advocates of exclusion now understood that their struggle's ultimate fate would be decided in Washington rather than Sacramento. Therefore, the legislature urged Congress in an 1872 resolution to negotiate a modification of the Burlingame Treaty in order to discourage future Chinese immigration.[38] Two years later, however, the effort to nationalize their campaign assumed a more urgent tone when attorneys for Ah Fong, a Chinese woman whom the commissioner of immigration had rejected as a person of unsavory character, challenged the 1870 antiprostitution law in a legal battle that ultimately led to the U.S. Supreme Court. The Court eventually nullified the legislation on the grounds that it violated existing treaty relations.[39] Responding quickly, the state senate adopted two additional resolutions. The first endorsed a federal bill sponsored by Cong. H. F. Page of California and intended to prohibit the employment of Chinese contract laborers.[40] The second called for the state's representatives in Washington to press for establishment of a new relationship with China.[41]

In the attempts to eradicate the "Chinese problem," California and its Republican Party depended heavily on Page, who maintained his seat in the House for ten years, largely at the expense of the Chinese. The Civil War had brought Republicans into the forefront of state politics, but the Democrats regained control only a few years after the war ended, primarily through their adoption of a strong anti-Chinese platform.[42] They used the issue to such advantage that by the early

1870s Republicans, attempting to recoup their losses, added denunciations of the Chinese to their own speeches. Page, as an anti-Chinese Republican, gained election to the House in 1873. Along with Sen. A. A. Sargent, another California Republican, he continually battled Democratic opponents in an effort to portray himself and his party as the best choices for resolving the issue of Chinese immigration—a portrayal Henry K. Norton has identified as the most critical for any individual who seriously aspired to public office in California.[43]

Clearly, his own tenure in office ultimately depended upon opposition to the Chinese, but Page's support of federal anti-Chinese legislation far exceeded the demands of political expediency. Although he left no papers or letters from which to build a clear analysis of his personal views regarding the Chinese, Page emerged not only as a reliable supporter of the exclusion movement but also as a champion of the cause. He had moved to California in 1854 and settled in Placerville, where he studied law. In addition to beginning his own practice after passing the bar, he engaged in several profitable business ventures. For the purposes of this study, his most notable entrepreneurial activity was in the state's mining industry, which during the second half of the 1850s had persuaded the state legislature to push the Chinese out of mining by enacting the foreign miners' tax.[44]

Before introducing the antiprostitution law, Page had already sponsored four anti-Chinese bills and three resolutions in the House. The first, which he presented on December 15, 1873, prohibited the employment of coolie labor and was referred to the Committee on Education and Labor, which never acted on it.[45] Next, on January 14, 1874, he received unanimous consent to submit a significant resolution requesting that the Committee on Foreign Affairs urge the president to renegotiate the Burlingame Treaty in order to "check or altogether prevent Chinese immigration."[46] Approximately two years later Congress would give its approval to a more reserved version of this resolution, eliminating the reference to exclusion, and appoint the joint investigative committee that traveled to California in 1876.[47]

By the fall of 1874, having established his credentials as a champion of exclusion, Page joined other members of Congress from California in launching an intense lobbying effort against the 1868 treaty—one that would continue for the next five years. In the midst of a campaign for reelection, he had reason to fear that his constituents would quickly turn to alternative leadership unless they could be given some kind of interim victory. Therefore, after convincing voters to send him back to the House for a second term, Page wasted little time initiating such an attempt at quick success. On December 8 he introduced another resolution, which his colleagues approved and sent to the Committee on Foreign Affairs: "Resolved, That the Committee on Foreign Affairs be instructed to inquire whether any legislation or other action on the part of the Government of the United States is necessary to prevent the immigration or importation of coolies under contract for servile labor, and Chinese women brought to the United States for the purpose of prostitution; and that said committee report by bill or otherwise at its earliest practicable convenience."[48]

Because the state's fortunes in the *Ah Fong* case had turned downward in U.S. Circuit Court less than three months earlier, Page hoped to replace the doomed state law with a federal equivalent.[49] To his disappointment, the House committee endorsed reevaluation of the Burlingame Treaty's provisions regarding immigration but refused to support his bill, to endorse exclusion, or to alter the bans against coolie immigration contained in the 1868 treaty.

Recognizing that a revision of the treaty placed all of its contents in jeopardy, Page presented two more bills to the House, both designed to protect its one anti-Chinese element. Fearful of Charles Sumner's impending effort to revise naturalization law, California senators had managed to exchange their votes in favor of ratification for a clause expressly prohibiting Chinese immigrants from becoming citizens.[50] Because Page was now calling for the treaty's alteration, he apparently wanted to ensure that the clause would not be deleted. To that end, first on December 22, 1874, and again on January 13, 1875, he proposed legislation that would disqualify the Chinese from naturalizing.[51]

He was calling for reinforcement of the formal precedent established by the Burlingame Treaty. Had he managed to achieve the passage of either bill, a revised treaty could not have made citizenship possible for Chinese immigrants unless it contained a clause explicitly granting the right of naturalization—a most unlikely development. Although both bills died in committee, Page's precautions proved unnecessary. The prohibition contained in the Burlingame Treaty was preserved in its successor. The Chinese would not receive the right to become naturalized citizens until passage of the Magnuson Bill in 1943.

Although his efforts on behalf of the exclusionists, like the bills prohibiting Chinese naturalization, had produced few results before 1875, that year marked the turning point for Page and the anti-Chinese movement. The House Committee on Foreign Affairs had rejected his calls for an exclusion act and refused even to expand the prohibition of coolie immigration contained in the Burlingame Treaty, but its response to the issue of Chinese females proved far more satisfactory. Prostitution and moral corruption were issues of national concern in the 1870s and 1880s, a reality that encouraged the committee to endorse Page's resolution of December 8, 1874. Their accompanying report recommended that Congress protect American moral values by establishing a process of individual interrogation for all Chinese women attempting to leave China for the United States. There would be stiff penalties for those found guilty of violating the law.

Even though he refused to accept anything short of exclusion, Page sponsored the committee's proposed legislation, which he regarded as a positive step toward his final goal. Cautiously worded to stay within the Burlingame Treaty's provisions for "free" Chinese immigration to America, the bill would succeed where its predecessors on the state level had failed, chiefly because it possessed the necessary restraint to secure the support of members of Congress not yet solidly aligned with the exclusionists. By 1875 Page had already built his political career around a strong anti-Chinese reputation, and the movement was steadily gaining national momentum. He could afford to wait for exclusion while presenting his constituents with a much-needed victory.

On February 10, 1875, as he addressed Congress on the subject of American treaty relations with China, Page introduced his bill and emphasized its interim nature.[52] His speech, however, contained three important elements. Although they revealed that he considered the legislation a compromise measure on the way to total exclusion, those elements reflected the concerns of capitalists and moral crusaders. First, and most important, Page stated that organizations within the Chinese underworld sponsored the overwhelming majority of Chinese immigrants in exchange for their services as coolie laborers bound to their benefactors by a quasi-slave contract. Such an arrangement violated the moral conscience of Californians and undermined the state's economic future. Second, he argued that until an agreement could be reached on a proper method of exclusion, government officials should enforce the Burlingame Treaty's bans against coolie immigration with all strictness. Finally, supported by the testimony of several American missionaries, he asserted that 90 percent of the Chinese females residing in the United States worked as prostitutes. Telling colleagues that a people whose immigrants consisted of coolies and prostitutes deserved exclusion, Page insisted that Congress could do no less than make his bill into law, thereby providing an immediate and effective end to the importation of Chinese moral decadence.[53] Thus, he proposed a law that addressed American moral and health concerns, provided a means of restricting dependent immigrants, and furthered the cause of exclusion.

The contents of the Page Law closely mirrored the provisions of California's 1870 attempts to prohibit the immigration of coolies and prostitutes from China. In regard to the immigration of male laborers, it fell slightly short of its predecessor, duplicating the maximum jail sentence of one year for persons convicted of transporting contract laborers but limiting the fine to no more than $2,000. In its penalties against the importers of Chinese prostitutes Page's bill exceeded the severity of the 1870 state law:

> The importation into the United States of women for the purpose of prostitution is hereby forbidden; and all contracts and agreements in relation thereto, made in advance or in pursuance of such illegal importation and purposes, are hereby declared void; and

whoever shall knowingly and willfully import, or cause any importation of, women in the United States for the purposes of prostitution, or shall knowingly or willfully hold, or attempt to hold, any woman to such purposes, in pursuance of such illegal importation and contract or agreement, shall be deemed guilty of a felony, and, on conviction thereof, shall be imprisoned not exceeding five years and pay a fine not exceeding five thousand dollars.[54]

With the exception of California's unconstitutional exclusion law, this section of the bill made it the most severe anti-Chinese legislation enacted in the United States before 1882.

Remembering the fiasco created by attempts to enforce this kind of restriction at the state level, Page carefully worded its title. Because any attempt to overreach the provisions of the Burlingame Treaty could not stand the test of constitutionality in the Supreme Court, he officially designated the Page Law as "An Act Supplementary to the Acts in Relation to Immigration." Thus, by casting his proposal within the framework of legislation already compatible with American-Chinese treaty relations, Page hoped to avoid a challenge to its legitimacy. The record indicates that this effort proved successful; no one formally questioned the law's constitutionality during its tenure.

With the Page Law, California's anti-Chinese forces reversed the strategy followed in their attempts to prohibit Chinese immigration at the state level. The earlier campaign had quickly enacted an exclusion law and then tried to impose immigration restriction after its judicial nullification. When restriction also fell to defeat they realized that Chinese immigration could only be stopped through national action—and then only by accomplishing a modification of the Burlingame Treaty. In the meantime, a federal restriction law, carefully placed within the context of the treaty's existing provisions and vigorously enforced, would both boost morale and enhance the exposure of the exclusion movement in areas outside the Pacific Coast. Moreover, the combined desires of employers and moral crusaders—to prohibit dependent immigration while eliminating the threat of social corruption and physical disease—provided broad support for antiprostitution legislation.[55] Because the bill did not violate American treaty relations with China, prohibiting only the immigration of coolies and prostitutes, Congress enacted it into law with virtually no opposition. Inspired by such easy victory, Page and the other exclusionists pursued their efforts to renegotiate the Burlingame Treaty.

The intensified campaign was aided in 1876 by the California legislature, which placed anti-Chinese lobbyists on the government payroll by authorizing the city of San Francisco to appropriate money from its general fund for the expenses of a delegation appointed to voice the state's grievances in Washington.[56] During the following year, however, the exclusion movement acquired a new and troublesome ally that necessitated a restructuring of its rhetoric. Intense labor unrest dominated both California and the nation in 1877 and spawned two important events, each occurring in July: the eastern railroad strikes and, of greater importance to this study, the formation of the Workingmen's Party in California.[57]

On the state level, a new political party threw established lines of support into disarray, especially among the Democrats, and both major parties sought to neutralize voter desertions by reidentifying themselves with California's white workers. Most of the infant party's platform—issues such as the eight-hour day, better wages, and dissolution of private monopolies—would alienate business and industrial leaders, so Republicans and Democrats sought their identification with labor in the anti-Chinese movement and, in so doing, changed its focus.

In voicing opposition to the immigration of Chinese laborers the Workingmen's Party claimed that the immigrants served as the tools through which employers depressed wages and deprived white workers of the opportunity to better themselves. Although political leaders such as Horace Page had also mentioned the harmful effects of Chinese immigration on white workers, their major emphasis before 1877 had been that immigration posed a moral and medical threat to white society.[58] They had portrayed Chinese prostitution as the worst element in an enterprise that hampered California's ability to attract honorable families to the state, denouncing male laborers as both coolies and the primary supporters of Chinese prostitutes, opium dens, and tongs. Still, they had at least referred to the Chinese as a threat to "American" labor and therefore could easily assume a pro-labor posture by recasting the exclusion movement's moral focus into one that emphasized the economic problems associated with Chinese immigration. Moreover, by placing the blame on the Chinese themselves, they could urge Congress to prohibit future immigration without echoing the antimanagement rhetoric of the Workingmen's Party.

Neither the Republicans nor the Democrats publicly acknowledged their accommodation to the California labor movement, but their continuing effort to force a renegotiation of the Burlingame Treaty produced a sequence of events that began in the winter of 1877 and reflected an effort to portray the two major parties as friends of workers. On December 12 of that year, seventeen thousand members of the newly formed Workingmen's Party, headed by Dennis Kearney, petitioned both Congress and the president to negotiate a revision of the Burlingame Treaty.[59] Nine days later the California legislature pushed Kearney and his followers from the spotlight by calling for a state referendum on the Chinese issue thirty days before the next general or special election.[60]

Although no one doubted that voters would express overwhelming opposition to Chinese immigration, state leaders hoped to use this landslide decision as leverage in the push for a revised treaty: "The governor shall prepare a memorial from the people of the State of California, attested by the secretary of state, with the great seal attached, setting forth in brief the question submitted to the electors and the vote thereon, and send copies thereof to the President and Vice-President of the United States, to each Cabinet minister, Senator, Member of the House of Representatives, and the governor of each State and Territory."[61]

By placing this forceful statement of California's opposition to Chinese immigration in the hands of so many elected officials, the legislature accomplished two objectives. First, it informed every aspiring presidential candidate, as well as every governor and representative seeking support for his own causes, that California's allegiance depended upon a new treaty with China. Then, it suggested to the white workers of the state that their interests could be best protected by Democrats and Republicans without the need for a radical third party.

Page and the anti-Chinese forces in Congress used these resolutions and referenda to launch a second line of attack in the battle for exclusion: passage of additional federal legislation that would force the president to initiate a renegotiation of the Burlingame Treaty. Early in 1879, apparently for the purpose of protecting the anti-Chinese reputations of those members of Congress from California who shared his party affiliation, Democrat Albert Willis of Kentucky led the House Committee on Education and Labor to join Page in sponsoring a bill that would prohibit all shipmasters from transporting more than ten Chinese passengers to the United States, in any combination of men and women, on a single voyage.[62] Willis also portrayed the committee's recommendation as a means to sensibly end the undesirable immigration of an inferior race. Citing the government's previous "failure" to peacefully assimilate Indians and blacks into American society, he urged the Congress to restrict the future immigration of the Mongolian, "who has neither the docility and humility of the one [the African] nor the consciousness of inferior civilization which distinguishes the other [the Indian]."[63] Thus, his public statements suggest that Willis, besides seeking to bolster the popularity of his party in California, supported the exclusionists from the perspective of a former pro-slavery Democrat.

The committee's proposal initially received a less than favorable response from many members of Congress for at least two reasons. First, such a restriction, although not directly opposing the right of Chinese citizens to immigrate to America, clearly violated the spirit of the Burlingame Treaty by making it extremely difficult for Chinese immigrants to migrate freely to the United States.[64] Second, the proposal, if allowed to become law, would mark the end of mass immigration from China and severely cripple the profits of American shipping companies. As he appealed for their approval, however, Page reminded colleagues of the petition submitted to them by the Workingmen's Party (although never directly referring to its source). Reading its full text, he then urged Congress to support the bill "in the interest of society, for the preservation of the purity, order, and prosperity of the intelligent communities that make up the great commonwealths of our free Republic; . . . in behalf of the industrial development of the Pacific States; . . . and in the interest of the workingmen of our own section and of our whole land."[65]

Some House members continued to speak against passage, but a delicate balance of political power characterized the Congress between 1876 and 1880.[66] As reflected in the disputed victory of Rutherford B. Hayes in the presidential election of 1876, near parity existed in both houses of Congress, with the Republicans holding a slight majority in the Senate and the Democrats an equally slim advantage in the House. In 1879, needing every vote to ensure passage of their own bills, most Republicans and Democrats could not afford to risk alienating California in support of immigrants banned from the political process, especially when opposed by such apparent unity. Therefore, after raising the passenger limit to fifteen, the bill gained House approval by more than a two-to-one margin, with the Senate following suit.[67]

By identifying exclusion as a labor issue Page had protected himself from the threat of opponents in the Workingmen's Party, whose candidacy could have eroded his labor support and given some future election to a Democrat. Yet when President Hayes received the legislation, he faced exactly the dilemma that California's anti-Chinese forces had hoped to create for him. He could not ignore the law's contravention of the Burlingame Treaty, but congressional opposition to the document had reached a magnitude that demanded his immediate and decisive response. Seeking to find middle ground, Hayes vetoed the bill as a violation of treaty relations with China but signaled his acquiescence to the anti-Chinese movement by pledging to order a renegotiation of the Burlingame provisions regarding immigration.[68] Page and his allies had achieved the triumph they desired. They knew that the possibility of a federal exclusion act depended on a revised treaty and not on a restriction law that the Supreme Court would eventually nullify. Therefore, the president's veto was not challenged.

Honoring his promise, President Hayes instructed George F. Seward, U.S. minister to China, to solicit the increased cooperation of Chinese authorities in suppressing the emigration of undesirable people and inquire about China's willingness to revise the Burlingame Treaty.[69] In response to Seward's efforts, the Chinese government pledged full support in halting the emigration of "criminals, lewd women, diseased persons, and contract laborers" but insisted that its treaty relationship with America remain unaltered.[70] Hayes realized that this position would not satisfy Congress and appointed a special commission to negotiate a restructuring of the 1868 treaty.

Arriving in Peking on September 27, 1880, the representatives insisted that China agree to such a modification on the grounds that the United States possessed the right to "decide to what extent and under what circumstances that immigration is wholesome and to stop it when it becomes injurious."[71] Although Chinese officials for more than a month refused to alter their position, the commission's persistence, and its assurance that America would enact laws restricting Chinese immigration only as a last resort, finally produced a revised treaty on November 6.[72]

The 1880 treaty deviated dramatically from the immigration provisions of its predecessor, replacing them with language that would permit passage of the Exclusion Act less than eighteen months later.

> Whenever, in the opinion of the government of the United States, the coming of Chinese laborers to the United States or their residence therein affects or threatens to affect the interests of that country or to endanger the good order of the said country or of any locality within the territory thereof, the government of China agrees that the government of the United States may regulate, limit, or suspend such coming or residence, but may not absolutely prohibit it. The limitation or suspension shall be reasonable and shall apply only to Chinese who may go to the United States as laborers, other classes not being included in the limitations. Legislation taken in regard to Chinese laborers will be of such a character only as is necessary to enforce the regulation, limitation, or suspension of immigration, and immigrants shall not be subject to personal maltreatment or abuse.[73]

Thus, the new treaty empowered Congress to stop the flow of Chinese laborers in any way it deemed necessary, providing the legislation was not permanent. Yet even that stipulation mattered little because no chronological limits were established for such a temporary restriction.

Because the Treaty of 1880 recognized the authority of Congress to suspend Chinese immigration, anti-Chinese forces moved toward passage of their long-awaited objective: a federal exclusion act.[74] The campaign for exclusion had gained so much momentum by 1880 that the presidential platforms of both political parties included a promise to restrict Chinese immigration.[75] On January 26, 1882, the Senate Foreign Relations Committee reported its unanimous support of a proposal to suspend the immigration of Chinese laborers for a period of twenty years.[76] Careful not to undermine their recent victory in the 1880 negotiations, the bill's sponsors entitled their proposal "A Bill to Enforce Treaty Stipulations Relating to Chinese." For more than a month the Senate debated whether twenty years exceeded the requisite bounds of "reasonable" suspension, but the bill passed easily on March 9, and the House approved it within hours of its introduction two weeks later.[77]

Cheng Tsao-ju, the Ch'ing minister plenipotentiary in Washington, echoing the Senate debate, formally protested that a twenty-year exclusion violated the 1880 treaty's promise of moderation. In response, President Arthur vetoed the legislation because of its duration, and the anti-Chinese bloc could not override his veto.[78] On April 12, 1882, however, Page introduced a substitute bill "to execute certain treaty stipulations relating to Chinese" that reduced the period of immigration suspension to ten years.[79] Within five days the House had overwhelmingly approved the new proposal, and the Senate concurred before month's end by more than a two-to-one margin.[80] Although Chinese officials once again voiced opposition, President Arthur, faced with a two-thirds majority in the Senate, signed the Exclusion Act into law on May 6.[81] Ironically, this hard-won success signaled the end of Page's political career. Most California voters now considered the problem solved, and they abandoned the champion of exclusion in the November congressional election. Shortly after his defeat Page left the state altogether to practice law in the nation's capital until his death in 1892.[82]

Placed within the context of America's historic movement toward Chinese exclusion, the Page Law united economic, moral, and public health concerns to achieve the exclusionists' first sustained triumph, thereby erecting the foundation upon which they transformed the Chinese question into a national political issue. It promised, if vigorously enforced and applied according to prevailing anti-Chinese stereotypes, to restrict both the immigration of prostitutes and the development of families in the Chinese American community. By preserving the instability of Chinese settlement, the law gave the exclusion movement time to gain momentum and add labor advocacy to its moral emphasis. Thus, the 1875 legislation provided a valuable stopgap measure and represented the strongest possible immigration restriction allowed by the Burlingame Treaty. It was the only restriction bill, before the treaty's revision in 1880, ever to escape nullification by the Supreme Court.

4

The Hong Kong Consuls: Erecting Barriers

In the 1870s the American consular service acted primarily as the country's commercial representative in foreign territory. Consuls inspected the cargoes of ships bound for the United States, established official estimates of their tonnage, and collected the appropriate import duties. In addition, they supervised the operation of homes for destitute sailors, arbitrated disputes concerning goods or personal property damaged on American ships, and served as executors for the estates of Americans who died in the areas under their jurisdiction. They performed no regular diplomatic duties but were often used in that capacity because of their convenience to foreign governments and acquaintance with local authorities. Officially, they represented the State Department, but they also submitted quarterly commerce reports to the Department of the Treasury.

Shipping lines frequently accused the consuls of overestimating the weight of a vessel's cargo or assessing extra charges for their services. Most of these complaints remained unsubstantiated, however, and the State Department rarely disciplined its consular officials for engaging in improper activities. In fact, the department generally permitted the collection of personal fees, averaging from $5 to $10, as a means of supplementing the salaries of the consuls.[1] Thus, the integrity of the American consular service during this period is difficult to evaluate. Some appointees no doubt used their positions for economic gain and in ways that Americans living in the late twentieth century—or even the early twentieth century—would not accept from their country's diplomatic representatives, but these officials were not diplomats. As commercial agents, whom the government paid little but allowed to share in the profits generated by America's foreign trade, their job was to protect the overseas commercial interests of the United States rather than serve as ambassadors for American democracy. In that capacity they received little respect at home and often ran afoul of shipping companies that resented their authority to collect personal fees for their services, but the State Department generally approved of and appreciated their actions.

Confronted with this ambivalent record of consular integrity, Mary Coolidge and her successors have based their disregard for the Page Law on the alleged corruption that characterized the American consuls in Hong Kong. Along with their other duties, the commercial focus of American consulates also made them responsible for authorizing the departures of people seeking to immigrate to the United States from foreign ports. Thus, the Page Law required all Chinese emigrants to undergo an examination by the American consul at their port of departure. The consul determined the nature of this examination, which he reported to the State Department for approval, but through it was expected to determine the legality of each person's emigration and ferret out prostitutes among the female applicants.[2] Those whom he certified as acceptable then received clearance to the United States, while persons failing to meet the Page Law's standards of morality lost the privilege of emigration. Because State Department records show that "all Chinese emigration to the United States is from Hong Kong," the consular official in that city assumed the role of chief interrogator for all prospective Chinese emigrants.[3] In that capacity, although American port authorities and judges provided some supplementary support, primary responsibility for enforcing the law lay squarely on the consul's shoulders.[4]

Recognizing the Hong Kong consul's central role as enforcer of the Page Law, Coolidge has characterized the holder of that office in 1875 as a talented extortionist. According to Consul John Mosby, his official successor, David Bailey generated several thousand dollars of additional income each year through an elaborate system of bribes. In addition to the ship captains and merchants who regularly paid him "extra money" for reduced tonnage duties and required shipping vouchers, Consul Mosby reported that Bailey also charged Chinese women an additional fee of $10 to $15 for processing their emigration applications.[5] These charges of dishonesty led Coolidge to conclude that David Bailey's efforts to fulfill the responsibilities given to him by the Page Law were merely attempts to "cover up maladministration in office by an appearance of zeal."[6] Lucie Cheng Hirata, writing seventy years later, also cited corruption in the Bailey administration as the central reason for her conclusion that the law's effectiveness remains doubtful.[7] More recently, Benson Tong, although much kinder in his assessment of Bailey's character, has sustained this condemnation of consular performance.[8]

Neither Coolidge nor Hirata attempt to account for the decline in female immigration from 1875 to 1882 despite the purported corruption of consular authorities. Tong, however, has acknowledged this substantial reduction and portrayed Bailey as one who "seemed enthusiastic in checking the trafficking" while refocusing his accusations of dishonesty on Sheldon Loring, interim consul following Bailey's departure.[9] Yet both perspectives depend entirely on reports filed by John Mosby, suggesting that the nature and effect of alleged consular corruption requires further investigation. If Mosby exaggerated or fabricated his charges, then the Page Law may have exerted a much stronger prohibitive force than Mary Coolidge, Lucie Cheng Hirata, and Benson Tong have recognized. Therefore, a comprehensive measurement of the law's impact can only be obtained by comparing the administrations of all three of the men who enforced the Page Law: David Bailey, Sheldon Loring, and John Mosby.

David H. Bailey: 1875–77

Despite accusations that he disregarded administrative ethics, David Bailey's relation to the Page Law was one of champion and crusader. Upon receiving word of its passage, Bailey remarked to his superiors that he hoped to "be able to put a stop to the traffic in women immigrating to the United States for lewd and immoral purposes."[10] He also spoke of his "strong and radical views . . . as to the relation of the sexes in emigrating from China to foreign countries" and was reported by one Hong Kong newspaper to have claimed almost singular responsibility for the law's enactment.[11] Indeed, Mary Coolidge herself has noted that anti-Chinese congressmen quoted Bailey more than any other authority.[12] Thus, as he read his orders concerning enforcement of the statute, he had played an important role in securing its passage.

Although a desire to draw attention away from his other activities may have motivated Bailey's commitment to the Page Law, his zeal proved to be much more than an appearance. The fact that at least two hundred female applicants had appeared at the consulate on the same day he received the announcement of the law's passage prevented Bailey from having the time to plot an elaborate strategy for evaluating their character. He responded to this inconvenience, however, by subjecting each woman to a rigid interrogation consisting of the following questions:

> Have you entered into any contract or agreement with any person or persons whomsoever, for a term of service within the United States for lewd and immoral purposes?
> Do you wish of your own free and voluntary will to go to the United States?
> Do you go to the United States for the purposes of prostitution?
> Are you married or single?
> What are you going to the United States for?
> What is to be your occupation there?
> Have you lived in a house of prostitution in Hong Kong, Macao, or China?
> Have you engaged in prostitution in either of the above places?
> Are you a virtuous woman?
> Do you intend to live a virtuous life in the United States?

> Do you know that you are at liberty now to go to the United States, or remain at home in your own country, and that you cannot be forced to go away from your home?[13]

Bailey did not report the number of women rejected after this first examination, but he then took the remaining applicants to the harbor master of the British colonial government to seek his aid in ascertaining their virtue. This officer asked the same questions, cross-examining each applicant and employing secret detectives to expose impostors.[14] Consul Bailey then reported that "those who passed a satisfactory examination, so as not to come within the class prohibited by law, were allowed to go on board the steamer."[15] Finally, after she boarded the ship, the consul questioned each woman once again.[16] Those who were successful in enduring all three ordeals received certificates of morality to be presented to the port authorities in San Francisco. The consul never indicated the exact number of applicants who prompted this first attempt at enforcing the Page Law but informed his superior in Washington that "a considerable number were rejected at the first and second examinations." Still, 173 were granted clearance to sail for California.[17] Bailey then lamented, "I am not entirely satisfied with the result of this first case arising under the recent Act; but every effort was made that could be, in so short a time, to enforce the law."[18]

The American consul quickly converted his dissatisfaction into action. First, he solicited a guarantee of cooperation from the British colonial authorities. In seeking their help, he no doubt found willing partners. Hong Kong officials had recently embarked on their own effort to suppress not only the emigration of prostitutes but also the buying and selling of human beings for any purpose.[19] Moreover, Bailey supplemented this support by enlisting the aid of the Tung Wah Hospital Committee, an association of the most prominent Chinese businessmen in Hong Kong.[20] The organization had petitioned the government to prosecute the suppliers of emigrant prostitutes as early as 1872, subsequently employing its own detective staff to investigate possible abuses.[21]

Although Coolidge suggests that Consul Bailey had merely accepted the Tung Wah Committee's independent offer of help, articles from both the *China Mail* and *Hong Kong Press* confirm his initiation of their discussions on the issue.[22] Through such meetings the two parties formulated a joint plan for halting the emigration of Chinese prostitutes, tightening the "leniency" of Bailey's first attempt. Their strategy was to require from each woman an official declaration of purpose in emigrating and personal morality, which she would submit to the American consul along with an application for clearance to America.[23] After the completion of these requirements, the onerous process of approval began.

> The Declaration when filled in, will, in each case, be submitted at once to the Committee, who will after a careful examination report the evidence as to character to me. A

list of the intending immigrants will be sent at the same time to the Colonial Government for investigation. The day before the sailing of the vessel, an examination of each applicant will take place at the Consulate. On the day of the sailing, an examination will be had at the Harbor Master's office and again on board the ship, just before sailing . . . photographs will be used as a means of identification.[24]

Bailey supplemented his series of investigations with Tung Wah intelligence activities, which helped him detect the smuggling of uncertified women. He also sent telegrams to San Francisco port authorities to warn them of the imminent arrival of those who had eluded detection.[25]

In his maintenance of this complex system, the consul also proved diligent. Indeed, his letters show that he used every branch of the examination network he had established. To the British colonial secretary, he sent correspondence constructed in the following format:

I have the honor to enclose for the information of the Emigration Office a list of Chinese females who propose to emigrate to the United States on the 17th instant by the Steamer "Quang Si."

I shall feel extremely obliged if possibly I can be informed whether or not they are going to the United States under contract for lewd and immoral purposes, in contravention of the Act of Congress approved March 3rd 1875.[26]

In addition to his continued solicitation of British aid, correspondence with the Tung Wah Hospital Committee dominated Bailey's official letter writing, and it was in response to their reports that he sent the telegrams to San Francisco warning of the expected debarkation of fraudulent immigrants.[27] He also secured protection for women who were sent back to China by American missionaries after their rescue from Chinatown brothels.[28]

After he had completed all areas of the examination process, Consul Bailey sometimes sent letters ahead of the steamers to the collector of customs in San Francisco, urging him to conduct his own thorough investigation because the Chinese were "exceedingly deceptive" in their attempts to circumvent the law.[29] Thus, the evidence of both Bailey's reports to the State Department and documents that record the performance of his duties suggest that he made preventing the emigration of Chinese prostitutes from Hong Kong a priority assignment. Moreover, the State Department did not require Consul Bailey to establish conclusively that a prospective female emigrant was a prostitute but permitted him to reject any woman he suspected of immigrating for "lewd and immoral purposes." Thus, with the burden of proof placed on the applicants, and given Bailey's judgment regarding the Chinese proclivity for deception, his enforcement of the Page Law would have complicated the immigration of Chinese wives and daughters as well as prostitutes.

In regard to the extra fee Bailey was alleged to have collected from prospective female emigrants, Coolidge relies upon John Mosby to substantiate her claims that the bribe served as the actual means through which certificates of character were granted. In his report of the extra charge, however, Mosby failed to mention that the bribe was not offered at the close of the examinations but at the time of application.[30] Female emigrants still faced the rigorous interrogations of the British harbor master and Tung Wah Hospital Committee in addition to Bailey's own examination, and no female emigrant was known to have received a certificate of character without the agreement of all three investigative elements.[31] Thus, rather than a means of avoiding detection as a prostitute, the bribes that Chinese women reportedly paid to Bailey would have served as guarantees that their applications would receive proper consideration. Therefore, the consular bribe, although illegal if it existed, would have represented yet another hardship that Bailey placed upon prospective emigrants—a hardship that would have created a greater problem for the wives of laborers, who possessed limited resources, than for the wealthy tongs whose traffic in prostitution Bailey had claimed responsibility for stopping.[32]

Throughout his administration, American port authorities accused David Bailey of improperly enforcing the Page Law on only one occasion. On February 1, 1877, Thomas Shannon, collector of customs in San Francisco, wrote a letter of complaint to the consul because Bailey had failed to forward certificates for the women who had recently arrived on two consecutive steamers.[33] Shannon colored even that criticism, however, with appreciation for the consul's previous efforts to enforce the law, asking him, "Have you abandoned your admirable plan for prevention of importation of women for immoral purposes, or is the non receipt of the photos and certificates due to some irregularity in the mails[?]"[34] Bailey responded by blaming the oversight on a clerical error and assuring the collector that he had examined each of the women and found them to be respectable.[35] Neither man gave any indication that he suspected the women whose credentials were not forwarded of being prostitutes.

Thus, although the available documentation neither confirms nor refutes Coolidge's charges of corruption in the Bailey administration, his record regarding the Page Law reveals a consistent commitment to its enforcement. Moreover, if he did collect bribes from Chinese women seeking to immigrate to the United States, the evidence suggests that these additional fees made the journey more, and not less, difficult. The persistence of the consul in regard to curbing prostitution appears to have been part of a more broadly focused commitment to eliminating the overseas transportation of all Chinese citizens against their will. Robert Irick's study of the coolie trade has also credited him with attempting, as early as 1871, to lobby the Spanish and Portuguese governments on behalf of Chinese laborers ensnared by this enterprise.[36] The State Department must not have regarded his overall administration of the consulate as irregular. Although Mary Coolidge fails to mention it, Bailey received a promotion to vice-consul general and moved to Shanghai in 1878.

In the presidential election two years earlier, Rutherford B. Hayes had made opposition to governmental corruption a central element in his campaign. Shortly after taking office, he had ordered all executive departments to make appointments on the basis of merit only while continuing to advocate civil service. In 1877, as part of his reform effort, he had even removed Chester A. Arthur and Alonzo B. Cornell, both well-connected members of his own party, from their positions in the Treasury Department. Given Hayes's scrutiny, officials in the Department of State must have judged Bailey innocent of wrongdoing in his administration of the Hong Kong consulate. Otherwise, in light of Mosby's formal accusations, one would expect Secretary of State William Evarts to have dismissed him from the post of vice-consul general or to at least have reprimanded him. Indeed, David Bailey had been appointed to the consular service during Ulysses S. Grant's administration—the very target of the reform campaign that had made Hayes president. Had the evidence supported allegations of corruption brought against Bailey by his own appointee to the Hong Kong consulate, it is unlikely that the president would have missed such an easy opportunity to bolster his reformist image by failing to take punitive action.[37]

Like many others in his position, Bailey no doubt had taken advantage of the department's leniency toward consular attempts at supplementing inadequate salaries with "extra" income from foreigners. Yet the persistent charges levied against him may have stemmed primarily from the decision of his official successor, for reasons certain only to himself, to launch a vicious attack on the consul's reputation. Perhaps that kind of vendetta accounts for the even more egregious character assassination that Mosby unleashed on the man who served during the interim between Bailey's departure and his arrival.

H. Sheldon Loring: 1877–79

When Bailey nominated him for vice-consul in 1877, Sheldon Loring was returning to a position that he had initially assumed four years earlier. Having served as a Union colonel in the Inspector General's Department during the Civil War, he was first appointed head of shipping and emigration at the consulate and then elevated to the post of vice-consul in 1873.[38] Complaints about his mishandling of State Department funds allocated for the compensation of discharged seamen, however, had led to his removal from office in 1875.[39] Then, when a subsequent investigation found Loring innocent of such charges, the State Department reinstated him in response to Bailey's nomination. Shortly after his assistant's return,

Consul Bailey requested an extended leave of absence and left Loring in charge of the consular duties. At the end of the following year Bailey finally resigned his office and briefly left the consular service. The State Department then elevated Colonel Loring to the rank of acting consul, a position he held until John Mosby's arrival in February 1879.

Upon assuming his post, Mosby described the acting consul as a dishonest and inept pirate, whose chief function under Consul Bailey had involved the collection of revenues from bribes and other illegal sources—a description that has led such scholars as Elmer Sandmeyer to identify the year of his appointment as the point at which the prostitute trade resumed.[40] Although such "vital" issues as the improper numbering of consular dispatches abound in Loring's official correspondence, supporting this portrayal, further study suggests that Mosby exaggerated his evaluation. His difficulties with the State Department's numbering system do raise a certain doubt about his competence, but Loring's military experience suggests that he was far more than the bungling cutthroat described by Consul Mosby. Furthermore, a more detailed examination of the documents relating to the administration of his office shows that Colonel Loring performed his duties with dedication and at least minimal efficiency.

In regard to Chinese immigration, the surviving evidence indicates that Acting Consul Loring did not neglect his responsibility for enforcement of the Page Law. Indeed, he diligently informed port authorities in San Francisco of intelligence reports regarding women suspected of possessing forged certificates while warning the representatives of steamship companies that he would deal severely with those who tried to circumvent the statute. For example, Loring sent the following message to a Pacific Mail agent after a steamer belonging to his company arrived in San Francisco with more than twenty-five uncertified Chinese passengers:

> It is hardly necessary for me to call your attention to the fact that this is a breach of law and one that at this time the Courts of the United States are not inclined to view with any degree of leniency when brought before them.
>
> I have therefore to request that you will please aid me in the execution of the law, and the carrying out of my instructions as to cases like the one in point, by warning the officers and others employed on the various steamers of the line of the serious nature of such illegal practices, and of the penalty that is certain to follow, both as to themselves individually as well as the Company that employs them.[41]

Thus, Mosby's charge that Sheldon Loring either lacked the ability to perform the duties of acting consul or made no attempt to carry them out loses much of its credibility when compared with historical evidence. Colonel Loring may not have distinguished himself as an unusually capable consular official, but his training and the record of his service suggest that he was both qualified and responsible.

The question of Loring's honesty emerged from his frequent association with illegal activities, such as the allegations that led to his earlier dismissal as vice-consul and Mosby's scathing report of his performance as acting consul. Yet the State Department never judged him guilty of wrongdoing, and the only primary evidence related to Colonel Loring's alleged improprieties supports his integrity. When the assistant secretary of state questioned him concerning a complaint that he had violated an executive order by charging a $5 fee for the verification of landing certificates, Loring offered a straightforward answer:

> In reply, I beg respectfully to refer you to my No. 444 bearing date December 17, 1877 addressed to the Hon. F. W. Seward, and to his reply thereto No. 188 bearing date 28 January 1878, received at this office March 29. Immediately on the receipt of this dispatch with Circular enclosed, I ceased to charge the $5.00 as provided in Paragraph 333 Fee No. 30 Consular Regulations 1874.
>
> With reference to my disposition of the fee of $5.00 collected in the case referred to, I beg respectfully to refer you to my reports for the 1st Quarter 1878. In the record of Treasury fees under date of February 16th 1878 item No. 235 you will find the fee of $5.00 in full credited to the Government.[42]

Although this one defense does not conclusively exonerate Loring, it still contradicts Mosby's portrayal of him as an unscrupulous criminal—a portrayal the consul never reinforced with substantive evidence. At worst, Sheldon Loring appears to have been guilty of doing no more than following the practices of many other consular officials who often charged extralegal fees in order to gain additional income.

In addition to the lack of incriminating documentation contained in Loring's records, Mosby undermined the veracity of his reports through his own actions as consul. Upon arriving in Hong Kong, for example, he decried the incompetent negligence of his predecessor by accusing Loring of totally abandoning the consular examination of prospective female emigrants, originated by Bailey. In a later report to the State Department, however, Consul Mosby characterized his own interrogation as "superfluous" considering the rigidity with which the British authorities conducted their investigations.[43]

Colonel Loring had inherited from his former superior an effective system of cooperative examination by American and British officials and by the most prominent Chinese businessmen in Hong Kong. Scarcity of resources makes the level at which he maintained this system impossible to determine. Yet some scant information does provide a dim reflection of the acting consul's activities. During the only quarter for which a record of his correspondence has survived, the second quarter of 1878, he received no letters concerning female emigration and sent three (6.8 percent of his total correspondence). All of the letters were mailed to the Tung

Wah Hospital Committee.[44] If one regards that quarter as normal, then Loring clearly failed to participate in the examination system with the same intensity as his predecessor. Still, he did not abandon the system altogether.

Perhaps hindered by declining American commitment to uncovering attempted emigration by prostitutes, the other two components in Bailey's plan continued to administer their interrogative functions.[45] Furthermore, an additional group of Hong Kong businessmen had created their own organization in the fall of 1878, adopting elimination of the prostitute trade as one of its major goals.[46] No doubt both aided and prodded by such assistance, Loring also remained at least an active part of the process. Although the period in which he served as acting consul coincided with an increase in the number of Chinese women arriving in the United States from 77 in 1877 to 354 in 1878, nothing, despite Sandmeyer's statement to the contrary, indicates that the increase was composed of prostitutes.[47]

Because none of the consuls ever reported the number of women whom they rejected as unfit immigrants, the multiplicity of arrivals may reflect no more than a rise in the number of Chinese female applicants. Although lamenting the inability of local endeavors to succeed in eradicating the prostitute trade, Elizabeth Sinn has suggested that they were thwarted during the late 1870s by expanding Chinese immigrant communites in the Straits settlements that offered more secure profits for the industry than did an increasingly hostile United States.[48] When Col. John Mosby arrived there in February of 1879 on his self-proclaimed mission to bring a renaissance in the integrity and efficiency of the Hong Kong consulate, he in fact found the Page Law still performing its role in preventing a balance of the sexes in Chinese American society.

John S. Mosby: 1879–82

John Mosby had served as a Confederate cavalry officer during the Civil War. In 1863 Gen. J. E. B. Stuart appointed him commander of a guerrilla unit known as "Mosby's Partisan Rangers"—a position in which he distinguished himself, having risen to the rank of colonel and emerging as one of the leading officers in the southern cavalry by the war's end. After the South's defeat, he had returned to his native Virginia and taken up the law practice that was his occupation before the war. He then followed the lead of Gen. James Longstreet, Lee's second in command, by becoming a Republican and supporting Grant for the presidency. Then, in the final quarter of 1878, he was appointed American consul to Hong Kong as a part of President Hayes's reform program. Shortly after assuming his duties, Mosby began to gain for himself the reputation of being a great rehabilitator of the consular service.

Upon his arrival at the consulate in February 1879, Mosby began to search for abuses with relentless determination. When he decided that Sheldon Loring had participated in illegal activities, he forced the vice-consul to resign. He then reported to the State Department that he had uncovered a scheme in which thousands of dollars were annually collected from shipping firms as extra wages for the consul. He then fired Peter Smith, the shipping master in charge of collecting and disbursing the wages of a lodging house for destitute sailors.[49] Mosby also turned his reformist attention toward female emigration, eliminating the bribe that his predecessors had allegedly collected as part of the application process.[50] In addition to this action, he took upon himself the responsibility of personally interrogating every Chinese woman who sought to leave for the United States and intensified an already active relationship between the consulate and the Tung Wah Hospital Committee.[51]

As a result of his efforts—probably made successful by following David Bailey's policy of expecting dishonesty when dealing with the Chinese—Mosby could report to his superior that "during my residence in Hong Kong of over three years less than two hundred Chinese women have gone from here to the United States."[52] In compiling this successful record of restriction, however, he had created no new procedure. In fact, he maintained essentially the same relationship with the Chinese merchants that Bailey had created and Loring had used: "I do not issue (a certificate) to any woman going to the United States unless they are bonded for by the 'Tung Wah Hospital Committee,' (which is an association of the most respectable Chinamen here), or some other person known to me who knows the woman."[53] Yet despite that nearly identical plan, Mosby presented his program to the State Department as though he had originated it, making no mention of how he came into contact with the "Tung Wah" men or the process by which they bonded emigrants. Perhaps such self-promotion explains why Mary Coolidge inaccurately memorialized him as the man who "accepted the services of the Tung Wah Hospital Committee in ascertaining the character of women emigrants and was thanked for his cooperation in suppressing the export of prostitutes by the Chinese Consul-General."[54]

John Mosby's desire to appear more of a consular reformer than he actually was casts a cloud over criticisms of his predecessors. Although consistently condemning them as pirates and incompetents, he made many of their practices his own. For example, in addition to retaining the old system of emigrant examinations, Mosby complained to the assistant secretary of state that, because previous policy had allowed Bailey and Loring to keep revenue from emigration fees, a new directive requiring him to remit it to the Treasury Department was unfair.[55] Furthermore, he had decried Loring's practice of granting certificates to women cleared by the colonial harbor master without conducting his own examination, yet in 1882 he wrote to the State Department and port authorities in San Francisco to tell them that he would no longer examine Chinese women desiring to emigrate on foreign vessels. After commenting about the thoroughness of British investigations, Mosby sought to justify this refusal by arguing that the Page Law only required certificates of character from Chinese women traveling on American ships.[56]

When anti-Chinese forces in the United States began to protest his actions, the consul brought his denunciation of the men who came before him to an ironic conclusion. In a June 21, 1882, letter to the San Francisco collector of customs, Mosby, who since arriving in Hong Kong had launched repeated attacks against their alleged laxity, now defended his own abandonment of the consular examinations by accusing them of extralegal severity:

> The whole apparatus and machinery of photographs, descriptive lists, sureties, and passports which were devised by my predecessor without any authority of law, I have now abolished. I continued these after assuming charge of this Consulate without any charge for the trouble from deference to established precedent and because it was a sort of obstructive proceeding which, while it did no harm, kept some of the worst characters from going. A clamor having been raised in San Francisco on account of some irregularity in the form of some of these papers, I have determined to grant no more and to do only my legal duty in the matter.[57]

The pronouncement occurred too near implementation of the Exclusion Act to exert an impact on Chinese female immigration. Still, over the course of three years Consul Mosby had accused his predecessors of both criminal failure to enforce the Page Law and overly zealous efforts to ensure its effectiveness. In each case he referred to the same actions by Bailey and Loring but charged them with negligence in order to justify his reform rhetoric and with undue severity when facing complaints about his own dereliction of duty.

Such inconsistencies render the consul an unreliable witness and call his entire evaluation of the Bailey and Loring administrations into question. Throughout his tenure at the Hong Kong consulate, Mosby acted like a reformer with no issue for reform. He accused the previous consuls of corruption where none existed and exaggerated charges that may have been genuine. After exhausting those allegations, he then launched a campaign to clarify the difference between official and unofficial consular activities.[58] Next, he turned to the task of submitting his formal reinterpretation of the Page Law. In fact, nearly all the consular dispatches Mosby sent to Washington from 1879 to 1882 consisted of complaints. When lacking incentive to argue legal issues he expressed his criticisms on the method of sending mail to the consulate, or the shortage of official stationery in his office, or the conduct of other consuls in China. One of his most frequent grievances was that the secretary of state or the president had not answered his last letter of complaint.[59]

Mosby's obsession with finding fault coincides with his propensity to misrepresent administration of the Page Law under Bailey and Loring. With the remarkable exception of his obviously unpublished reference to their overly zealous methods of enforcement, he portrayed both men as unscrupulous opportunists who saw every consular responsibility as a chance to extort money from those who would be affected by its fulfillment. That description could have emanated from any one, or a combination, of at least three factors. First, the consul may have sought to discredit Bailey and Loring merely as a means of validating his own actions. Second, his apparent instability may suggest that they represented the most logical "first targets" in his self-appointed crusade for reform. Finally, bitterness over the Civil War might have motivated him. Both Bailey and Loring had served as Union officers during the war and become colonels without distinguishing themselves in battle. Mosby, however, had elevated himself to the same rank in the Southern cavalry through heroism and had served under perhaps the most flamboyant and controversial general in the Confederate army. Thus, as he sat writing reports from a relatively insignificant British colony, the humiliation of two men whom he regarded as both inferiors and enemies may have represented his attempt to gain a measure of revenge.

While the motives for its creation remain uncertain, Mosby's caricature of his predecessors clearly misled Mary Coolidge and produced such a convincing portrait that even some contemporary historians have merely followed her error in their descriptions of the Page Law and its enforcement. Had the consuls who preceded him actually distinguished themselves only in the areas of corruption and ineptitude, then the statute would have proven ineffective in preventing either legitimate immigrants or prostitutes from coming to America. Yet the best available evidence suggests that he grossly misrepresented the truth on this matter and therefore that his allegations should be discounted. Furthermore, the failure of the 1875 law to satisfy its sponsor's desire to protect his state from the dangers of Chinese immigration should not be regarded as a basis for doubting its effectiveness. No matter how faithfully U.S. consuls in Hong Kong had enforced it, the legislation could never have prevented, or even delayed, passage of the Exclusion Act. Page and the other exclusionists had adopted as their primary objective the prohibition of Chinese male immigration. Although providing an effective deterrent against women, his antiprostitution law offered no practical means of stopping the men. Given that shortcoming, he and his colleagues still would have pressed for the enactment of severer legislation, even if the Page Law had entirely excluded female immigrants.

Finally, consular records indicate that Consul Bailey, rather than destroying the law's effectiveness through his reported corruption, made it a central element in the work of his administration. Sheldon Loring, his temporary successor, failed to match Bailey's zeal but did continue to enforce the statute. In fact, the only documented breakdown in the Page Law's enforcement occurred when Consul

Mosby decided to ignore seven years of State Department policy and reinterpret his role in its implementation. With the brief exception of Mosby's action, consular officers in Hong Kong consistently represented a formidable barrier for Chinese females attempting to join their husbands and parents in the United States. Moreover, the period from 1875 to 1882 appears to have also marked the years in which both Hong Kong's colonial officials and Chinese leaders demonstrated their greatest vigilance in combating the would-be suppliers of women for Chinese American brothels.[60]

Faced with such a powerful combination of deterrents, the communication lines that connected emigrants to their home villages undoubtedly informed families of the unique perils awaiting female applicants in Hong Kong. Women denied certificates at the consulate would have recounted their experiences upon returning to the homes of their parents-in-law, whereas repatriating emigrants would have brought stories about the subsequent troubles of those who had passed the consular examinations. Therefore, in addition to turning away applicants, consular efforts to enforce the Page Law likely convinced many Chinese wives and daughters not to attempt emigration at all.[61] In the final months before exclusion Consul Mosby's refusal to issue certificates lessened the initial trauma for those Chinese women courageous enough to board the steamers, but his action produced a strong response in San Francisco to the resulting rise in female immigration.[62]

The experiences of Chinese women in the United States indicate that Hong Kong did not contain all the barriers hindering their immigration. Similar obstructions crossed the ocean with them. The customs collector's examination replaced that of the consul, and state and federal judges repeated the interrogations conducted by American and British officials and the Tung Wah Hospital Committee. Unlike their ordeals on the other side of the Pacific, the new obstacles would ultimately collapse. When carried back through the normal channels of village and clan ties, however, they must have represented yet another psychological hurdle for women who were contemplating the attempt. When they reached the San Francisco docks, Chinese female immigrants, who had already run a gauntlet of consular examinations, found getting off the steamers a less difficult but equally disturbing adventure.

5

The San Francisco Port Authorities and Judges: Reluctant Liberators

In the letter to Consul Mosby on August 28, 1879, Thomas Shannon, then collector of customs in San Francisco, congratulated Mosby for having stopped the flow of "lewd women" to his port. Shannon then exhorted the consul to continue his pivotal role in enforcing the Page Law, reminding him that "the fact . . . you have succeeded demonstrates the truth of my theory hitherto expressed to your predecessor, that vigilance and activity on the part of the Consul at Hong Kong was the proper way to enforce the law."[1] Therefore, as this statement suggests, port officials fluctuated in their attitudes toward the 1875 statute, voicing unqualified support while cautiously attempting to minimize their responsibility for making it effective. In seeking to account for such an ambivalent posture, the evidence suggests three complimentary factors.

First, although they shared in the desire to restrict Chinese female immigration, efforts to aid the enforcement of the Page Law created a great deal of extra work for customs officials. Upon receiving word of the new law's enactment, the port surveyor found himself ill-prepared to conduct thorough examinations when faced with large numbers of female arrivals. A letter to the secretary of the treasury, dated April 20, 1875, complained of serious understaffing at his office and requested permission to hire temporary female inspectors who could conduct the required physical examinations of Chinese women. In endeavoring to illustrate the need for additional personnel, the surveyor provided a rare glimpse of the landing of Chinese women at the San Francisco docks: "I beg leave to report that at this Port it occasionally happens that there will arrive in vessels on Steamers female passengers, and in the Steamers from China as many as two hundred at one arrival. It also occasionally happens that the only lady inspector at this port (and there is but one) is detained from her duties by sickness or casualty."[2] Fearful of the increasing volume of Chinese female immigrants coming to America during the late 1860s and early 1870s, port authorities depended upon the American consul in Hong Kong to limit their numbers and thereby ease the burden of examination in San Francisco.

On top of the problems associated with investigating large numbers of Chinese women, rejection of prospective female immigrants created much greater difficulties for customs officials than for the consuls in Hong Kong. Although the Page Law empowered the customs collector to refuse a landing to any female arrival who failed his examination of character, it also permitted those whom the collector rejected to file a petition for a writ of habeas corpus and overturn his decision. Until the desperate months between exclusion's passage and implementation, no women sought to make use of that judicial means of gaining their liberty, perhaps because of the financial burden that such a process entailed. Still, John Mosby, in one of his efforts to clarify the statute's interpretation, illustrated the dilemma that San Francisco authorities confronted:

> When an application is made to a Consul by a Chinese woman intending to emigrate to the United States, the burden of proof devolves upon her to prove a good character as a condition precedent to granting the certificate . . . [but] after a China woman arrives within the jurisdiction of the United States she is *prima facie* a woman of good character, even without a Consul's certificate, and it devolves upon the government to prove that she belongs to the prohibited class before she can be sent back.[3]

Thomas Shannon's correspondence with both Mosby and Bailey implies a sincere desire to aid in the enforcement of the 1875 law. Yet, given the embarrassment that would have resulted from a defeat in the courts, it is not surprising that he refused to act upon any but the most reliable information in denying Chinese women the right to disembark. As a reflection of this understandable caution, the customs collector responded with limited enthusiasm when Otis Gibson, a Chinatown missionary, warned him of the imminent arrival of prostitutes:

> I am in receipt of your letter of the 10th instant advising that you have creditable information that about one hundred Chinese women are expected to arrive by the incoming steamer from China and that they are imported for sale as prostitutes in violation of the recent Act of Congress.
>
> In reply I have to say that while I deem it my duty to take prompt action to carry out the provisions of the law, yet as I am liable for damages if I detain any person in consequence of suspecting him or her to belong to the prohibited class, and it should be decided by the court that such person is not of the class referred to, I have to request that you furnish me with such data or specific evidence in regard to the one hundred women or any one of them, that will enable me to sustain my detaining them should they appeal to the court.[4]

Shannon's concern about liability stemmed from the fear that a ruling against his detention of female immigrants might entitle them to sue the Treasury Department for damages. Such a lawsuit would have presented no personal financial danger to the collector but could have resulted in reprimand, demotion, or dismissal for him. Although no suit of that kind was ever filed, the verdict of the American consul regarding an applicant's suitability for emigration was virtually irreversible. Judges in San Francisco, however, could set aside any action taken by the collector of customs, so the prospect of legal repercussions caused city officials to look toward Hong Kong as the center of authority for suppressing the immigration of Chinese women.

Finally, because similar local and state ordinances had consistently failed to pass the test of constitutionality in federal courts, port authorities hesitated to risk an appeal of their decisions. Fearing a repeat of the fiasco created by their attempts to enforce the 1869 and 1870 California laws and by the series of trials that led to eventual nullification, port authorities preferred to rely upon the American consul's judgment of moral character. As Port Surveyor Giles Gray testified before the California Senate Special Committee on Chinese Immigration in 1876, "The law is practically worthless, so far as this portion of it is concerned [that of the port authorities' right to refuse entry to Chinese women suspected of prostitution]. When they present this certificate here we cannot go beyond that [accepting the consular certificate as proof of good character] from mere suspicion."[5]

Thus, whether resulting from local officials' fear of embarrassment or the monetary limitations of Chinese immigrants, San Francisco courts conducted no habeas corpus trials for Chinese women between 1874 and 1881. Consul Mosby's decision of 1882, however, which allowed female emigrants to board foreign vessels without certificates, stirred both port authorities and the Chinese American community into action. From March to June of that year, as the Exclusion Act's implementation approached, women challenged their deportation in three separate trials that took place in U.S. district and circuit courts.

From the testimony compiled in the first of these trials, the story of fourteen-year-old Loy How emerges. Traveling in the company of four other prospective female immigrants, she had come to San Francisco to join her parents, who had left home together five years earlier. After the port surveyor examined her, however, he discovered that the girl's certificate did not match the one forwarded from Hong Kong. His subsequent actions were undertaken without explanation, but perhaps he suspected the discrepancy to be the work of Chinese tongs. Conceivably, such an organization might have been attempting to smuggle her into the country for service in a Chinatown brothel by paying a woman of reputable character to apply for emigration at the consulate in her place. Upon successfully com-

pleting the requisite examinations she could have then obtained the consul's
certificate and passed it on to Loy How before she boarded the China steamer.

Such a scenario might seem plausible, but evidence does not support its probability. In an interview with the *Daily Press of Hong Kong,* dated August 10, 1875,
Consul Bailey had identified substitution as a major concern in his efforts to prevent the emigration of Chinese prostitutes from Hong Kong. He also pledged to
solicit the help of Chinese and British leaders in devising a plan that would eliminate the problem.[6] True to his word, he had incorporated the British colonial government and the Tung Wah Hospital Committee into the process of investigating
female applicants. Thus, Bailey had designed—and his successors had maintained—an examination procedure aimed specifically at eliminating substitution.

As dictated by his system, Bailey first processed the photographs of female applicants and received character reports from the British registrar general and the
Tung Wah Hospital Committee. Then, on the day before her scheduled departure,
the consul himself conducted a lengthy interrogation of each prospective emigrant.
On the following day he questioned the women individually on two more occasions, once at the British harbor master's office and again on board the steamer
just before it departed Hong Kong for the United States. Only after the completion of the entire examination process did he grant consular certificates, with
photographs attached, to the women whom he judged to be acceptable.[7] It would
have been extremely difficult, if not impossible, for prohibited individuals to take
the place of approved applicants. Yet although they were almost certainly aware
of this procedure, customs officials ordered Loy How's detention as a suspected
prostitute, citing the erroneous certificate she had brought from Hong Kong as
proof that she had traveled to the United States for "lewd and immoral purposes,"
a line of reasoning made sensible only by the suspicion that she had acquired the
certificate by means of substitution.[8]

During the ensuing trial Loy How relied upon a court-appointed interpreter to
convey the following account of her arrival at the San Francisco docks:

Q: Where did she see her mother when she first came?
A: The first time I land on the shore I see her on the dock, on the wharf.
Q: Who was with her if anyone?
A: She says great many Chinamen there. I don't know who they were. I saw my mother.
Q: How did she know it was her mother?
A: Because I know it was my mother. I recognize her.
Q: By her dress? Was she dressed the same as when she saw her in China?
A: She says I don't recognize by dress but by her countenance, her face.
Q: Did she speak to her?
A: No sir.

Q: How near was she to her?

A: Not very far, but pretty far. I didn't talk to her.

Q: Why didn't she speak to her mother?

A: There was a man on board ship wouldn't allow her to talk to her.

Q: How would he stop her? Couldn't she say hello to her mother, speak to her?

A: When I arrived my mother approached me, and the watchman on the dock drove them away, of course I couldn't speak to them.

Q: She didn't speak to her mother?

A: No sir.

Q: Might she not be mistaken about that being her mother? Might it not be someone else?

A: No sir, no mistake. I recognize.[9]

Apparently, Consul Mosby, who had recently informed his superiors that the issuance of consular certificates was unnecessary, had caused Loy How's detention by providing her with a blank certificate and photograph and mailing an outdated certificate from prior examinations as that of the young emigrant.[10]

Despite the caution of customs officials in detaining Chinese women, the journey to America ended with the collector's deportation order for at least some. Although no digest of the number sent back to Hong Kong in this manner has yet been discovered, the few available references suggest that they almost certainly returned no less than a hundred, and possibly several hundred, prospective female immigrants. The *San Francisco Chronicle* reported on July 28, 1882, for example, that the collector of customs had refused to permit the debarkation of nine women from the steamer *Triumph*.[11] They never penetrated the courtrooms of San Francisco, which indicates that they did not appeal the collector's action. Furthermore, Col. F. A. Bee, the American consul for Chinese in San Francisco, testified at Loy How's trial that port authorities had refused the landing of "several" female immigrants during Thomas Shannon's tenure as port surveyor. Bee further intimated that the number of women returned to China after the Page Law's adoption was substantial.[12]

The families of Loy How—and of many other female Chinese who journeyed to San Francisco in the shadow of exclusion—refused to accept defeat. While their loved ones were forced to remain on board the ships that would return them to China, husbands and fathers fled the docks to secure lawyers, who appealed the surveyor's decision, according to the provisions of the Page Law, by petitioning for the writs of habeas corpus in American courts. Those attempts to gain their freedom brought the petitioners before judges who, sharing the popular conviction that prostitutes composed most of Chinatown's female population, regarded their guilt as a foregone conclusion and subjected them to additional interrogations. Although the process sometimes included transferal from the steamers to more oppressive accommodations in the county jail, defense attorneys and steamship companies generally joined forces to overturn such decisions.[13]

At first glance, one might find the owners' support surprising, but the explanation is a fairly simple one. Courts prohibited vessels from leaving port until it could be determined whether they had transported prostitutes in violation of the Page Law. An adverse ruling would not only mean that companies must assume financial responsibility for return of the women but that prosecutors might also file criminal charges against them, which could potentially result in heavy fines and even the loss of their shipping licenses. Therefore, the advantage of monitoring access to their passengers—and of offering eyewitness challenges to any charges of improper actions during the course of the trial—rendered the expense of continuing to house and feed them negligible by comparison. The women, however, could gain freedom only by enduring yet another humiliating ordeal.

The trial of Loy How and her four companions took place in March of 1882. The customs collector had detained all five because they carried incomplete certificates.[14] Determined to contest that action, their families had secured the services of Leander Quint, a prominent San Francisco attorney. As legal counsel for the Pacific Mail Steamship Company (the firm that had transported them to America), Quint had represented the twenty-three female immigrants who gained their freedom through the 1874 trial that produced the Court's *Chy Lung* decision (chapter 3).[15] A British chartering service owned the steamer on which Loy How and her companions had emigrated, however, and no legal relationship existed between Quint and that firm. He had agreed to defend the petitioners as a result of the solicitation—and money— of their loved ones and the Chinese Six Companies, the collection of immigrant benevolent associations representing geographic districts in China and whose leaders served as Chinatown's quasi government. His reputation and success in the earlier case made him a logical although undoubtedly expensive choice. Upon learning of his involvement in the case, District Attorney William Teare responded to the prospect of defeating such a reputable foe in such a popular cause by deciding to present the government's case personally rather than rely on his assistants.

Following the same route traveled by its predecessor eight years earlier, the petition first came before Judge John Hunt in the superior court.[16] District Attorney Teare focused upon the character of the eldest of the women, a returning immigrant named Wah Ah Chin (Wong Ah Chin in some documents) who was thirty-eight. She had first come to America with her husband and eldest child. After establishing a small fishing business in San Francisco, the couple had decided to complete their family's move to the United States. Therefore, her husband had sent Wah Ah Chin back to Canton to collect their two smaller children and then return to San Francisco on one of the Hong Kong steamers.[17] After securing her children's passage, she had been preparing to complete her mission when the grandfather of Loy How, whom she had known for several years, asked her to look after the girl until she could be reunited with her parents at the docks.[18]

Teare used this supervisory relationship to substantiate his charge that Wah Ah Chin had gone to China to purchase a fresh crop of girls for Chinatown brothels. Relying on testimony from the interpreter who had assisted port officials in examining her, the prosecutor noted the older woman's watchful care over her children and her friend's granddaughter, attempting to portray her as an agent for their tong owners.[19] The interpreter described Wah Ah Chin as a wily matron endeavoring to smuggle her employers' slaves into the country. When Judge Hunt asked him to account for the discrepancy between the petitioners' certificates and the information obtained in their interrogations, the interpreter brought the desired picture into focus:

Q: The name she gave to you in conversation was different from that in the paper?
A: The old woman did not differ much but the young ones differed altogether, pretty near no question alike in the paper.[20]

Thus Wah Ah Chin, as a veteran of earlier consular examinations, appeared to have presented a well-rehearsed story, and her charges had exposed their deception when separated from her direction. Teare then sharpened the image by establishing that all of the young girls had given Wah Ah Chin their tickets, depending upon her to deliver them to the ship's captain before their arrival in San Francisco.[21] Finally, Teare called each of the girls, and the younger woman also on trial, to the stand and demanded to know their relationship to the older woman. Although all the petitioners steadfastly denied any indenture to their companion, an excerpt from the woman's testimony reveals the extent to which the prosecutor had etched his portrait into the judge's mind:

Q: By the Court—You might ask her if she knows who paid her passage money.
A: I don't know, my father-in-law or my husband. I don't know about that business.
Q: Ask her if she knows how much was paid?
A: No sir, I didn't ask.
Q: Never asked who paid the passage?
A: No sir, I didn't pay no attention. My husband or my husband's father attended to all that business.
Mr. Teare: Does she know how much her passage money was?
A: She says somewhere about $35.
The Court: Ask her if her husband had in China, money amounting to $300 in American money when they came to this country?
A: I don't know anything of the kind.
Mr. Teare: Ask her if she knows this woman (Wong Ah Hing) [Wah Ah Chin, whom he had accused of being an agent for the importers of Chinese prostitutes]?

A: Never knew her before.

Q: Did she ever see her before?

A: No sir.

The Court: Which woman is that?

A: The oldest lady.[22]

Thus, as the district attorney continued to probe into Wah Ah Chin's relationship to the witness, Judge Hunt had already assumed the role of a "second prosecutor," following to the letter Teare's argument that she had purchased the younger women, and had brought them to San Francisco as Chinatown prostitutes.

Quint attempted to overcome the judge's prejudice by proving that the female immigrants were, in fact, the wives and children of Chinese men living in the city. He launched this effort by noting that the petitioners had presented the Hong Kong consul's certificates of character to the ship's captain.[23] Because they had sailed on the British steamer *Anjer Head,* however, Consul Mosby's decision to forego examinations of immigrants traveling on foreign vessels had caused the discrepancy between these documents and the women's statements to customs officials.[24] A letter from the consul to San Francisco customs collector E. L. Sullivan, dated June 21, 1882, would later clarify his role. Responding to complaints about incomplete certificates, Mosby expressed surprise at the difficulties Chinese female immigrants had experienced over the past months and complained, "As the women had the legal right to go without any certificate from me, I can't see what harm was done by their going with a blank one."[25] Thus, as their attorney clearly demonstrated and subsequent documentation confirmed, improper papers carried by Chinese females who immigrated in 1882 had been intentionally issued by the consulate and reflected no attempt on their part to deceive the government.

After transferring blame to John Mosby, the defense then called Wah Ah Chin as its first witness, presenting her as a dedicated wife and mother who had cared for a friend's granddaughter during the perilous journey to join the girl's parents.[26] Quint brought this testimony to a close by directing his client to identify her husband. When she succeeded, he began preparing for a future appeal to higher courts by moving for the immediate discharge of all five women. Judge Hunt immediately rejected his motion and ordered the hearing continued—a reaction which, although not at all unusual, anticipated the ultimate result of the trial and the need for an appeal.[27]

Through their own testimony the defense attorney had tried to establish that all of the women were either wives joining husbands or children joining parents. He even brought the people who had been waiting for their loved ones in San Francisco to the witness stand to corroborate their testimony. Ah Po, who had come on the steamer with his wife, told the court how the ship's crew had separated them on the voyage and then detained her on board when they reached port, forcing him to leave her on the steamer and search for help.[28] When Teare asked him to identify the purpose of bringing his wife to America he responded by illustrating their desire to earn a living together.

Q: What did his wife come here for?
A: I took my wife, come here. I try to go to business and wherever I go—If I go fish my wife go fish—Monterey or Santa Cruz. Lots of Chinamen down there fishing.[29]

Finally, when this testimony failed to impress the judge, Quint desperately attempted to arouse his sympathy by placing Loy How's mother on the stand and directing her to repeat the heart-rending story of the aborted dockside reunion with her daughter.[30] Still, none of these efforts proved successful, and Judge Hunt ordered the women deported on the grounds that they had immigrated for the purposes of prostitution.[31]

As their families, who had not been allowed to talk to the women during the entire trial, watched them leave the courtroom in tears and return to the steamer, the immigrants found themselves trapped in what must have seemed like a nightmare of unending separation.[32] They had survived the system of examinations in Hong Kong. They had even endured days of seasickness and crossed an ocean. But they failed to overcome the barrier of a San Francisco courtroom. Turned away from their families, they appeared destined to land once again in Hong Kong.

Only their lawyer's persistence reversed this tragic course. Drawing on the experiences that had led to his victory in 1874, Quint appealed the decision to Judge Ogden Hoffman of the U.S. District Court. Hoffman had moved from New York to California in 1850 as a means of furthering his legal career by exploiting the infant state's developing judicial system. At twenty-nine, less than a year after his arrival, he had used well-placed political connections to secure a federal judgeship in the district court.[33] Since his appointment the judge had demonstrated a fierce independence and willingness to render unpopular decisions. Although he personally "favored the restriction of Chinese immigrants and regarded them as racial inferiors," Hoffman's record indicates that he did not judge the merits of their petitions on the basis of that opinion.[34] Indeed, as occasional detentions under the Page Law were replaced by routine ones under exclusion, thousands of habeas corpus cases would fill the district court's docket in subsequent years, and Hoffman's rulings in those trials reflect an unexpected compassion for separated Chinese families.[35] The stories of Loy How, Wah Ah Chin, and the other petitioners likely found a receptive ear in Judge Hoffman, and his independent spirit neutralized intimidation brought to bear by anti-Chinese forces. After hearing the same testimony that had produced Hunt's ruling, he found the prosecutorial evidence to be inadequate and released the women.[36] The *Anjer Head* wives and daughters had at last won their freedom.

Chou See Ti You v. R. J. C. Todd

The second habeas corpus trial produced by the "Mosby dictum" took place in May of 1882. Chou See Ti You, the twenty-eight-year-old wife of a Chinese laborer (or tailor, according to some press reports), and six other female immigrants "failed" the port surveyor's examination and were denied a landing in San Francisco. Again, while these women were detained aboard the steamer *Glamis Castle,* their families obtained the assistance of a prominent lawyer in the city, Samuel H. Dwinelle.[37] Dwinelle had served as judge for California's Fifteenth District from 1867 to 1880, having won election to his final term with only two dissenting votes.[38] The reapportionment of state judicial districts, however, combined with public disfavor over an unpopular ruling, had forced him to return to his law practice.[39] Now in old age, Dwinelle sought to add one more victory to an illustrious career. Realizing the futility of taking his case through the state courts, he submitted the petition for his clients' release directly to Judge Lorenzo Sawyer of the U.S. Circuit Court.

In choosing Judge Sawyer as the recipient of his petition, Dwinelle had made a somewhat risky decision. Like Ogden Hoffman, Sawyer had come to California in 1850 as part of the same gold rush that had produced the state's first wave of Chinese immigration. Yet, in contrast to his colleague, Sawyer initially moved west to pursue instant wealth and spent his first months of residence looking for gold. Then, as dreams of a big strike faded and winter approached, he returned to the legal profession, opening a practice in Nevada City.[40] From this rather humble position as a boom town lawyer, he devoted the latter half of the 1850s to unsuccessful political campaigns, first as the Whig candidate for city attorney in San Francisco and then as the Know-Nothing nominee for district judge.[41] Finally, after joining the Republican Party, Sawyer received an appointment to the California supreme court in 1863.

As a justice, Lorenzo Sawyer established a strong record for championing individual rights, which he brought to the Ninth Federal Circuit in 1869 when President Grant nominated him for the judgeship.[42] In federal court he added to this judicial principle a vigorous commitment to the primacy of national law over states' rights: "However quickly other men retreated to the familiar comforts of states' rights after the Civil War, Sawyer had 'stricken the word "Federal" from [his] vocabulary' for he believed it 'the parent of many heresies.' He told H. H. Bancroft in an interview late in his life that he 'would not find the word ["federal"] as applicable to the U.S., in any of my opinions or writings within the last twenty-five years . . . I use the word "National" in its place.' "[43] His attempt to bring California more tightly under "national" control had frequently led the judge to rule in favor of Chinese immigrants who sought relief in the circuit court from discriminatory local and state legislation.[44]

Relying on a series of articles written less than a year after his arrival in California for publication in what she has described as "newspapers back home," Linda
Przybyszewski has attempted to portray Lorenzo Sawyer as a pro-Chinese judge:

> Rather than seeing the Chinese as unassimilable exotics, as un-republican supporters
> of despotism, as economic depressants willing and able to destroy the wage standards
> of free white labor, as amoral pagans, or as spreaders of Asiatic disease, Sawyer noted with
> approval their "industriousness, grave and dignified" deportment, and how the Chinese
> took a "deeper interest in our institutions than any other people." Defying the usual
> wholesale condemnation by whites, Sawyer pronounced himself "the most favorably
> impressed with the Chinese" of all the people he had seen.[45]

Such commentary may show that Sawyer had moved to California with a predisposition to like the Chinese, but later statements reveal that although he was still
appreciative of their work habits he eventually revised his assessment of their relative worth as an immigrant group.

Composed in 1886, a more specific letter to historian H. H. Bancroft suggests
that Sawyer's decisions favorable to the Chinese had emanated from a desire not
to champion their cause but to establish his court's dominance over the state legislature. He regarded the wives of Chinese laborers as especially undesirable immigrants:

> The Chinese are vastly superior to the negro, but they are a race entirely different from
> ours and never can assimilate and I don't think it desirable that they should. . . . If they
> would never bring their women here and never multiply and we would never have more
> than we can make useful, their presence would always be an advantage to the State . . .
> so long as the Chinese don't come here to stay. . . . When the Chinaman comes here and
> don't bring his wife here, sooner or later he dies like a worn out steam engine; he is sim-
> ply a machine, and don't leave two or three or half dozen children to fill his place.[46]

Considering that the articles to which Przybyszewski refers were written more
than thirty years before the trial of Chou See Ti You and her companions and the
letter to Bancroft only four years after, the issue of whether they had immigrated
as prostitutes or wives may well have been of secondary importance to Judge Sawyer. At least by 1886, he apparently regarded wives—and the sense of permanence
they might bring to the Chinese American community—as a more profound threat
to white society.

While Dwinelle might have aroused Ogden Hoffman's compassion by demon-
strating how the port surveyor had prevented his clients from reuniting with their
families, the Ninth Circuit Court clearly offered a patently unsympathetic arena
in which to plead their cause. Furthermore, because the women appearing before
his court had been detained through the enforcement of a federal law, a desire to
limit states' rights could not be counted on to counterbalance Sawyer's contempt

for Chinese family-building in California. Still, based on their years of association, Samuel Dwinelle apparently knew that the judge would not disregard judicial ethics in order to prevent Chinese female immigration. He needed only a little proof and even less persuasion to rule against the petitioners—and would make use of every legal means available to help the government win its case—but he would not ignore the Page Law's evidenciary requirements.

Perhaps in order to avoid another embarrassing defeat, District Attorney Teare chose not to oppose the likes of Samuel Dwinelle and left this case in the hands of his assistant, A. P. Van Duzer.[47] Van Duzer argued for deportation according to the same strategy Teare had used in the earlier trial. He presented the oldest of the women, a returning immigrant named Lin Quai, as an agent overseeing the importation of Chinese prostitutes—a charge he enhanced by revealing that she had once worked as a prostitute in San Francisco's Chinatown.[48] Noting that she was thirty-eight, Van Duzer sought to establish that her owners had "promoted" Lin Quai to purchasing agent. If he could expose her continued involvement in the prostitution business, the assistant district attorney expected Judge Sawyer to agree with his argument that the younger women were "guilty by association" and order their return to China. Yet despite ruthless cross-examination he could uncover no taint on the characters of the other immigrants, nor could any of his parade of witnesses testify to anything more than Lin Quai's former life as a prostitute.[49] No one could identify her as the present employee of a Chinese brothel.

Dwinelle countered with his own examination of the eldest of his clients. Lin Quai confessed to her former occupation but insisted that she had ceased to work as a prostitute after her marriage to Quen Ti Pon, a San Francisco trader. Subsequently, she had given birth to a daughter and accompanied her husband on a return visit to China. At the completion of their stay, Quen Ti Pon had crossed the ocean once again to set his home in order, and she and her daughter were attempting to rejoin him when the port surveyor had refused to allow their debarkation.[50] Five other petitioners then followed her testimony by identifying themselves as married women; the sixth, nine-year-old Choy Chook, said that she was the niece of Chou See Ti You.[51]

Some of the women joined Chou See Ti You in testifying that they had been detained by customs officials as their husbands looked on helplessly from the dock. Upon hearing that the men were present in his court, Judge Sawyer devised a plan for exposing the dishonesty of their purported wives.[52] After clearing all Chinese spectators from the room, the judge asked each woman to state her husband's name. He then ordered all the Chinese men waiting outside to reenter the courtroom and challenged the petitioner to identify her spouse. Finally, following such identification, Sawyer required the man to write both his own and his wife's name.

Much to the court's disappointment, every woman whose husband was present passed the test.[53]

Three of the petitioners could not use Sawyer's method to demonstrate their innocence. Their husbands had followed job opportunities into the countryside, relying upon the immigrant benevolent associations representing their home districts to provide for the newcomers until they returned to San Francisco. Dwinelle asked the court to recess for several days so these men could be located and brought back for identification by their wives. Judge Sawyer denied the motion, however, remarking "that it was not for him to await the pleasure of the petitioners until they could scour the country for husbands."[54] The decision implied that the women were using their husbands' purported absence to gain enough time for the coaching of impostors. Yet two recent historical studies support at least the plausibility of their claims.

As part of her study of Chinese agricultural workers, Chan has described the standard means through which Chinese male immigrants embarked upon a career in mining. Upon arriving in San Francisco, the men "were met by a small number of their fellow countrymen—usually merchants or their agents—who immediately took them to their lodgings. . . . [where] they were allowed to rest for a few days and were then outfitted for the gold fields and sent on their way."[55] Discussing the settlement patterns of male immigrants to Nevada, Sue Fawn Chung has noted that some who brought wives "left the women in safer Chinatown communities, while they worked in towns with a questionable reputation, such as the lawless Virginia City of the 1860s."[56]

Of even more significance to the *Chou See Ti You* case, Yung has explained the living arrangements established in California by her maternal great-grandparents. When his wife joined him in California, "Chin Lung. . . . continued to farm in the Sacramento Delta . . . [while] Great-Grandmother stayed in San Francisco Chinatown, where she gave birth to five children, two girls and three boys."[57] Thus, although nearly all Chinese immigrants entered California at San Francisco, many used the city as a hub from which to search for economic gain. Husbands pursuing such interests would likely have sent for wives without knowing whether they would be at the docks to meet them. They could rely upon "merchants or their agents" to care for the new arrivals and provide them with a place to stay and employment in Chinatown until the husbands returned to San Francisco.

Despite the handicap of Sawyer's predisposition to side with the prosecution, Samuel Dwinelle had erected a masterful defense that reduced all damaging testimony to the realm of hearsay. Reluctantly, Judge Sawyer pronounced the inevitable verdict but with the following explanation: "The Court should be satisfied without a doubt that these women were imported for immoral purposes. Though there were suspicious circumstances in the case, showing that they were imported for the purposes of prostitution, it had not been proven."[58] With that lament over the lack of conclusive evidence, he effectively proclaimed the immigrants' likely guilt at the same time he liberated them from the county jail.

The Application of Wong Wing

The final trial of Chinese female immigrants under the Page Law convened in June of 1882. Once again, the district attorney placed the case in the hands of A. P. Van Duzer, pushing him into a final confrontation with Leander Quint. As in the first trial in March, Quint filed the petition in the name of a Chinese man, Wong Wing, a friend of one of his two clients and her husband.[59] This time, however, he proceeded directly to what had proved a successful avenue of appeal in that case and sought the writ of habeas corpus from Judge Ogden Hoffman of the U.S. District Court.

Both the prosecution and the defense presented arguments similar to those used in the other two cases. Witnesses identified Chan Si, the older of the two women, as a former Chinatown prostitute, which prompted Van Duzer to charge that highbinders (tong agents) had sent her back to China to procure the services of additional women. He then claimed that the second defendant, Ng Si, was one of the woman's purchases and rested his case after describing the petitioners as "lewd and immoral women." Quint dismissed Chan Si's past as irrelevant and established that both women were married and had come to build homes with their husbands in San Francisco. Finally, as in the earlier trials, Judge Hoffman eventually ordered the immigrants released to pursue their new lives in the city.[60]

Despite such similarities, several unique circumstances marked the experiences of Chan Si and Ng Si. First, Van Duzer and the port authorities unveiled a new plan of attack by releasing ten other Chinese women without habeas corpus proceedings, thereby focusing on those immigrants against whom the evidence seemed most damaging.[61] Through that strategy, the assistant district attorney hoped to avoid the mixture of stronger and weaker cases and, by gaining a victory, to establish a precedent for deporting Chinese immigrants through administrative means. Second, the main body of testimony against the women consisted of allegations that they had engaged in specific illicit activities with members of the ship's crew.[62] Those charges constituted the government's first attempt to present more than circumstantial evidence in seeking to expel prospective female immigrants.

Judge Hoffman's decision to hold the women in custody on board the steamer without bail while he completed a vacation constitutes a third unusual characteristic of the trial. In addition to creating a terrible hardship for both the women and their families, the delay enabled Van Duzer and the port surveyor to assign undercover investigators to the docked ship in an unprecedented effort to catch their suspects in an immoral act. Although the ensuing investigations proved comically inept, they produced such charges as those made by Louis Tong Ling, a teacher who claimed to have seen "the two women and a man in suspicious proximity."[63]

Chan Si and Ng Si had come to San Francisco on the *Anjer Head,* the same steamer that had brought the petitioners detained in March.[64] As a result of his second involvement in a case accusing him of importing Chinese prostitutes, interest in the ship's master, Capt. Alfred Roper, diverted some public attention from the women. Roper's troubles with the law eventually went beyond his suspected association with the prostitute trade and temporarily overshadowed coverage of the trial in the San Francisco press; Van Duzer also charged him with illegal construction of passenger bunks and overloading his ship with human cargo.[65] Later confrontations caused by Roper's frustration over his multiple legal problems prompted additional charges: interfering with the duties of three separate customs officers and assaulting one of them.[66] A veritable caricature of the briny sea captain, Roper ultimately captured the sympathy of both the court and the press, continually stealing headlines from the women.

Finally, Judge Hoffman's reasons for releasing the petitioners focused on the distinction between the voluntary and involuntary immigration of Chinese prostitutes—a point that never appeared in the other habeas corpus proceedings. Upon granting the writ, Hoffman declared that "he was satisfied from the evidence that the elder woman was 'obviously a strumpet.'" He then expressed the opinion that the Page Law did not prohibit her voluntary immigration and ordered her release on that basis.[67] Although his judgment echoed an interpretation offered by some Hong Kong newspapers when the law was first enacted, American authorities from the consulate to the federal courts had never before decided a case on the basis of that distinction.[68] Still, although its logic remains a mystery, Judge Hoffman's ruling once again produced a happy ending for the immigrants.

In all three habeas corpus proceedings the prosecutors focused their cases on the oldest petitioner, which illustrates the virtually impossible task that confronted wives and daughters attempting to distinguish themselves from female immigrants brought into the country for prostitution. Both the trade in prostitutes and in *mui tsai* (young girls purchased to serve in the homes of prosperous families, in factories, or in brothels) often depended on female go-betweens.[69] Those agents, operating either as commissioned employees of Chinatown tongs or as independent dealers, made periodic buying trips to China and then returned with their human merchandise to the United States. Given the existence of such women, nothing more than anti-Chinese sentiment was necessary to convince port surveyors and judges that any group of female passengers who had reached San Francisco aboard the same ship constituted a go-between's latest cargo. Judicial principles might eventually compel judges such as Hoffman and Sawyer to rule in the immigrants' favor, but those rulings were still interpreted as triumphs of deception rather than innocence.

Although their legitimacy would never be acknowledged, Chinese women seeking to land in San Francisco between 1875 and 1882 could look to the experiences of earlier female immigrants as evidence that they were likely to succeed. The American consul in Hong Kong had represented the only serious obstacle to overcome, and port surveyors enforced the Page Law with extreme caution. They seldom turned away passengers cleared by the consul. Even if they did, American courts would likely overturn their decision. Still, the likelihood of victory did not make the struggle for one's release less frightening. The port surveyor separated husbands and wives, parents and children, almost at the moment before their reunions were realized and, at least sometimes, managed to deport female immigrants to China. Furthermore, although his attempts usually ended in failure, appeals of the deportation order still drove female petitioners into San Francisco courtrooms, where lawyers, witnesses, and even judges ridiculed the wives and daughters of Chinese Americans and accused them of immorality before hostile galleries. Finally, habeas corpus trials required the aid of prominent lawyers such as Leander Quint and Samuel Dwinelle. Although his association with the Pacific Mail Steamship Company had frequently led Quint to represent Chinese interests, both he and Dwinelle no doubt charged substantial fees in exchange for this unpopular work.

Perhaps such legal costs were underwritten by the Chinese Six Companies or the Chinese consulate in San Francisco in the same way that the prostitution industry might have done for its detainees. If not, they would have ruined the aspirations of women who had emigrated from a home village to pursue economic opportunities with their husbands. At any rate, the financial risks—to whomever assumed them—would have aided the attempt to restrict Chinese female immigration. With returning emigrants telling of Chinese women being imprisoned on the steamers and forced to appeal for their release in American courts, the specter of this second ordeal no doubt convinced even more wives to stay home and their husbands, hearing the same stories in Chinatown, not to send for them. It was clear to families contemplating a reunion in San Francisco that the United States would resist the immigration of Chinese wives and daughters as well as prostitutes. Consuls, customs officials, and judges continually reminded them of that fact.

6

The San Francisco Press:
Catalyst and Mirror

In a letter to H. H. Bancroft on May 7, 1876, Christian missionary Augustus Loomis responded to the report of the California legislature's investigative committee on Chinese immigration. He offered a less than flattering evaluation of the committee's findings and of the integrity of the state's newspapers in their coverage of the investigative proceedings: "I may be partial—one-sided in my views—but I am sure that the Newspapers and the Senatorial Committee are extremely prejudiced—have presented the worst features of one side [the economic threat posed by Chinese labor and the moral threat posed by Chinese prostitution] and suppressed the favorable aspects of the other side [the contributions of Chinese labor to California's economic development and the growing number of Chinese wives immigrating to California]."[1]

Loomis's allegations can hardly be disputed; state representatives in Washington used the committee's report to influence Senate appointment of a federal investigative committee on Chinese immigration later in the year. Their success proved most damaging to the Chinese American community because the Senate report recommended a renegotiation of the Burlingame Treaty and in so doing paved the way for the Exclusion Act's eventual adoption.

Having recognized the significant role played by the state committee in furthering the cause of exclusion and Loomis's accusations regarding its anti-Chinese bias, one's attention is drawn to the second object of his charges—the California press. English-language newspapers exerted a less-direct influence upon Chinese American life than did the state investigative committee. After all, neither Chinese laborers nor their wives subscribed to them. At least for those white Californians who read them, however, newspaper portrayals of Chinese American society must have done a great deal to affect the way in which immigrants, both male and female, were viewed and treated. If taken seriously—and no doubt it was—the press in cities such as San Francisco, by consistently stating or even implying that the female population of Chinatown consisted almost exclusively of prostitutes, could have destroyed the reputations of Chinese women.

With the exception of lower-level customs personnel, the officials most important to Chinese female immigrants would have been among those most likely to read a San Francisco newspaper. For example, the Hong Kong consuls were regular subscribers and, along with the judges, possessed the kind of formal education likely to make them more than cursory readers. Although port surveyors won their posts through the spoils system rather than merit, their political connections may have made them more interested in the press than average white Californians. Of course, the degree to which newspapers influenced the opinions of these officials, or of anyone else who read them, cannot be measured. It is likely, however, that the press and its readers maintained a reciprocal relationship. The articles about the Chinese that the press produced molded and mirrored the attitudes and actions of the public.

Newspapers across the country sometimes carried negative stories about the Chinese and even about female immigrants.[2] Yet they were reporting on distant problems and contributed little more to the exclusionist cause than improved national credibility. When the California press, especially that of San Francisco, wrote about the Chinese, however, it addressed one of the state's and city's most volatile social and political issues. The character of its reporting, if Loomis's claims of bias were valid, may have directly influenced the hostility endured by Chinese women who attempted to enter the United States through the Golden Gate.

This chapter will examine the character of the stories on Chinese female immigrants from 1875 to 1882 in San Francisco newspapers. The issue is not whether they printed prejudicial material—anyone at all familiar with Chinese American history would expect them to have done so—but the consistency of its use. By presenting an exclusively negative portrayal of women who populated the city's Chinese district, newspapers may have influenced the exclusively negative opinion of these women demonstrated by officials charged with approving their debarkation from the China steamers.

Local reporting on Chinese female immigrants included assaults on their character before the Page Law's enactment. Although men such as Charles Crocker, who depended heavily upon male workers in projects like railroad construction, could often persuade the press to balance stories of ruthless tongs with others extolling the contributions of Chinese labor to California's economic development, the coverage of females required no similar positive counterweight. Newspapers like the *Daily Alta California* had freely applauded state legislation of 1866 that had attempted to punish both Chinatown brothels and white landlords, complaining only of its narrow focus:

The men who own, as well as the men who sub-let many of the notorious dens on Dupont, Pine, Bush, Sutter and adjacent streets are perfectly well known. Why are they not prosecuted? Some of the newspapers had a great deal to say because a Chinese house of prostitution was opened on one of the principal streets of the city, a few months ago, and the police authorities were warmly adjured to shut them up. They did, and the white prostitutes still stand in their doorways nightly, in the very same block where there was authority enough to compel the closing of the Chinese den. Will not the same power that shut up one do the same work for the others?[3]

Although such expansion of blame for the growth of prostitution deflected some hostility from Chinese immigrants, the press still offered only a single image of Chinatown's female population—that of the prostitute.

Also in 1870, the *San Francisco Chronicle* had printed extensive excerpts from proceedings of both the Fourth Ward Democratic Club and its Anti-Chinese Convention, each of which called upon the federal government to abrogate the Burlingame Treaty.[4] No doubt such coverage had helped create the kind of political momentum that would finally prompt the California legislature to present Congress with its similar resolution in 1872. Still, the newspaper had not yet committed to the necessity of a new treaty. Later in the year it had published without editorial critique an interview with Sen. Cornelius Cole, a Republican, conducted at San Francisco's Grand Hotel as part of his reelection campaign. Among many other topics, the interviewer asked Cole's views on Chinese female immigration:

> Senator Cole: "I have no fear of the Chinese overrunning this continent, and yet when I look upon a certain class of Chinese who come to this land—I mean the females— who are the most undesirable of population, who spread disease and moral death among our white population, I ask myself the question, whether or not there is a limit to this class of immigrants? There is, and Congress will so legislate, I am satisfied, as to prevent the importation of these female coolies, as well as the males. The question is growing in importance daily in the Eastern States by reason of the introduction of a few Chinese here and there."[5]

The Page Law would realize his prediction before the legislature would again decide whom to award this seat in the Senate.

Although eager to forecast the enactment of an antiprostitution bill, Cole made it equally clear that he opposed any restructuring of the 1868 treaty:

> Interviewer: "Why not take the bull by the horn? Abrogate the treaty!"
>
> Senator Cole: "And lose the trade of China? San Francisco commerce is languishing, you tell me, and yet you suggest a means to lop off our growing commerce with the very Power upon which we rely for wealth. The trade of China has been sought for, prayed for, fought for, for years and years. . . . I would not consent to any such proceeding. I would favor agitation that would tend to keep the Chinese where they are—at home, but I would not destroy our commerce because five hundred a month come to our shores."[6]

In offering such coverage, the *Chronicle* had provided readers with opposing perspectives on the issue of repealing the Burlingame Treaty. Conversely, its implications regarding Chinese women had remained invariable. Subscribers were informed that even Democrats and Republicans had agreed in condemning female immigration—a position the newspaper had both reported and helped to shape.

As Page moved his bill from debate, to enactment, to enforcement, the press never wavered in its approach to stories covering the segment of Chinatown's population targeted by the legislation. A thorough if not exhaustive review of the articles that San Francisco newspapers published about Chinese American women between 1874 and 1882 fails to reveal a single entry favorable to them. Moreover, in addition to contents that held them up to unrelenting ridicule, fully a third of the fifty-one stories dealing specifically with female Chinese also carried strongly negative headlines, for example, "Chinese Chattels," "The Chinese Houris," and "The Chinese 'Wives.'" The unanimity of such reports intensified the already established image of slave-prostitutes that was applied universally other than in accounts of the occasional wife or concubine of a merchant or diplomat.

The first of the stories appeared on August 28, 1874, just four days after the steamer *Japan* had brought twenty-three Chinese females from Hong Kong and the port surveyor had refused their landing on the grounds that they were prostitutes. Reporting on their subsequent habeas corpus trial in state district court (which eventually led to the Supreme Court's *Chy Lung* decision declaring the California law unconstitutional), the *Chronicle*'s article was headed "A Cargo of Infamy" and announced that when Judge Morrison ruled in favor of their deportation his decision was "greeted by applause from the audience."[7]

In 1875 city newspapers heralded the Page Law's passage and its promise to stop the immigration of "lewd and immoral women" from China, but their reports on the committee's investigations of 1876 offered the decade's most thorough treatments of Chinese female immigration. On June 5 the *San Francisco Bulletin* summarized its report of the California investigation by outlining the central thrust of the committee's findings, with special emphasis given to Chinese women: "The habits and manners of the Chinese immigrating to this country are of the lowest order of that people. Most of the males are coolies, and are brought here under contract for servile labor. The females, of whom there are several thousand in the state of California, are of the lowest and vilest class, and are brought here for the purposes of prostitution and corrupting the morals of the people and bringing disgrace upon enlightened civilization." Endorsing the committee's claims as its own, the article concluded with a reproduction of the committee's recommendation that "the immigration of this class of Chinese is a great evil, and one that must, sooner or later, call for prompt and efficient legislation to prevent it."[8]

In July, between the state and federal investigations, local authorities tried to use the Page Law to prosecute the keepers of Chinese brothels. Their attempt failed in the U.S. Circuit Court, where Judge Sawyer, reflecting his desire to restrict states' rights, ruled that the 1875 statute prohibited the immigration of Chinese women for the purposes of prostitution but did not give authorities the right to arrest women already working as prostitutes in the city. As it lamented his decision, the *Bulletin* reported the unsuccessful effort to misconstrue the law as the work of valiant men determined to stop the growth of an immoral industry.[9]

When the Joint Congressional Committee on Chinese Immigration convened in the fall, San Francisco newspapers, like the committee, presented a more balanced account of the Chinese issue than that produced in their coverage of the state investigation.[10] In just eighteen days, however, 129 witnesses were placed under oath, producing 1,200 pages of testimony. The press could not possibly include excerpts from each examination. Given the need to choose quoted material selectively, it is significant that the newspapers recorded only one genuinely positive statement regarding Chinese American women, that offered by Augustus Ward Loomis on November 10. In reporting his testimony regarding the evils of Chinese prostitution in San Francisco, the *Bulletin* included Loomis's statement that "at present the Chinese are bringing their wives here more generally."[11]

Although failing to echo that opinion, Otis Gibson, another missionary to the Chinese in San Francisco, did offer a guardedly optimistic word. Appearing before the committee on the same day as Loomis, he suggested that the number of Chinese prostitutes was gradually decreasing, largely due to his enlistment of San Francisco's Chinese merchants in financing the return to China of all prostitutes who had escaped to his mission house and expressed a desire to go home.[12] The *Bulletin* supplemented his testimony with evidence submitted by Port Surveyor Giles H. Gray regarding the Page Law's effectiveness in preventing the immigration of Chinese prostitutes: "The Page Law was enacted in 1875. The arrivals before that time were from two hundred to four hundred a vessel. The collector can furnish the whole number who have arrived. I think the authorities at Hong Kong are exercising diligence to prevent the immigration of Chinese prostitutes to this country." Citing a drastic reduction in the number of female arrivals since Consul David Bailey had initiated his examinations, Gray expressed the opinion that "the Page Law was working well, and had effectively stopped the immigration of lewd women."[13]

The testimony of Gibson and Gray would not have pleased exclusionists, who wanted to fan the flames of anti-Chinese hysteria with reports that all less drastic attempts to deal with undesirable immigration had failed. In their intimations regarding the relative improvement of Chinatown's moral character the two men might even be regarded as supportive of the Chinese. They offered nothing helpful to the image of Chinese women, however. Unlike Loomis, neither attributed the decline of Chinese prostitution in San Francisco to an increase in the number of wives immigrating to America. On the contrary, that decline was credited to subtraction rather than addition, purportedly stemming from the return of women to China and the general decrease in female immigration produced by Consul Bailey's rigid enforcement of the Page Law.

There can be little dispute about the negative tone of the remaining depositions summarized in city newspapers in respect to both female and male immigration from China. Samuel Dwinelle and his brother John, whose statements regarding the desirability of Chinese immigration appeared in the *Alta* on November 16 and 14, respectively, represented the more moderate side of the anti-Chinese movement. Thus, the nature of their testimony renders unnecessary a presentation of that offered by militant exclusionists. Samuel Dwinelle, as one might expect considering his later defense of Chou See Ti You and her companions in the U.S. Circuit Court, expressed the opinion that Chinese workers had made an important contribution to California's economy by providing a source of cheap labor when the state contained an inadequate number of white workers. He then added, "Personally my prejudice is very strong against the Chinese; I never employ them."[14]

If his brother's opinions regarding the Chinese remained somewhat ambiguous, John Dwinelle, a Republican member of the California legislature representing the eastern side of the San Francisco Bay, left no doubt as to his support of exclusion: "I do not think Chinese immigration is desirable; they will not assimilate with us. I think it would be better if we never would have had a Chinaman. I believe in the Fatherhood of God and the brotherhood of man, but don't look on the Chinaman as a man or brother. I think he is a human being, of a race that has ripened and is rotting out. I think we ought to restrain immigration."[15]

As the comments of both men reflect, Chinese males occupied a more central position in the congressional committee's investigation than Chinese women, although occasionally someone spoke, although guardedly, in the men's favor. Yet for Chinese women and their future in the United States the only clearly positive words recorded during the proceedings came in the form of Augustus Loomis's observation about what he perceived as a recent increase in the immigration of Chinese wives.

To their credit, San Francisco newspapers did at least publish the Loomis's testimony, but the whole of their remaining references to Chinese female immigrants carried the same tone as the committee's findings. For example, when summarizing the report in an article dated February 26, 1877, the *Sacramento Record Union* concluded that the Chinese "bring with them neither wives, families nor children. The female immigrants are bought and sold like chattels, and practice the most revolting vices and immoralities."[16] Thus, the press in both San Francisco and the state capital invariably portrayed Chinese women—and usually the entire Chinese

American community—in a manner concisely summarized by Samuel Dwinelle. At the conclusion of his testimony before congressional investigators, Judge Dwinelle observed, "In this city . . . the press is decidedly opposed to Chinese immigration."[17]

Following the federal hearings on Chinese immigration, Chinese women did not often appear as the subjects of reports in city newspapers until the habeas corpus trials of 1882. Until that time, the severe and unchallenged enforcement of the Page Law by American consuls in Hong Kong and customs officials in San Francisco had reduced the number of female arrivals to a level that depressed the interest of reporters.

Four articles published in 1877 represent the reports that did appear, however. First, in their reviews of *The Chinese in America* by Otis Gibson both the *San Francisco Post* and the *San Francisco Bulletin* gave extensive attention to the author's views on Chinese American women. Although only a small portion of Gibson's book was devoted to that topic, the *Post* focused upon his estimate that among the 2,800 females in Chinatown, 2,600 were "enslaved prostitutes."[18] The *Bulletin,* in turn, added to its critique an editorial comment that Gibson's "view of their character [that of Chinese female immigrants] does not differ materially from that generally held by intelligent citizens. Nine-tenths of them are held in a bondage worse than death."[19] In April the *Sacramento Bee*'s editor echoed the perceptions of his San Francisco counterparts: "Very few Chinese wives are brought to this country, the great bulk of the women who land here being, I presume, prostitutes."[20] Finally, on August 25, 1877, the *San Francisco Call* informed readers of the general character of Chinese women living within their city: "The Chinese females who immigrate into this state are, almost without exception, of the vilest and most degraded class of abandoned women. These women exist here in a state of servitude, beside which African slavery was a beneficent captivity."[21]

Thus, although few accounts of female Chinese were brought to their attention between 1876 and 1882, those San Franciscans who read one of the city's or the capitol's newspapers—whether private citizens, customs officials, or judges—were given one consistent analysis. The press unanimously informed them that nine of any ten Chinese women stepping off a steamer from Hong Kong were certain to be prostitutes.

The three habeas corpus trials conducted during 1882 brought Chinese American women onto center-stage. Moreover, with the increasing number of articles, San Francisco's newspapers continued to assail the virtue of Chinese female immigrants with the same vigor that had characterized their coverage of the previous decade. Such unwavering prejudice is best illustrated by tracing the treatment of the first group of petitioners by one of the city's most influential newspapers, the *San Francisco Chronicle.*

When the immigrants petitioned for their release in superior court, initiating the process of convictions and appeals that would prove necessary to gain their freedom, the *Chronicle* introduced its story on the proceedings with the headline "Chinese Chattels."[22] The article highlighted the testimony of Capt. Alfred Roper, who had, in this first case, attempted to blame the immigration of Loy How and the other alleged prostitutes confined aboard his ship, the *Anjer Head*, on Consul John Mosby's decision to cease granting certificates to women traveling on foreign vessels. Then, with their guilt clearly implied, the reporter depicted his subjects as unruly disturbers of the court who, after Judge Hunt ordered a recess until the following day, resisted their return to the steamer so vigorously that the deputy sheriff was forced to remove them one by one.

The *Chronicle* reported events from the trial's second day in an article headlined "The Chinese Houris," which resembled the coverage of a Knob Hill cotillion and described each woman's attire and the enamored reaction of the Chinese men in the courtroom to their appearance:

> The moon-eyed beauties, radiant in vari-colored suits, their hair plastered in the most approved Oriental style, their pedal extremities encased in gilt silken shoes, were the cynosure of their interested countrymen. At the further end of the bench in the lobby, sat an enamored Adonis, his eyes riveted on the youngest of the quartet, who perfectly oblivious of the commotion she was causing, contentedly toyed a small bamboo fan; Adonis, with alarming persistency, gave evidence of being thoroughly Americanized, and at regular intervals offered a subdued cough but to no purpose; the maiden was as yet unacquainted with such esthetic overtures.[23]

When the eldest woman, Wah Ah Chin, successfully identified her husband from among all other Chinese males on the premises, the paragraph relating this event was headed "A Husband for the Occasion" and interpreted her demonstration of integrity as a failure to "corner the madam." The extensive article then included Captain Roper's report that his steamship company had fixed the passage for females "at $300 and for males at $40, in order to aid in the discouragement of female immigration."[24] Thus, in spite of evidence to the contrary, the newspaper colored each article to reinforce the assumption that the women petitioning for their release as the wives or children of Chinese laborers were in fact prostitutes.

As the first hearing of the case reached a close, attention was directed toward Judge Hunt's welcomed verdict. The *Chronicle* related on March 21 that he had ordered the women returned to China on the basis of their conflicting certificates.[25] Both statements that Hunt attached to his ruling and the newspaper's reaction to them poignantly reveal disregard for the legal rights of the petitioners. In accordance with provisions of the Burlingame Treaty, the Page Law placed no restriction on the immigration of Chinese wives. In ordering their return to China, however, the judge informed the women that, if their husbands were genuine, they could post a $500 bond for their wives' release—a decision which, although patently in violation of federal statute, the *Chronicle* judged to be sensible and fair.[26]

After informing readers that their aborted attempt to enter the country illegally was totally the responsibility of the prostitutes and did not involve Captain Roper, the article described the petitioners' reaction to defeat: "After the decision of Judge Hunt, remanding the Chinese women to the custody of the official on board of the 'Anjer Head,' they were driven rapidly to the vessel and left to their sorrowful reflections. They seemed to understand their situation, and gave loud voice to their sorrows. No sooner had they been left in their bunks than they joined in a Chinese chorus of soul-stirring anguish that commanded attention for some distance along the seawall."[27]

Such a painful scene could not help but inspire additional commentary, and curious readers would not be disappointed. Using the services of a professed expert on Chinese culture, whom he conveniently found at the dock but failed to identify, the reporter claimed that moving to a closer vantage point had exposed the women as frustrated prostitutes:

> At the door of the cabin stood the veteran Chinese chaperon, with a countenance that resembled the desiccated maturity of a Kentucky tobacco plant, and behind her on the trunks were arranged in various positions the distressed houris writhing in the agony of inconsolable grief. To one not acquainted with the peculiar traits of Chinese character this scene would have been touching in the extreme. There was one thing very remarkable about their lamentations . . . they shed no tears. An expert on professional Chinese laments gave a very unkind explanation of this angular circumstance, claiming in language more forcible than polite that the old woman had imported the girls . . . and she was afraid of being left. In the opinion of the expert, she had instructed the girls to howl, and they were simply doing their best to carry out instructions.[28]

As in all its other articles about the women of the *Anjer Head,* the *Chronicle* never pretended to entertain the notion that they might have been innocent of the charges levied against them. Instead, agreeing with the "intelligent citizens" of San Francisco, the newspaper accepted as a foregone conclusion that these immigrants, like 90 percent of the female residents of Chinatown, were prostitutes.

When Judge Hoffman overturned the earlier decision because of insufficient evidence—much to the disappointment of the press and most of San Francisco—the immigrants' appeal to the U.S. District Court resulted in their release.[29] The *Chronicle* reacted to this reversal by noting the petitioners' hurried departure from the courtroom after being told of the verdict, and three days later published an article headlined "Chinese Chattels."[30] That story, which described the process by which prostitutes came to America, began with a lament: "Though the business of importing women from Canton and Hong Kong for immoral purposes has been carried on for nearly a score of years, it is only recently that any official action has been taken to prevent it, and the task so far has proven by no means successful." Without mentioning the recent trial, such a critique of the Page Law's effectiveness clearly implied that the acquittal of five women against whom no evidence existed had represented an evasion of the law by a criminal class in San Francisco's Chinatown.

Coverage of the second habeas corpus trial by three San Francisco newspapers, the *Chronicle, Morning Call,* and *Daily Alta California,* was remarkable for the unanimity of its prejudice against the female immigrants and anyone associated with their cause. The *Chronicle*'s first article on the petition of Chou See Ti You and her companions before Judge Sawyer, "Chinese Female Chattels," treated even Samuel Dwinelle with disdain. Noting that he had opened the defense of his clients by referring to them as "'nice, virtuous women,'" the reporter scornfully pointed out that they were besieged by admiring "husbands" immediately after Sawyer ordered them held over for trial and adjourned the preliminary hearing.[31] In its opening story, "The Female Cargo of the 'Glamis Castle,'" the *Call* exercised a more respectful tone toward the former judge, but, as the headline indicates, regarded the women as somewhat less than human.[32]

After indirectly assaulting Samuel Dwinelle's integrity, the *Chronicle* report also misinformed readers in such a way that called the conduct of Judge Sawyer into question, making him appear supportive of the women to a degree that most San Franciscans would have found unacceptable. Upon completion of opening arguments by both attorneys, Sawyer had ordered that the petitioners be detained in the county jail, where their lawyer could visit them only in the company of the port surveyor's interpreter. That restriction must have rendered confidential dialogues between Dwinelle and his clients virtually impossible, because it was the port surveyor who had first ordered their detention as alleged prostitutes.[33] Yet the newspaper reported that Judge Sawyer had granted full visiting rights to the men claiming to be their husbands, thus charging him with unprecedented leniency and leaving more suspicious minds to wonder about the seriousness of his desire to return the women to China.[34]

All three newspapers treated any claims of innocence by the women as acts of deception. The *Alta,* for example, offered the following summary of their testimony: "Owing to the poor memory of the women, considerable confusion was caused. For instance, one of them was asked through an interpreter if she knew Chong Moon Lee, and without an instant's reflection, declared that she did not. After some conversation with the interpreter, however, she suddenly recollected that it was her own name. The ladies are exceedingly proficient, even for Chinese, in the art of lying."[35] Although subsequent testimony clearly established that this apparent lapse had been caused by John Mosby, no mention ever appeared of the consul's decision to supply emigrants with certificates bearing the names and photographs of prior applicants. Furthermore, references to the women as wives were invariably enclosed in quotation marks, and, aside from appearing in the titles of articles, even such a mock reference to marriage was deleted.

Notwithstanding the distinct anti-Chinese tone of earlier stories, the three newspapers published their most venomous comments in response to Sawyer's reluctant granting of the writ. In an article dripping with sarcasm, the *Alta* reported that the discharged women were immediately "placed in hacks and driven to the Chinese quarter."[36] The *Call* chose instead to focus on Judge Sawyer's lament that "though there were suspicious circumstances in the case, showing that they were imported for the purposes of prostitution, it had not been proven."[37] The *Chronicle* issued a more condemning assessment: "Perjury has again proved triumphant in our courts. The release of prostitutes imported on the 'Glamis Castle' was ordered yesterday because 'no legal evidence' could be produced that the women were brought here for that purpose. It is a safe prediction to make that the women will be practicing their peculiar vocation in Chinatown before the expiration of a week."[38] That final report, contained in an untitled paragraph at the bottom of page two, reflected a growing frustration over the failure of the courts to issue rulings in support of what the newspapers regarded as common knowledge: Essentially, every Chinese woman immigrating to the United States had come as a prostitute.

In covering the third case to reach federal court during the final months before exclusion, the *San Francisco Chronicle* filled its summer editions with further ridicule of Chinese female immigrants. It had, however, initially greeted the petitioners detained aboard the *Anjer Head* with an unprecedented expression of sympathy: "A *Chronicle* reporter on board the steamer . . . was given the opportunity to compare the women and the photographs of them which they carried, and found that, so far as he investigated, everything was according to the law and that each woman had in her possession a certificate attached to her photograph, signed by the American Consul at Hong Kong."[39] Such a statement may well represent the first expression of even implicit support contained in a local newspaper's report on the immigration of Chinese women to America, but subsequent events would render its uncharacteristic fairness only temporary.

When the government expanded its charges against Capt. Alfred Roper to include crimes other than the landing of Chinese prostitutes in the city, he put up a defense so sensational that it momentarily thrust the habeas corpus trial into a corner. Still, the women did not remain on the periphery for long. When Roper accused the port surveyor's interpreter, Chan Pak Quai, of attempting to solicit a bribe in exchange for facilitating the debarkation of his female passengers, the interpreter countered by claiming that the captain had, in fact, offered him money in exchange for their immediate release.[40] In seeking to convince the court of his integrity, Chan attacked the character of the women, thus reestablishing them as the focal point for both the court and the press: "The interpreter . . . Kwai claims to be in possession of evidence that the women on board had illicit intercourse with the whites on the voyage; and that on last Sunday he caught the steward and one of the smallfeet women in the latter's apartment under suspicious circumstances."[41] Although it initially threatened the petition sought by Chan Si and Ng Si, Chan Pak Quai's testimony eventually proved helpful to the defendants. No shred of proof was offered in support of his accusations, and the interpreter had inadvertently released their trial from an extended postponement.

As attorney Leander Quint competed for attention with Captain Roper's personal legal problems, he had continued to petition the U.S. District Court for a hearing on his clients' case but without success. Moreover, during their confinement on board the *Anjer Head* a single article in the *Chronicle* had anticipated and discredited Quint's entire defense. Entitled "Chinese Chattels: Some Light" and purporting to reproduce a conveniently anonymous letter from an unknown Chinese merchant in Hong Kong, the report claimed to expose in detail an elaborate system of smuggling Chinese prostitutes into San Francisco. Supposedly, the tongs routinely employed older men or women, each of whom acted as the guardian of six to twelve slave girls. To accomplish their assignment, these agents bribed members of the Tung Wah Hospital Committee to vouch for the character of their wards, thus deceiving well-meaning consular and customs officials into approving their immigration.[42] The letter, dated May 13, 1882, then mentioned the *Anjer Head* specifically, alleging that the steamer had left for America with twenty-two women "'all of whom are imported for immoral purposes except three, who are respectable married women.'"[43]

Careful not to libel any government officials, either Chinese or American, the *Chronicle* had instead implicated the Tung Wah Hospital Committee and unnamed Chinese criminals as the sources of prostitute traffic. Yet Quint was preparing to inform the court that Chan Si had acted as Ng Si's guardian on the voyage in order to assure her safe arrival in San Francisco.[44] Although undoubtedly fictional, this "secret information" would most likely have convinced all those who read it of both the attorney's insincerity and the immigrants' guilt.

When Judge Hoffman interrupted the trial's progress a second time by leaving on vacation, Alfred Roper once again shared center-stage with the two women imprisoned on his ship. The *Chronicle,* in reporting clandestine attempts by customs detectives to catch the petitioners in an immoral act, investigated the captain's charges that one of these agents had forsaken his post to play poker with the crew.

The *Chronicle* quickly refocused on the women, however, emphasizing the detective's claim that Roper had invented the incident in an attempt to discredit his testimony against them.[45] Finally, as one might expect, the newspaper typically treated the eventual release of the female immigrants as an unfortunate dismissal of Chinese prostitutes against whom the assistant district attorney had failed to gather sufficient evidence to warrant their deportation.[46]

Of course, no one can measure the degree to which the newspapers influenced public attitudes toward Chinese women. Yet Henry Tsai has placed much of the blame for an outbreak of anti-Chinese riots that terrorized western Chinatowns during the 1870s and 1880s on the increase of "inflammatory news . . . in the San Francisco press."[47] Moreover, in addition to serving as a catalyst for such atrocities, newspapers often redirected white hostility toward judges who ruled in favor of Chinese claimants. Linda Przybyszewski has noted that Lorenzo Sawyer on at least three occasions complained to Judge Matthew Deady of Oregon that any appearance of leniency toward the Chinese subjected him to the "'unpleasant' attacks of the white public and press."[48] A letter in 1876 describing his unsuccessful attempt to persuade a *San Francisco Chronicle* reporter that his judgments had emanated from a faithful attempt to uphold national law, for example, concluded with the lament that "'decent men have no protection against such calumnies."[49] Then, in 1884, Sawyer wrote that press reports of a habeas corpus case in which he had ordered the release of a Chinese immigrant detained by enforcers of the Exclusion Act had consisted of "'unmitigated lying as to what we do, and a torrent of abuse founded on the lying.'"[50] Finally, in the same year the judge intimated to Deady that even the *American Law Review* had criticized his conduct in cases involving Chinese claims.[51] Given his experiences, one must assume that what public and press would have regarded as equally unacceptable decisions had exposed Judge Hoffman to similar attacks.

Whether they subscribed to the *Chronicle,* the *Alta,* the *Call,* the *Post,* the *Bulletin,* or any other newspaper published in the city, the citizens of San Francisco read a consistent supply of anti-Chinese articles. Each report informed—or at least reassured—them that virtually all female immigrants arriving in San Francisco from Hong Kong came as slave-prostitutes brought into the country illegally to labor in Chinese brothels. When combined with the visible presence of such women, who solicited customers from barred cubicles along the back alleys of Chinatown, this unified condemnation aroused white resentment of the judges who permitted their continued immigration. Therefore, given the personal views of Hoffman and Sawyer in regard to the Chinese, their decisions in the Page Law trials despite such constant pressure testify to both judicial integrity and innocence of the petitioners.

The inflammatory reports of San Francisco newspapers undergirded the exclusion movement, which by the late 1870s had defined itself as an effort to protect white workers from cheap Chinese labor and white society from the special medical and moral threat of Chinese prostitution. By assisting the exclusionist cause, the press helped to develop a social and legal climate most aptly described by John Mosby in an 1882 letter to the collector of customs in San Francisco: "It is a useless and superfluous task for me to undertake to investigate the character of female emigrants and to grant them passports which are treated as nullities in San Francisco on the mere presumption that every Chinese woman is a prostitute."[52] That presumption, reflected and aided by the manner in which local newspapers described Chinese female immigrants throughout the preexclusion period, must have amplified the intensity with which customs officials and judges sought to enforce the Page Law.

Faced with—and most likely sharing in—the frustration of the press over their inability to prohibit female immigration from China legally, authorities demanded relief from the American consuls in Hong Kong. Through their continued subjection of prospective immigrants to a series of hostile examinations, the consuls thus completed a system that between 1875 and 1882 made the entry of Chinese women into the United States a truly difficult accomplishment. That cooperative effort enabled the law to achieve much more than its language suggests. In so doing it helped preserve sexual disparity among the immigrants, thereby creating a Chinese community that Sucheng Chan has described as "socially incomplete."[53]

7

The Census Enumerators:
Completing a Cycle of Invisibility

For women who were not prostitutes and who succeeded in overcoming the barriers raised against their immigration, life in the United States presented a number of difficulties and also created new opportunities for expanded independence. Although servant girls, who came as part of the *mui tsai* system, suffered at least quasi-legal status as the property of employers, they found some protection from abuse through the intervention of Christian missionaries.[1] The wives of laborers worked long hours under difficult conditions in a variety of Chinatown industries, but their freedom from joint family control and their value to an overwhelmingly male community opened avenues of autonomy that were unavailable to their counterparts in China.[2] Yet regardless of the treatment they received from employers or husbands, the immigrants remained virtually invisible to the rest of San Francisco.

The Rev. Otis Gibson, who directed one of the rescue missions providing shelter to escapees fleeing abusive situations, illustrated the refusal to acknowledge diversity in the Chinese female population. He estimated that a female population which he placed at 2,820 contained 2,600 "enslaved prostitutes" and only 120 "respectable women."[3] Such assessments completely failed to anticipate, however, the findings of the federal census compiled just three years after publication of his book in 1877. In direct opposition to Gibson's claims, the 1880 enumeration reported a dramatic decline in prostitutes among a virtually unchanged Chinese female population (chapter 1).

The explanation that these unexpected statistics merely reflected the industry's descending fortunes should not be discounted. The numbers of prostitutes recorded by census enumerators in 1870, however, would likely have resulted in a serious oversupply, whereas those Gibson presented would have amounted to an act of economic suicide on the part of those who controlled Chinese prostitution.[4]

Tong has attempted to account for misidentified women in the 1870 and 1880 censuses, echoing Mary Coolidge's acknowledgement that the total number of prostitutes was no doubt overstated.[5] Building upon the potential for such exaggeration, this chapter will explore the likelihood that the 1870 census undercounted Chinese wives and other women who were not prostitutes and establish continuity between the census and its successor.

The 1870 Census: Two Censuses

Margo Anderson, in an analysis of the 1870 census, has noted that it "suffered from extremely poor field procedures and some badly worded questions."[6] Caught up in a conflict over the proper way to incorporate former slaves into the electorate in anticipation of the Fifteenth Amendment's ratification, efforts to improve the process had died in Congress.[7] Thus, the first federal enumeration to follow the Civil War was conducted under the authority of 1850 legislation, which officials of the Bureau of the Census would later characterize as "entirely inadequate to meet the changed conditions under which the census of 1870 would have to be taken."[8] For general population statistics, the only significant changes from its predecessor were an increase in compensation for assistant marshals working in sparsely settled western sections and the additions of "Chinese" and "Indian" as categories for identifying the "color" of respondents.

One of the more obsolete features of the older census legislation to survive through 1870 was its lack of attention to the special problems of accurately recording information about immigrants. Anderson has pointed out that approximately 6.6 million Europeans had migrated to the United States since 1840, most of them settling in rapidly growing urban centers. Although Chinese immigrants had entered the country in much smaller numbers, they did not begin to come in significant quantity until after 1850.

By neglecting to enact updated census laws, Congress failed to provide essential assistance for the enumeration of such immigrant populations. Instructions to assistant marshals, for example, directed them to "adapt their inquiries to the comprehension of foreigners and persons of limited education" but made no funds available for the hiring of interpreters.[9] To compound the problem, census guidelines also retained an outdated definition of "family":

> By "family" . . . is meant one or more persons living together and provided for in common. A single person, living alone in a distinct part of a house may constitute a family; while, on the other hand, all the inmates of a boarding house or a hotel will constitute but a single family, though there may be among them many husbands with wives and children. Under whatever circumstances, and in whatever numbers, people live to-

gether under one roof, and are provided for at a common table, there is a family in the meaning of the law.[10]

Thus, census enumerators were faced with the daunting task of accurately identifying the relationships among immigrants residing in urban boardinghouses—a group that accounted for the majority of both female and male Chinese Americans in San Francisco in 1870—while relying on ad hoc interpreters and possessing no effective means of identifying family connections among their subjects.

In addition to the inadequacies of census instructions, the 1870 effort suffered from a woeful labor shortage at the field level. The national enumeration was conducted by only 6,530 assistants under the supervision of 62 federal marshals.[11] For the Fourth and Sixth wards of San Francisco, in which almost all of that city's Chinese population lived, only two individuals bore responsibility for recording information about every resident. Moreover, federal instructions prevented the assistant marshals from enlisting deputies to help them: "The assistant marshals shall make the enumeration by actual inquiry at every dwelling house, or by personal inquiry of the head of every family, and not otherwise. The duty can not be performed by deputy or proxy."[12] Finally, the individuals chosen for this task were not required to meet any qualifications for their service but were appointed by the federal marshal in their district, who was under no obligation to offer a justification for his selections to census officials in Washington.[13] Therefore, one must commence any study of Chinese Americans in the 1870 San Francisco census with the recognition that the entire project was carried out by two people whose suitability for the job was determined by a single federal marshal whose own position had been awarded through senatorial recommendation in exchange for political loyalty.

Given the limitations of legal guidelines and excessive workloads, the performance of census enumerators assigned to San Francisco's predominately Chinese wards assumes paramount importance in assessing this source's reliability. For Ward 4, the responsibility fell to William Martin. Although most of his life remains buried in anonymity, a few shreds of information have survived. A native of Ireland, Martin had settled in the city sometime before 1860 and established a general merchandise business with a number of partners. The census schedules for that year suggest that he had achieved some success in his new place of residence, claiming a personal estate valued at $2,000 and another $4,000 in real property.[14] Thirty-one years old at the time of the enumeration, he and Jane, his twenty-six-year-old, Ohio-born wife, shared a home with two children: Benjamin O'Mera (age eight and born in England) and Alice O'Mera (age five months and born in California).[15] The reason the children did not bear his surname is unknown. Perhaps Martin was their stepfather, or maybe, in the interest of attracting a broader range of customers, he had adopted a business name that did not identify him as Irish.

Given the fact that Benjamin's place of birth was listed as England even though his father had left there more than ten years earlier, it is also possible that he and his sister were foster children.

In spite of his earlier prosperity, the 1860s had not treated William Martin with kindness. By the time of the next census, his business had gone bankrupt. At the same time he was conducting the enumeration of Ward 4, Martin and a former partner named C. P. Robinson were attempting to recover ownership of a corner lot at Jackson and Hyde streets by filing suit in district court against their erstwhile associates.[16] In response to the interview for his own family, he claimed ownership of no real estate, valued his personal property at only $125, and listed his occupation merely as "Census Taker."[17] His personal life had fared no better. Jane no longer lived with him, and although divorce may have been the cause it is more likely that she had died. Although Benjamin was also absent from the household, he may have established an independent residence after achieving his majority, perhaps as an expression of dissatisfaction with his father's new wife Fanny, a year older than William and also from Ireland.[18] Although none of these mysteries can be answered with any certainty, only Alice—whose surname was now listed as "Martin"—remained at home.

Notwithstanding such economic and family tragedies, William Martin had apparently maintained sufficient political connections to secure the financially lucrative appointment as enumerator for the Fourth Ward. No documentation exists to determine whether the person responsible for his selection, W. G. Morris, grand marshal for the district of California, acted out of party patronage alone or combined that motive with personal friendship. His reasons were sufficiently strong, however, to warrant disregard of the 1850 law's requirement that the enumerator for each census subdivision (in San Francisco, each city ward) "should be a resident therein."[19] Thus, without further information to the contrary, Martin most likely began his work in the Fourth Ward without the ability to speak Chinese, with limited knowledge of the community, and having secured the position as a means of rebuilding a portion of his lost wealth. Moreover, unless he differed from the majority of San Francisco's Irish Americans, he also brought to the enumeration a clearly defined bias against Chinese immigrants.

Even though no record exists of his personal views regarding Chinese immigration, one can speculate with more certainty that William Martin was unfamiliar with the community he was surveying. Without governmental provision for an interpreter to accompany him, the maze of boardinghouses must have presented a formidable obstacle. To help him navigate through the ward in time to meet deadlines, census instructions permitted the estimation of information such as age and offered assurance that he was "under no obligation to give any man's occupation just as he expresses it."[20] Thus, when hindered by difficulties of language he could expedite the process of recording vital statistics by writing down what he could understand and accept as true and then guessing at the rest.

Martin most often took advantage of the "best approximation" option by choosing the diminutive term *Ah* to accompany the surnames of his respondents (and incorrectly recording it as their surnames), employing it for more than 99 percent of the Fourth Ward's Chinese female residents.[21] Moreover, the enumerator appears to have approached other areas of his work with an equally reckless commitment to expediency. Although nationally the Chinese community contained well below one hundred females per one thousand males in 1870, the Fourth Ward's females-per-thousand ratio was 409. The number rose to 730 when limited to dwellings that contained both genders.[22] Such remarkable parity does not in itself indicate that nuclear families were misidentified, but Martin's negligence increased the likelihood of such occurrences.

Among the seventeen people (ten males and seven females) who lived in an average dwelling containing both female and male residents, Martin managed to identify on average a fraction above two families and generally divided them according to sex.[23] Because groups of men and women would have no doubt congregated together, that enumerative tendency likely made the work go faster but was wholly inappropriate for identifying family relationships. Therefore, although his choice of "Prostitute" as the occupational category for nearly 90 percent of Chinese females over the age of twelve may have been the correct one, it offers little more promise of accuracy than does the identification of their surnames as Ah.[24]

Significantly, Sue Fawn Chung has discovered a similar failure to decipher living arrangements in the Virginia City, Nevada, census for 1870, which identified ninety-four of the community's 103 Chinese females as prostitutes: "A single woman living in a household with more than one male was not necessarily a prostitute, since kinsmen tended to live together under the care of a husband and wife team."[25] Attempting to account for the cultural ignorance of the local enumerators, Chung has proposed a significant downward revision of the totals of prostitutes in 1870: "By subtracting the twenty-three women who were probably married and living with their spouses from the number of women designated as prostitutes, the number of Chinese women involved in sexual commerce drops dramatically to seventy-one (70 percent of the former total). Assuming that there were married women who were missed by the census taker, the ratio of prostitutes to married women might be even lower."[26] Given the likelihood of inflated numbers of prostitutes in Virginia City's relatively small Chinatown, one can assume even greater probability of such misrepresentation in San Francisco, which contained the country's largest and most important Chinese community.

Although conclusions about the character and attitudes of William Martin are limited to informed conjecture, one may portray the assistant marshal for Ward

6 with more confidence. A native of England, Henry C. Bennett had not yet migrated to San Francisco at the time of the 1860 census but, like Congressman Page and Judge Sawyer, had first settled in gold country. By the beginning of the Civil War he had established an abolitionist newspaper in Nevada City and, although electing not to establish such an enterprise after moving to the coast sometime in the latter half of the decade, still listed his occupation as "Editor" on the 1870 census schedule.[27] In city directories he had also identified himself as both a federal pension agent and secretary of the Chinese Protection Society. Fifty-six when he began to fulfill the duties of an enumerator, Bennett was a resident of Ward 6. He lived on Clay Street with Harriet, a Massachusetts-born wife twenty-one years his junior, and their five children, all of whom were natives of California: Harry, fourteen; Eugenia, twelve; Joseph, nine; and Reuben and George, four and one, respectively.[28] Even though the family did not own their residence, Henry listed his personal estate at a fairly substantial $2,500. Perhaps as a result of that relative prosperity and his political activism, Marshal Morris had awarded him the lucrative dual positions of enumerator and compiler of the city's full census report.[29]

On May 21, less than two weeks before commencing his enumerative duties, Henry Bennett presented a lecture at Mechanics Institute Hall in support of continued Chinese immigration. In that presentation, he argued that Chinese labor had greatly benefited the region, creating demand for the job skills of white workers rather than undercutting their employment opportunities.[30] Accordingly, in the introduction to his address, Bennett announced, "'I shall assume the office of counsel for the defense of the Chinese, not so much for their sake as for the sake of the white workingmen of California.'"[31] Describing China as "the purest democracy existing," he cited as proof "its fundamental principle . . . 'that the will of the people is the law of Heaven,'" the possibility for upward mobility afforded through it civil service system, and the prevalence of at least functional literacy among its population. Claiming the support of congressional leadership dedicated to protecting the interests of white workers, he then argued that "it was the destiny of the republic to utilize [Chinese] labor as a means of converting them to Christianity, and that California should reap the advantages and honor of making the conversion."[32]

Although supportive of Chinese immigration in general, Bennett conceded that "much, and well-grounded complaint is made against the importation of a class of Chinese females, who are a danger and disgrace to this community."[33] He blamed the importation of Chinese prostitutes on white traffickers, however, and predicted that the enterprise would soon be halted by governmental cooperation between the countries of origin and destination: "With reference to the Chinese women, he showed conclusively that they were not brought here by the Chinese, who had protested and petitioned against their being allowed to land, and had actually paid the fare of hundreds of them back to China. They were brought here by white men, in defiance of law, decency and popular opinion. The lecturer stated that no more of this class of Chinese women would be brought here, as the Governments of the United States and China had taken such steps as would prevent them."[34] Bennett held his convictions strongly enough to broadcast them before an audience that responded to his speech with frequent interruptions, periodic attempts to wrest the podium from his control, and what one reporter who covered the event characterized as "three groans for Bennett."[35]

Near the end of June, as his work for the census continued, the Chinese Protection Society awarded Bennett a medal in recognition of his service to the city's Chinese community.[36] In its account of the ceremony, the *Evening Bulletin* verified his identity as the society's secretary.[37] Mary Coolidge would later single out this group as an especially important guardian of immigrant safety: "In 1869, the abuse had become so flagrant and the police so indifferent that a Chinese Protection Society was organized among merchants and humanitarians in San Francisco, which employed a staff of special police to patrol the city day and night and to arrest those molesting the Chinese."[38] For documentary evidence to support such recognition, Coolidge cites an article appearing in the *Sacramento Daily Union* on November 27, 1869. Its author was Henry Bennett.

As executive head of the society, Bennett had attempted in his article to present a comprehensive description of San Francisco's Chinese population. Following a statistical analysis of their economic contributions to the city and the state of California, he had argued that "aside from prejudice, which proceeds from ignorance, there is nothing in the habits or customs of the Chinese calculated to injure the morals or business of any American community."[39] Although providing an estimate of the number of immigrant females, he made no mention of prostitution. He had chosen to conclude the account, however, with an indictment of San Francisco's Irish American community, of which William Martin was a part: "It is a significant fact . . . that every person arrested [by Chinese Protective Society officers] was an Irishman, and the children who give the officers the most trouble are of Irish parentage."[40] Responding to Bennett's assertions in a separate article, the *Union* noted that his report was "quite interesting" and commended it "to the careful perusal and study of our readers."[41]

In contrast to Martin, Henry Bennett's role as an advocate for San Francisco's Chinese American community afforded him a significant advantage as he approached the assignment of surveying the Sixth Ward. Armed with his record of courageous support for Chinese immigrants, Bennett likely found willing volunteers to serve as interpreters in a section of the city where he made his home. Perhaps as a result of that familiarity and assistance, he used *Ah* only 67 percent of the time and, unlike Martin, in its proper position following the surname.[42] Working against his ability to delineate nuclear families was a ratio of only 155 females per thousand males, which increased to 422 per thousand when confined to mixed-gender dwellings.[43] Still, Bennett identified nearly three families per dwelling among an average of fourteen residents.[44] Moreover, the benefit of interpretive aid apparently enabled him to recognize relationships between females and males rather than simply resort to his colleague's artificial divisions based on gender.[45]

Unfortunately, census schedules do not lend themselves to a comprehensive analysis of differences between the Chinese residents of Wards 4 and 6. Therefore, one cannot discount the possibility that the former contained a significantly larger proportion of prostitutes among its Chinese female population. Yet the relative credibility of each enumeration can be judged with far more confidence. By every available criterion, the trustworthiness of Henry Bennett's work exceeded that of William Martin's. Perhaps Martin's attitudes toward Chinese immigrants differed from those of most Irish Americans living in San Francisco. Still, even if anti-Chinese sentiments did not influence his performance, census schedules at least suggest that he approached his work with little regard for precision.

Bennett, however, had established an impressive public record of support for the immigrants while never acting as an apologist for the prostitution industry. Moreover, from among all the city's enumerators, Marshal Morris had selected him to serve in the critical role of compiler of the San Francisco census. Although nothing more than political patronage was required to secure the post of census taker, errors in the final compilation sent to Washington could delay payment for services and necessitate unremunerated recounts.[46] Such an unpleasant possibility offered sufficient grounds to warrant placing the task in the hands of the most skilled rather than the best connected official. Thus, all available evidence supports the reliability of Bennett's survey, depicting a Chinese American community in which 47 percent of females over the age of twelve were not employed in the prostitution industry.[47] Conversely, the same documentation casts doubt on the problematically high prostitute count that Martin reported.

The 1880 Census: Efficiency and Speculation

Although the 1870 census suffered from bureaucratic obsolescence, later officials declared that its successor marked "the beginning of the third era in census taking in this country."[48] As the result of legislation passed in 1879, the superintendent of the census received direct supervisory authority over the entire enumerative process, which enabled him to remove the responsibility for field research from the hands of federal marshals. In preparation for that task, Superintendent F. A. Walker appointed 150 field supervisors and 31,000 enumerators, selected on the basis of their qualifications, to do the work that had been performed by only 62 marshals and 6,530 assistants in 1870.[49] For San Francisco's Chinese community, thirty-three enumerators completed the task Martin and Bennett had performed by themselves ten years earlier.[50]

Beyond the benefits of a dramatically increased workforce, the 1880 census also featured an improved information set in its schedules. In addition to the old requirement of assigning a number to each dwelling, enumerators were instructed to record street addresses. Columns were also added for the purpose of identifying marital status and familial relationships. Supplementary to such improvements in format, an eleventh-hour modification in the rules of appointment clarified the circumstances under which the 1850 law's residency requirement for enumerators could be set aside:

> It is provided by law that enumerators shall be selected solely with reference to their fitness, and without regard to their political or party affiliations. Enumerators are required to be residents of their respective districts, with the following exception, to wit: That "in case it should occur in any enumeration district that no person qualified to perform, and willing to undertake, the duties of enumerator resides in that district, the supervisor may appoint any fit person, resident in the county, to be an enumerator in that district."[51]

That stipulation guarded against awarding positions in exchange for political support while replacing the ward system with much smaller enumeration districts. It also made the appointments far less financially rewarding—and therefore far less attractive—than they had been in 1870.

As a byproduct of the position's less lucrative nature, indexes in the census schedules do not reveal the location of the 1880 enumerators. Those discovered by chance during the course of searching the schedules for Chinese Americans were not heads of their own households. When entrusted with the task ten years earlier, Martin and Bennett had already lived to middle age, raised families, experienced the unpredictability of fortune, and established valuable political relationships. In contrast, Edward Wadhan, the official responsible in 1880 for surveying residents of the Second Ward's Enumeration District 21, was only nineteen and lived with his parents.[52] Because Anderson has noted that Superintendent Walker "turned to the new universities to recruit his special agents and higher-grade staff," perhaps field supervisors had followed his example and offered enumerator positions as summer employment for students at the nearby University of California.[53]

Despite the great advantage of increased personnel, directors of the 1880 census achieved mixed results in efforts to purge obsolete or ill-advised regulations from statutes that governed their work. Although retaining their requirement that "the work of enumeration must be done by the enumerator in person, and can not be performed by proxy," they revised the definition of "family" to account for the distinct environment of urban boardinghouses: "The word family, for the purposes of the census, includes persons living alone, as previously described, equally with families in the ordinary sense of that term, and also larger aggregations of people having only the tie of a common roof and table. A hotel, with all its inmates, constitutes but one family within the meaning of this term. . . . In the case, however, of tenement houses and of the so-called 'flats' of the great cities, as many families are to be recorded as there are separate tables."[54] Thus, the enumerators of 1880 could not duplicate William Martin's strategy of dividing the residents of Chinese boardinghouses into two families according to gender. Instead, they were expected, in keeping with the schedules' new column for listing familial relationships, to identify all nuclear families within a given dwelling.

Regrettably, such wise retentions and revisions were sometimes counterbalanced by poorly reasoned policies. For example, the federal government still failed to allocate funds for interpretive assistance in districts containing high immigrant populations but gave enumerators even more freedom to "correct" what they regarded as dishonest responses to their questions: "It is further to be noted that the enumerator is not required to accept answers which he knows, or has reason to believe, are false. He has a right to a true statement on every matter respecting which he is bound to inquire; and he is not concluded by a false statement. Should any person persist in making statements which are obviously erroneous, the enumerator should enter upon the schedule the facts as nearly as he can ascertain them by his own observation or by inquiry of credible persons."[55] Without interpreters to assist their efforts, even better qualified enumerators might be expected to have relied upon their prejudices for or against the Chinese in judging the veracity of responses about female occupations. Moreover, amid the exclusion fervor energizing San Francisco in 1880 such prejudices were more likely to have fallen on the anti-Chinese side.

Given this mixture of improvements, ill-advised carryovers, and unwise revisions, the general reliability of the 1880 census is difficult to ascertain. In balance, the value of information recorded on its schedules exceeds that contained in earlier efforts, but the issue of probable inaccuracies revolves once again around the actual performance of field enumerators. Unfortunately, their relative youth eliminates the feasibility of providing personal histories to compare with those of Martin and Bennett. The more manageable size of enumeration districts, however, minimizes the importance of such missing evidence. Not only did their abbreviated assignments afford a distinct advantage over the ward divisions in terms of workload but they also minimized the impact of individual prejudices on the composite results. Whether supportive or hostile toward Chinese immigrants, each worker gathered information for roughly 10 percent of the numbers he would have surveyed under the earlier system. Whereas William Martin had been responsible for shaping public perceptions regarding nearly 50 percent of San Francisco's

Chinese American community—and more than 75 percent of its females—none of the 1880 enumerators wielded even a substantial fraction of his influence.

Although their diminished roles lessened the individual significance of census takers in 1880, the results of their collective effort are both important and accessible. Perhaps owing to the less daunting task assigned to them, the surveyors of enumeration districts in the Fourth and Sixth wards resorted much less often than had Martin, or even Bennett, to the use of *Ah* in identifying Chinese residents—only between 4 and 6 percent of the time.[56] Furthermore, despite demographic changes that no doubt made their task more difficult, the census takers identified a dramatically higher number of nuclear families than had either of their predecessors.

In Ward 4, a substantial increase in the male population had combined with a smaller decline among females to create a per-thousand ratio of only 254, which grew to but 407 when limited to dwellings containing both genders.[57] Yet in the Sixth Ward, although the rate of female population growth had significantly outdistanced that of its male counterpart since 1870, the number of males cohabiting with females had more than tripled. Thus, the latter's increased ratio of 223 per thousand had actually fallen to only 293 in sexually integrated residences.[58] Furthermore, even though the number of people residing in an average Fourth Ward dwelling remained at seventeen, only five were now likely to be female, a figure that remained virtually constant in Ward 6 but was typically accompanied by sixteen males.[59] Yet enumerators in 1880 still managed to distinguish three to four families per dwelling in each ward.[60]

Although these statistics suggest a movement toward the level of accuracy demonstrated by Henry Bennett, no one enjoying a similar degree of friendship and trust among Chinese Americans served as an enumerator for the 1880 census. Federal officials' apparent reliance upon educated young people, however, likely improved the precision with which information made its way from mouth to paper. Yet lack of social experience may have put them at a disadvantage in comparison with both of their 1870 counterparts when faced with contradictory impressions. Exercising the authority to correct suspect answers, field-workers in several wards seemed particularly inclined to note alternative occupations for female respondents. For example, Tallmadge Norwood's survey of Enumeration District 54 in the Sixth Ward discovered an inordinate number of women who claimed to be dressmakers. For 143 of them, most of whom were whites born in either Europe or the United States, he wrote "Dressmaker?" in the occupational box.[61] Similarly, enumerators for three districts in Ward 4 recorded "Prostitute?" for 147 Chinese women, even though 58 of them were married and living with their husbands.[62] Unfortunately, the listing for "Relationship to Head of Household" focused solely on a single individual whom enumerators judged to have authority over a particular group of people as "ostensible head of the family."[63] Thus, the record identifies most married women who lived in boardinghouses as "Lodger" or "Boarder." Still, seventeen of the women were given some variation of "Wife?/ Prostitute" in the relational and occupational categories.[64]

White respondents, all but one of whom were single, divorced, or widowed, might have issued "Dressmaker" claims to frustrate a young census taker for their own amusement. Yet regardless of Norwood's likely ability to perceive tone and mannerisms as well as language, compilers of the final census tabulation dismissed his suspicions and counted none of the women as prostitutes. Conversely, when the group of Chinese females in Ward 4 identified themselves as the wives of males within the same family units, enumerators who could not speak Chinese judged themselves competent to expose deception. Their presumption also saddled eighty-nine single women in the same ward with the analogous designation "Prostitute?"[65]

Thus, on the basis of nothing more than ill-informed hunches, enumerators had placed 13.6 percent of the ward's Chinese female population over the age of twelve on their list of permanent suspects. Moreover, in contrast with their non-Chinese counterparts, the census schedules' final tabulation indicates that all the women were included in the prostitute total. If one removes them from the count for lack of conclusive evidence—as was apparently the case with the white dressmakers of Enumeration District 54—the percentage of Chinese prostitutes residing in the Fourth Ward drops from 33 to 20 percent of the female population over twelve, moving it significantly toward the 10 percent recorded in Ward 6, where none of the "Prostitute?" variations were used for Chinese respondents.[66]

In the fulfillment of their recording duties, 1880 census takers appear to have demonstrated a level of reliability—at least relative to San Francisco's Chinese American community—that fell somewhere between the performances of Henry Bennett and William Martin. Like Bennett, their ability to record more than the surnames of respondents corresponded with a smaller percentage of prostitutes in their report of the female population. Yet the propensity of some Ward 4 workers for "correcting" the occupations of Chinese women reflects the same kind of apparent anti-Chinese bias that brings Martin's prostitute count into question. Although not contradicting the contention of other scholars that Chinese prostitution remained an important industry in San Francisco throughout the preexclusion period, a critical analysis of the two censuses suggests that both likely exaggerated its significance. Enumerators no doubt overrepresented the number of prostitutes and at the same time failed to acknowledge a rising percentage of those who were not prostitutes in the Chinese female population. Such probable distortion lends new credence to the generally ignored assertion that Loomis made in response to H. H. Bancroft's letter of inquiry in 1876: The more recent pattern of Chinese female immigration to the United States had been characterized by a growing number of wives.[67] If Loomis was right, as this study's analysis suggests, census data represented yet another element in the character assassination of San Francisco's Chinese American women.

Because the 1870 and 1880 censuses offer the only comprehensive pictures of Chinatown between ratification of the Burlingame Treaty and passage of the Exclusion Act, the apparent errors in the enumerations are unfortunate. In 1870 a pair of individuals wielded enormous power in shaping both public and governmental perceptions, and the disparity of their reports cannot be dismissed. In his survey of Ward 4, William Martin may or may not have applied the anti-Chinese bias held by most of his fellow Irish Americans. The record of his work indicates, however, that language barriers operated in conjunction with a desire to complete the project as expediently as possible. The result was a poorly compiled census that appears to have relied more on the quick application of popular stereotypes than on a serious attempt to gather data.

Such shortcuts, as well as their results, are even more troublesome when compared with Henry Bennett's survey of the Sixth Ward. Perhaps the geographic area assigned to Bennett merely contained all of Chinatown's "respectable" women, or maybe his advocacy in behalf of Chinese immigrants inspired a distortion of the facts for the purpose of rehabilitating their public image. Neither assertion can be disproved or validated with the available evidence, but the comparative superiority of Bennett's work argues against them. In terms of thoroughness, whether recording vital statistics for prostitutes or wives, his survey of Ward 6 represents the best enumeration of Chinese Americans compiled during the preexclusion period. Thus, the myriad occupations among the ward's female residents—especially given the demonstrated reluctance of San Francisco officials and newspaper reporters to acknowledge any such diversity—suggests that women who were not prostitutes had already immigrated in significant numbers by 1870.

The succeeding census greatly reduced the influence of census takers while demanding of them a similar degree of professionalism to that which Henry Bennett had voluntarily demonstrated. Yet new legislation also permitted a flexibility that made the record's corruption more transparent. Although biased suppositions also targeted non-Chinese women at the field level, officials at the Bureau of Census purged their potential impact from their final tabulation. For the white population, "Dressmaker?" was reduced to nothing more than a curiosity for scholars conducting research on the enumeration schedules. Conversely, the designation "Prostitute?" accounted for approximately a third of the Chinese women "officially" reported as engaged in that occupation.[68] One cannot discount the possibility that enumerators in Chinatown may have been right in their instincts, but an equal application of such speculation would have also resulted in a much higher non-Chinese prostitute count. Therefore, racial selectivity in the compilation process clearly skewed the 1880 findings in a manner adverse to the reputations of Chinese Americans.

The historical record of these Chinatown censuses calls to mind observations made by Robert Irick upon concluding his study of the Ch'ing government's attempts to protect emigrant laborers from abuse. Irick argues that previous studies had unfairly labeled imperial officials as unconcerned about the fate of their overseas citizens. He then calls into question the wisdom of basing such an assessment on the claims of foreign observers, who are both ignorant of the cultural subtleties underlying Chinese actions and predisposed to assume their insincerity:

> I have tried in the foregoing pages to outline the Chinese policy toward the coolie trade as presented in the Chinese documentation. It was not always an effective or even rational policy from a modern point of view, but the picture that emerges is far more positive than the ones of disinterest, ineptitude, corruption, and nonaction that are usually presented. It causes me to question seriously the validity of relying solely on the observations and descriptions of contemporary foreigners, even though they may have been intimately concerned with the problem and familiar with the Chinese. We must always allow for prejudice on the part of the observer, but the suspicion must go even deeper, to the point of questioning whether or not the cultural, racial, and religious biases of the nineteenth-century foreigner in China made it impossible for him to understand Chinese motives and actions. If the same applies to other problems of Chinese diplomacy in the nineteenth century, then our whole conception of the period must be seriously revised.[69]

For Chinese American females living in San Francisco in 1870 and 1880, the same tainting of records appears to have characterized the evaluation of their occupations and familial relationships contained in the federal censuses. Therefore, to borrow Irick's words, perhaps "our whole conception of the [preexclusion] period must be seriously revised."

If one accounts for questionable census data, it is probable that at least a thousand of San Francisco's Chinese females were not working as prostitutes in 1870 and that the number had grown to nearly 1,700 ten years later. With the notable exception of Henry Bennett, however, field-workers collecting raw data for these final two censuses before exclusion appear to have allowed societal—and perhaps personal—prejudices to obscure the existence of resident women who met the Page Law's criteria for admission into the country. In so doing, they both followed and fueled a multilayered system that severely inhibited the ability of such legal immigrants to reunite with their husbands and parents. Enumerators entering Chinatown's boardinghouses tended to see what local newspapers and government officials prepared them to see, and their reports provided "objective evidence" that strengthened the case of both Horace Page in 1875 and the sponsors of the Exclusion Act seven years later. Thus, they constituted the final link in a circular chain of discrimination that reinforced the original pattern of gender imbalance in the Chinese American community.

8

The Task of Restoring
Female Visibility

Regardless of their true reasons for coming, Chinese women who immigrated to the United States both during and after exclusion suffered from negative stereotyping of their sexual habits. Stuart Miller has traced this image of immorality to the early nineteenth century, when Protestant missionaries began working in China and depicted all of China, especially the peasant classes from which most immigrants came, as morally corrupt. One missionary, writing in 1830, for example, described Chinese villages as places where "'girls scarcely twelve years old were given up to the beastly passions of men. Parents prostituted their daughters; husbands their wives; brothers their sisters—and this they did with diabolical joy.'"[1] Journalists also joined in denunciations of Chinese decadence. Horace Greeley asserted in 1854 that "the Chinese are uncivilized, unclean, and filthy beyond all conception without any of the higher domestic or social relations; lustful and sensual in their dispositions; every female is a prostitute of the basest order."[2]

Of course such depictions of Chinese prostitution did contain at least a kernel of truth. Impoverished families sometimes sold female children to purchasing agents, who might then market their property to brothels. In addition, a significant number of Chinese women, faced with severely restricted opportunities for financial independence, chose to use their ability to provide sexual services as a means of attaining a measure of autonomy. Such diversity in the process through which prostitutes had entered into the industry produced an equally complex social hierarchy among them. Gail Hershatter has identified perhaps as many as ten layers in this structure at different points in China's history.[3] Because others have noted that overseas communities as a whole possessed much more compressed social frameworks than did their urban counterparts at home, it is safe to surmise that a simpler hierarchy also existed among San Francisco's immigrant prostitutes.[4] Still, even a truncated catalog of differences in both their initial recruitment and position within Chinese society would no doubt have confounded the interpretive efforts of journalists and other writers.

Although most of the white prostitutes in Chinatown voluntarily entered their profession in response to limited employment options, some had been forced into prostitution. Published descriptions of the women emphasized the latter condition over the former, however, and writers consistently presented white slave-prostitutes as unfortunate victims of deception and perversion, implying that they would not have voluntarily sold themselves. Most followed a pattern similar to the account of a *New York Times* reporter, who, in 1873, visited an opium den in his city's newly developing Chinese community: "To the reporter's inquiry about 'a handsome but squalidly dressed young white girl' present in an opium den, the owner replied 'with a horrible leer, "Oh hard time in New York. Young girl hungry. Plenty come here. Chinaman always have something to eat, and he like young white girl, He! He!"'" The article warned, "This was no empty boast; many white girls were lured into these opium dens."[5]

Conversely, although Chinese prostitutes were also depicted as slaves, American writers regarded their bondage as exclusively monetary in nature and announced that they readily engaged in sexual intercourse for money. Indeed, one missionary reported that "girls in China prostituted themselves at four and five years of age."[6] Therefore, in contrast to the methods necessary to entrap whites, the owners of Chinatown brothels had not lured the women into immoral lifestyles but had lured immoral women into positions of economic slavery through false promises of profit: "'The unfortunate girls were also deceived. They were led to believe that when they arrived in San Francisco they would get $1,000 a year, which the cunning importers falsely promised them.'"[7] The distinction separated Chinese prostitutes from their white counterparts and preserved their image as unusually harmful to the country's moral well-being.

Governmental officials usually joined newspaper editors and missionaries in decrying the negative impact of all prostitution on San Francisco society, but all three singled out the Chinese as especially dangerous threats to white families. Attracted by irresistible stories of these lustful experts at seduction and sexual pleasure, husbands and sons often visited Chinatown brothels, bringing disgrace upon themselves and the women who waited for them at home. Near the time of the Page Law's enactment, new medical theories on the transmission of diseases added the fear of contamination to these feelings of shame. Miller has revealed the strength of this second concern in his account of the American Medical Association's research on the spread of syphilis.[8] Despite the association's conclusion that Chinese immigrants had not imported a special strain of the disease, its director asserted in 1876 that Chinese syphilis represented a major health hazard to the families of white men and boys who used the services of Chinatown prostitutes:

No less a figure than J. Marion Sims of New York, president of the AMA and world-famous gynecologist, sounded the tocsin of Chinese syphilis in 1876. In his official address at the centennial jubilee of the AMA, Sims warned that the spread of syphilis had already reached epidemic proportions. He indicted the "Chinese slave" used for the purpose of prostitution, who "breeds moral and physical pestilence" on the West Coast. There, "even boys eight and ten years old have been syphilized by these degraded wretches."[9]

Although the 1870–71 *San Francisco Directory* had listed 446 white prostitutes among that city's population, Sims's speech demonstrates that even the eastern medical community had charged Chinese houses of prostitution with almost exclusive responsibility for the spread of venereal diseases in California—and that anti-Chinese forces had sought to establish a specific, noneconomic reason for eliminating Chinese female immigration before 1875.[10]

Horace F. Page, in a speech before the Congress on February 10, 1875, expressed the particular concern of white women over the perceived threat that the immigration of Chinese females posed to their security: "I hope, sir, that it [the evidence he had presented in support of restricting female immigration from China] will have the effect to place a dividing line between vice and virtue; that it will send the brazen harlot who openly flaunts her wickedness in the faces of our wives and daughters back to her native country."[11] Chinese women, whom white society had almost universally branded as immoral seductresses, threatened family health and security by compromising the moral integrity of white males.

Faced with the identification of these female immigrants as dangerous moral and medical threats to American society, Congress acceded to the demands of western legislators for a bill that would prohibit them from entering the country. Thus, the Page Law did not exist as a mere appendage in the fight to exclude Chinese labor but sought to address the concerns of a powerful and diverse coalition united only in its opposition to Chinese female immigration. While ineptly attempting to prohibit the immigration of coolies the legislation mobilized American consular and port authorities in a vigorous effort to stop Chinese women from endangering the nation's physical and ethical well-being. Moreover, although the law limited its official focus to prostitution, enforcement officers expanded it in a way that could also protect those who employed Chinese labor from the threat of increased wage demands due to dependent immigration. By using a common assessment of Chinese womanhood, held at least since the 1830s, they could turn away the wives and daughters of workingmen as "immoral women," thereby excluding virtually all prospective female immigrants.

With the exception of John Mosby's 1882 histrionics, the records of consular attempts to enforce the legislation indicate that they exercised uncommon diligence in its implementation. David Bailey initiated a remarkably thorough procedure for preventing Chinese women, suspected of emigrating as prostitutes, from reaching port in San Francisco. Sheldon Loring may have lacked Bailey's personal interest in the law, but he still maintained the system of enforcement established by his predecessor. Finally, although formally charging that Bailey and Loring had handled the statute with mercenary ineptitude, Consul Mosby adopted their method of screening prospective female emigrants.

Even though U.S. consuls in Hong Kong vigorously fulfilled the Page Law's requirements of them, the statute neglected to address the concerns of organized labor, which composed the heart of America's anti-Chinese movement. Labor demanded general exclusion, and representatives such as Horace Page, who depended increasingly upon such support for reelection, intended from the beginning to replace the 1875 law with a federal exclusion act. Thus, Page's legislation merely represented the best immigration restriction possible under the guidelines of the Burlingame Treaty. Its focus on prostitution would pacify moralists within the anti-Chinese movement until a revision of the treaty could be secured, which would then permit passage of the first Exclusion Act.

Of all the ordeals faced by those who immigrated to San Francisco before exclusion's implementation, their experiences during the habeas corpus trials of 1882 constituted the strongest contradiction of the prostitute charge. In each hearing, prosecutors pressed for deportation before judges supportive of their efforts. Sometimes even helping district attorneys with their questioning, none of the judges ever expressed doubt that the petitioners in their courtrooms had come to the United States for the purposes of prostitution. Yet despite the aid of such biased referees, the government never won a case. Its only evidence consisted of the commonly held conviction that any Chinese woman who arrived at the city's docks, other than the wife or concubine of a merchant or member of the "educated elite," was a prostitute. Although the judges all announced agreement with that assessment, conscience was blamed for preventing them from issuing deportation orders without the benefit of more substantive and specific defamations of character. Impelled by fidelity to the law, they expressed regret over allowing the entry of immoral women and then ordered the petitioners released. Had there existed any factual basis for concluding that these immigrants were anything but the wives or daughters of Chinese American laborers, the likelihood of such a scenario taking place defies belief.

In contrast to the courts, San Francisco newspapers were not bound by evidenciary restraints in subjecting the Page Law's enforcement to public scrutiny. Inspired by the ethical and medical fears that had given life to the statute, city reporters universally portrayed newly arrived females as an additional load of prostitutes whose presence would corrupt white men and spread disease throughout the population. Whenever women came with valid certificates of character, the press still refused to acknowledge their legitimacy. Instead, they branded consular officials in Hong Kong as either the victims of Chinese deception or the accomplices of Chinese tongs, criticized the customs collector for permitting prostitutes to land, and lamented the undermining of their state's health and moral fiber. Faced with such relentless supervision, both the consuls and port authorities made enforcement of the Page Law a priority.

Even when rigid consular examinations resulted in the issuing of certificates of character to emigrant women, port surveyors followed the reasoning of the press. On some occasions they rejected the certificates as the product of deceit or bribery, refusing to grant the female immigrants a landing. When challenged in court, however, such action placed federal judges under the same pressures of public exposure experienced by the consuls and customs officials. San Francisco newspapers regularly accused Lorenzo Sawyer and Ogden Hoffman of showing undue leniency toward Chinese petitioners and, as Sawyer discovered, sometimes fabricated their stories. Their decisions to release the women brought before them—in spite of personal opposition to Chinese female immigration—demonstrated great courage. Still, the judges always attempted to redirect public censure toward Congress, decrying their powerless positions as guardians of a defective law. In so doing, they helped the press transform unpopular decisions into testimonials supporting the cause of exclusion.

At the beginning of each decade, reports from census workers also boosted the exclusion effort. Significantly, however, San Francisco's political leaders did not cite the enumerators' 1880 findings as evidence of diligence. Considering the tremendous drop in Chinese prostitutes since 1870, one would expect the officials to have pointed proudly to their successful campaign against the prostitution industry. Yet newspaper articles and campaign speeches from the period make no mention of the decline and generally point to Chinese prostitution as a growing rather than lessening problem. The failure to acknowledge such a striking reduction in the prostitute population no doubt reflects the intensity of California's anti-Chinese movement, which refused to recognize any positive change in a community it was determined to remove from the state. At any rate, because the Page Law had forced Chinatown's female population to remain essentially the same size, inflated prostitute figures in 1870 may have rendered the change much less dramatic on the streets than on paper.

American consuls, port surveyors, and judges failed to leave an exact record of their impact on Chinese female immigration. By recklessly enforcing the Page Law, however, they clearly erected a formidable barrier. Regardless of the actual number of Chinese wives and daughters turned away or discouraged by the legislation, its existence helped perpetuate the importance of prostitution within the economic and social structure of American Chinatowns. Because the law virtually excluded their spouses from joining them, unattached men continued to pour into the country during the third quarter of the nineteenth century, thereby reinforcing a business that Lucie Cheng Hirata and Benson Tong have designated as one of that period's most lucrative Chinese American enterprises. The tongs operated numerous brothels in cities along the Pacific Coast, especially in San Francisco. Occupying layered social positions that designated the identities of their patrons, this collection of businesses serviced both Chinese and white customers, producing tremendous profits for the owners and creating a difficult problem for the leaders of states such as California that were attempting to attract families from the eastern United States and Western Europe.[12]

In addition to undergirding the institution it sought to eliminate, the Page Law severely inhibited the development of American Chinatowns. Nothing exerted a stronger impact on the evolution of Chinese American society than the shortage of women. A legislative history that followed female exclusion with a general ban on working-class immigration "meant that Chinese laborers, who constituted the majority of the Chinese immigrants, could not establish conjugal families in the United States."[13] Through the middle of the twentieth century, men without families dominated this ethnic community, helping sustain a sense of transience much longer than in others in which earlier immigration had been characterized by sojourners.

Although hardships such as California's special taxes on foreign miners and its cubic air laws (designed to harass boardinghouse residents by jailing them for being packed too tightly into their crowded rooms) damaged the quality of life for male Chinese Americans, the scarcity of women weakened their desire to overcome such difficulties and build more stable lives in a new country. Separation from the support of either joint or nuclear families compounded the effects of ill-treatment, making Chinese laborers more likely to regard their sojourn in the "Golden Mountain" as an ordeal rather than a new beginning. Prostitutes helped to ease the sojourners' loneliness yet did little to enhance the permanence of Chinese settlement in the United States except when they left brothels and married after either fulfilling their labor contracts or escaping from their employers. The future of America's Chinese community lay in the immigration of wives not prostitutes, but the Page Law prohibited both groups from immigrating in significant numbers after 1875.

Scarcity of data limits an assessment of the statute's precise impact to the speculative realm of what might have been. Although such conjecture must be acknowledged as unreliable, it at least serves the purpose of illustration. Had no restriction of their immigration been enacted—and had their numbers increased at the same rate experienced from 1869 to 1874 (626 per year)—then 3,285 additional Chinese females would have entered the United States by 1882.[14] That projection does not account for the likelihood that a much larger than usual group would have joined their male counterparts in the push to immigrate before implementation of the Exclusion Act. Still, even an ordinary pattern of female immigration would have held the gender ratio fairly stable during the resulting explosion of male arrivals. The 1880 census recorded a Chinese American population consisting of 100,686 males and 4,779 females. At a rate of 626 per year, 3,756 new female immigrants would have entered the United States between 1875 and 1880, yet the actual total during that period was only 1,504. By adding the difference between these two figures (2,252) to the total recorded in the census, which would account for repatriations, one can project a Chinese female population, without the Page Law's interference, of 7,031.

That number of females would have limited the expanding sex ratio to about seventy per thousand instead of the forty-seven per thousand that was experienced. Moreover, new female immigration produced a net population gain of only 213 between 1870 and 1880, meaning that 1,288 female Chinese either died, repatriated, or moved to other immigrant communities. Because increased hostility usually produced more return migration, the 1875 law may, therefore, have helped limit actual net gain in addition to restricting immigration. Finally, America's Chinese male population experienced a net growth of about 30 percent from 1880 to 1882. Total female immigration during those two years totaled only 219, however, meaning that the number of females either remained stagnant or declined due to departures. Had the female population increased at the same rate as the male, it would have exceeded nine thousand by the time of exclusion and held the sex ratio at 1880 proportions.[15] Furthermore, the record of Chinese settlement in Hawaii and Malacca suggests that the ratio likely would have narrowed when the 1882 legislation cut off the flow of new immigrants.

Despite the enactment of general restrictive legislation, Hawaii's Chinese continued the family-building process, and the proportion of females to males grew during the immigration declines that characterized Malacca's years of economic decline. Unattached men moved on to more favorable environments, but families tended to weather the hardships and stay. Thus, in the aftermath of exclusion, America's Chinese male population plummeted to fewer than sixty-seven thousand by 1910, whereas the number of females had almost fully recovered from an initial drop by the same year.[16] Had the Page Law not prevented female immigration from maintaining its 1869 through 1874 rate, the exodus of sojourners likely would have reduced the Chinese American sex ratio to nearly 120 females per thousand males—possibly much lower, depending on the extent to which women participated in the great immigrant wave of 1882.[17] Such projections, although potentially well off the mark and hardly approaching parity, suggest that the development of nuclear family units in America's Chinese community would likely have followed a pattern similar to that of Hawaii, remaining slightly behind due to

America's substantially greater distance from the Chinese mainland. Although one can only guess at its precise effect on family development, the Page Law did at least prevent Chinese Americans from settling in the "normal" manner reflected by their immigration to other parts of the world.

My assumption has been that the law's negative effect on family immigration resulted accidentally through the misapplication of prevalent anti-Chinese stereotypes. Cheng and Bonacich, however, have noted that capitalist interests often persuade their governments to pass legislation designed to prohibit women and children from immigrating, thereby preserving a low-cost labor force by excluding dependents: "Immigration law can select for able-bodied young men while excluding all dependent populations, such as women, children, the elderly, the sick, and paupers. When they are not permitted to bring families, they can be housed in bunkhouses, compounds, or other substandard housing, while educational facilities need not be supplied, and so on."[18]

One cannot discount the possibility that politically powerful employers of Chinese labor such as the railroad companies at least secretly supported the Page Law while publicly opposing exclusion. Surviving records, however, render more defensible the interpretation that moral and medical paranoia joined with negative stereotyping of Chinese women to produce, inadvertently, the same kind of selective exclusion those scholars have described.

Despite the likelihood that female exclusion was an unintentional byproduct of the Page Law, Judge Lorenzo Sawyer's observations about the limited desirability of Chinese immigration offer at least some justification for applying the Cheng and Bonacich model to this legislation. Maintaining the opinion of Chinese work habits he had formulated in 1850, Judge Sawyer took exactly the position they would have predicted. He rejected the assertion that Chinese workers threatened the economic future of the West and relied on racial stereotypes to assert their superiority in comparison to at least one other minority group: "The Chinese are vastly superior to the negro, but they are a race entirely different from ours and can never assimilate and I don't think it desirable that they should; And for that reason I don't think it desirable that they come here. . . . the objection is the dissimilarity of races, and so far as the mere labor is concerned it is a great advantage to the country. What we complain of, what the public complain of is really a virtue, their industry, their economy, their frugality and perseverance."[19] Sawyer then outlined the conditions under which the future immigration of Chinese workers might prove useful:

> If they would never bring their women here and never multiply and we would never have more than we could make useful, their presence would always be an advantage to the State [as a source of cheap labor]. . . . so long as the Chinese don't come here to stay, [keeping responsibility for the reproduction of labor in the immigrants' homeland] their

labor is highly beneficial to the whole community. . . . the difficulty is that they are beginning to get over the idea that they must go back. . . . Then [with the weakening of the sojourner mentality] they will begin to multiply here and that is where the danger lies in my opinion. When the Chinaman comes here and don't bring his wife here, sooner or later he dies like a worn out steam engine; he is simply a machine, and don't leave two or three or half dozen children to fill his place [preservation of cheap labor by prohibiting the immigration of a dependent sector].[20]

If the judge's observations did, in fact, represent a common viewpoint among capitalist interests in California, then the Page Law may belong to a distinct genre of legislation created by a coalition of exclusionary zeal, bourgeois morality, and moneyed economics rather than the antimonopolists whom Bonacich has credited with authorship of the Exclusion Act.[21]

Regrettably, insufficient documentation exists to test the validity of this supposition. Still, it would explain the subordination of labor-oriented rhetoric in speeches supportive of the 1875 statute as well as organized labor's failure to embrace its passage as a positive step toward exclusion. At any rate, although California capitalists may have resisted a general exclusion of Chinese workers, they offered no formal opposition to restricting female immigration. Their silence suggests that they may have at least recognized the potential economic advantages of a misenforced antiprostitution law.

Since publication of the article in which I first argued for the Page Law's importance in 1986, enactment of this legislation has achieved general recognition as a critical event in Chinese American history.[22] Yet the first thirty years of Chinese immigration too often remains a story of sojourners and prostitutes and is divided into three distinct periods: 1852 to 1882 (the period of voluntary sojourning); 1882 to 1943 (the period of forced sojourning); and after 1943 (the period of transition from sojourners to families). Within that interpretive framework, attempts to account for the shortage of females during the first of these periods still tend to rely excessively on the sojourner mentality of male immigrants. Those who emphasize the importance of this mindset have asserted that Chinese immigration between 1852 and 1882 remained overwhelmingly male because commitment to sojourning, nurtured and sustained by rigid cultural restraints, reduced the United States to nothing more than a place where one could seek his fortune.

Regardless of their destination, sojourning men dominated the initial settlement of Chinese immigrant communities. Yet even before the discovery of mitigating factors such as the Page Law, sojourner theorists themselves expressed some discomfort over their dependence on an unusually persistent cultural impediment. Stanford Lyman, while concluding that Chinese men had freely chosen to immigrate without their families between 1852 and 1882, has suggested that they would have eventually developed more "normal" communities had the Exclusion Act not closed the door to future immigration.[23] Lucie Cheng Hirata has also voiced concern over the sojourner theory's inability to adequately explain the shortage of women in American Chinatowns. After discussing the importance of tradition to the development of sojourner communities, she notes that "equally, if not more important, was the racist hostility of white society."[24] Tracing the development of anti-Chinese legislation from the unconstitutional California laws through the Page Law, the Exclusion Act, and the 1891 decision to detain Chinese immigrants on Angel Island, she at least implies that these legislative restraints may have discouraged the immigration of Chinese wives.

A more comparative examination of the historical record corroborates the intuition of such scholars. In Singapore and Penang, where British authorities encouraged the immigration of Chinese families, the female population steadily increased. Nuclear families gradually eroded the sojourner's dominance. Hawaii experienced a similar initial pattern of Chinese immigration, but the arrival of female family members occurred at a much slower rate that corresponds with early passage of restrictive immigration legislation.

Unlike British officials in Singapore and Penang, the Hawaiian government began to enact periodic anti-Chinese legislation shortly after the population of sojourning males reached significant proportions. Moreover, Hawaii's annexation to the United States in 1894 extended the Exclusion Act's jurisdiction to the islands, making the immigration of both male and female Chinese extremely difficult. Before 1894, however, legal restrictions always targeted male laborers while welcoming female immigration. Thus, Hawaiian laws had represented a colonized society's attempt to limit the presence of a particularly exploitable labor force rather than capital's endeavor to prevent the establishment of a dependent class. Given that direction of its legislative restrictions, Hawaii proved a much less hospitable environment than the settlements along the Malay Peninsula but still offered Chinese women the opportunity to either sojourn or establish permanent homes with their husbands—and, gradually, they did.

U.S. response to Chinese immigration differed far more significantly from that of Singapore and Penang. Government officials in California acted to restrict volume even more quickly than in Hawaii. Their attempts to impose these immigration restrictions, however, violated American-Chinese treaty relations and therefore could not pass the test of constitutionality in the courts. The nullification of such state laws provided a brief respite for both females and males who sought to immigrate, but anti-Chinese leaders on the Pacific Coast eventually succeeded in securing federal restrictions. While, as Edna Bonacich has noted, the Exclusion Act served the antimonopolistic interests reflected in the Hawaii and California efforts, the first of these federal laws—the Page Law of 1875—satisfied the concerns of exclusionists, moralists, and monopolists who, for different reasons, especially feared the immigration of Chinese women. Indeed, Karen Leong has observed that through this legislation "the Chinese Question was . . . re-established on a common ground that forged a united West Coast while appealing to the nation's ideals of gender and sexuality."[25]

Unfortunately, comprehending the motives behind gender-specific exclusion does not solve the problem of incomplete or inaccurate evidence. For scholars seeking to reclaim the history of Chinese American women, corruption of the census records engenders particularly stubborn difficulties in this regard. The failure of the 1870 census to denote familial relationships or recognize the existence of multiple nuclear families in urban boardinghouses limits any attempted identification of such families to the speculative realm. Furthermore, the enumerators' overuse of *Ah,* especially in Ward 4, frustrates searches for specific families from one census to the next. Finally, oppressive workloads at the field level, as well as regulations permitting the approximation of ages and intuitive recording of occupations, call the reliability of registered information into question. The 1880 census remedied some of those shortcomings but still authorized enumerators to estimate age and afforded them even more freedom to "correct" the answers of respondents. In addition, the names written on census schedules usually represented transliterations of Chinese by individuals who did not speak the language and possessed no official guidelines for the task. Even those persons who appear in each census may do so under different names and with inconsistent age listings.[26]

When taken together, the 1870 and 1880 censuses reveal that field-workers were more likely to identify women as prostitutes in wards where dwellings contained a higher ratio of females to males. Although such a phenomenon might seem counterintuitive at first, perhaps it illustrates yet another characteristic of the surveyors' approach to carrying out their duties. More effort would have been required to ascertain family relationships in mixed-gender dwellings that contained a larger number of female residents. Thus, census takers—notably, William Martin in 1870—were determined to finish the job as quickly as possible and may have felt a greater need to rely on their prejudices in such instances. They could move through the process of connecting husbands and wives with relative speed when confronted with only one or two women, especially if the male head of household belonged to the upper layers of Chinese American society. Such a hypothesis could be tested in relation to the 1880 census at least by dividing results according to enumeration districts rather than wards.

In addition to scholars whose interests focus on Chinese Americans, the performance of enumerators also warrants examination by specialists in women's history. Although more males than females were probably engaged in illegal or undesirable enterprises when the 1880 census of San Francisco was conducted, evidence indicates that field-workers placed self-imposed restrictions on the exercise of their freedom to correct false answers. Indeed, what has amounted to a nearly exhaustive review of the city's census schedules uncovered no examples of listings such as "Tong Leader?" or "Smuggler?" for male respondents. Although universal in principle, the right of correction appears to have been applied in a gender-specific manner. While officials responsible for compilation of the raw data in San Francisco expunged assumptive queries from their summaries for everyone but the Chinese, one cannot help but wonder whether different mixtures of racial and gender bigotry similarly affected the census schedules of other communities. If so, the "official" portrayal of San Francisco's Chinese female population may reflect a larger problem worthy of its own research.

Notwithstanding their limitations, existing documents reveal that Chinese immigrants, whatever their destinations, created communities of sojourning males during the first fifteen years or so of settlement. Moreover, inhibited by the joint family structure, Chinese women could not be expected to correct that sexual imbalance through a mass exodus from their husbands' ancestral villages. Instead, having won the approval of parents-in-law for a variety of reasons, wives—some initially accompanied by daughters and others sending for them when life was more settled—left slowly and in relatively small numbers. Along with the concubines, *mui tsai,* and prostitutes who also made the journey, these pioneers gradually became integral parts of each Chinese emigrant community.

Economic booms sometimes brought waves of new sojourners into a particular settlement, but, unlike nuclear families, most soon left in pursuit of other opportunities. When unhindered by external obstacles, the erosion of the sojourner's dominance consistently took place. Governmental interference, especially when it came in the form of female immigration restrictions such as the Page Law, slowed or reversed the trend, however. Fewer women came, transforming the sojourner into an institution rather than a fading symbol of the community's maturation. In the United States the process took place in two steps. First, the 1875 law arrested a slowly developing pattern of family-building and then exclusion cemented that reversal. Although some wives and daughters courageously endured the ordeal of consular examinations and habeas corpus trials, an unknown number of them were still turned away. More important, a much larger group of would-be emigrants undoubtedly possessed neither the will nor the economic incentive to risk the attempt.

Scholars exploring the lives of prostitutes have made valuable contributions to both Chinese American and women's history. Still, future studies must correct a tendency to disregard the contributions that women who were not prostitutes made to the development of immigrant communities before 1882 and often up to the twentieth century. As early as 1870 half of the Chinese females living in San Francisco were likely not engaged in prostitution, and that segment of the population deserves at least equal attention. Failures to recognize the existence of these women have subjected interpretive structures to the all too common problem of transposing female experiences into male categories. Thus, because federal law did not impose significant immigration restrictions on men before 1882, most studies of the preexclusion period have followed Coolidge's lead and designated these as the years of "free immigration." For women, however, significant governmental barriers had already been erected by 1875.

Judy Yung has rightly noted that female lives were "doubly bound by patriarchal control in Chinatown and racism outside."[27] Gender-specific legislation clearly reinforced the internal constraints that held many wives in the villages of their parents-in-law by focusing racial hostility in a manner that discouraged both nonconformists and those whose emigration might otherwise have received joint-family endorsement.[28] In order to "unbind" the legacy of Chinese American women comprehensively, future studies of the years before 1882 must adopt at least two new approaches. First, they must conceptualize the periods of female immigration according to the outline first introduced in chapter 1:

1852–68	The period of male sojourning
1869–74	The period of unrestricted family immigration
1875–82	The period of female exclusion
Post-1882	The period of general exclusion.

Second, subsequent examinations of both documentary and oral resources must transfer the burden of proof from the immigrants to the institutional forces that obscured their diversity. They must start with believing the women, asking questions that will bring their stories to light and incorporating them more fully into what is emerging as a multidimensional chronicle of female participation in the formation of Chinese community life in the United States.

In the words of Judge Lorenzo Sawyer, females who attempted to enter the United States between 1875 and 1882 faced a federal government that remained favorable to Chinese immigration "if they don't bring their women here." The exact impact of that single caveat on Chinese American family and community development defies measurement. Such gender-specific exclusion also established the prototype for female experiences under exclusion and as such informs examinations of these issues that concentrate on the period from 1882 to 1943. Ultimately, the Page Law of 1875 explains why Chinese American history followed the pattern of neither Chinese immigrant communities in other parts of the world nor sojourning groups of different ethnic heritage. Thus, its role was no less than foundational, and the recognition of its importance represents an essential ingredient in the ongoing cause of restoring to visibility those pathbreaking women—whether prostitutes or not—who made the long voyage from China to the United States in the years before exclusion.

Appendix

Document 1: An Act Supplementary to the Acts in Relation to Immigration (The Page Law)
[sec. 141, 18 Stat. 477 (1873–March 1875]

Be it enacted by the Senate and House of Representatives of the United States of America in Congress assembled, That in determining whether the immigration of any subject of China, Japan, or any Oriental country, to the United States, is free and voluntary, as provided by section two thousand one hundred and sixty-two of the Revised Code, title "Immigration," it shall be the duty of the consul-general or consul of the United States residing at the port from which it is proposed to convey such subjects, in any vessels enrolled or licensed in the United States, or any port within the same, before delivering to the masters of any such vessels the permit or certificate provided for in such section, to ascertain whether such immigrant has entered into a contract or agreement for a term of service within the United States, for lewd and immoral purposes; and if there be such contract or agreement,the said consul-general or consul shall not deliver the required permit or certificate.

Sec. 2. That if any citizen of the United States, or other person amenable to the laws of the United States, shall take, or cause to be taken or transported, to or from the United States any subject of China, Japan, or any Oriental country, without their free and voluntary consent, for the purpose of holding them to a term of service, such citizen or other person shall be liable to be indicted therefor[e], and, on conviction of such offense, shall be punished by a fine not exceeding two thousand dollars and be imprisoned not exceeding one year; and all contracts and agreements for a term of service of such persons in the United States, whether made in advance or in pursuance of such illegal importation, and whether such importation shall have been in American or other vessels, are hereby declared void.

Sec. 3. That the importation into the United States of women for the purposes of prostitution is hereby forbidden; and all contracts and agreements in relation thereto, made in advance or in pursuance of such illegal importation and purposes are hereby declared void; and whoever shall knowingly and willfully import, or cause any importation of, women into the United States for the purposes of prostitution, or shall knowingly or willfully hold, or attempt to hold, any woman to such purposes, in pursuance of such illegal importation and contract or agreement, shall be deemed guilty of a felony, and, on conviction thereof, shall be imprisoned not exceeding five years and pay a fine not exceeding five thousand dollars.

Sec. 4. That if any person shall knowingly and willfully contract, or attempt to contract, in advance or in pursuance of such illegal importation, to supply to another the labor of any cooly or other person brought into the United States in violation of section two thousand one hundred and fifty-eight of the Revised Statutes, or of any other section of the laws prohibiting the cooly-trade or of this act, said person shall be deemed guilty of a felony, and, upon conviction thereof, in any United States court, shall be fined in a sum not exceeding five hundred dollars and imprisoned for a term not exceeding one year.

Sec. 5. That it shall be unlawful for aliens of the following classes to immigrate into the United States, namely, persons who are undergoing a sentence for conviction in their own country of felonious crimes other than political or growing out of the result of such political offenses, or whose sentence has been remitted on condition of their emigration, and women "imported for the purposes of prostitution." Every vessel arriving in the United States may be inspected under the direction of the collector of the port at which it arrives, if he shall have reason to believe that any such obnoxious persons are on board; and the officer making such inspection shall certify the result thereof to the master or other person in charge of such vessel, designating in such certificate the person or persons, if any there be, ascertained by him to be of either of the classes whose importation is hereby forbidden. When such inspection is required by the collector as aforesaid, it shall be unlawful, without his permission, for any alien to leave any such vessel arriving in the United States from a foreign country until the inspection shall have been had and the result certified as herein provided; and at no time thereafter shall any alien certified to by the inspecting officer as being of either of the classes whose immigration is forbidden by this section, be allowed to land in the United States, except in obedience to a judicial process issued pursuant to law. If any person shall feel aggrieved by the certificate of such inspecting officer stating him or her to be within either of the classes whose immigration is forbidden by this section, and shall apply for release or other remedy to any proper court or judge, then it shall be the duty of the collector at said port of entry to detain said vessel until a hearing and determination of the matter are had, to the end that if the said inspector shall be found to be in accordance with this section and sustained, the obnoxious person or persons shall be returned on board of said vessel, and shall not thereafter be permitted to land, unless the master, owner, or consignee of the vessel shall give bond and security, to be approved by the court or judge hearing the cause, in the sum of five hundred dollars for each such person permitted to land, conditioned for the return of such person, within six months from the date thereof, to the country whence his or her emigration shall have taken place, or unless the vessel bringing such obnoxious person or persons shall be forfeited, in which event the proceeds of such forfeiture shall be paid over to the collector of the port of arrival, and applied by him, as far as necessary, to the return of such person or persons to his or her own country within the said period of six months. And for all violations of this act, the vessel, by the acts, omissions, or connivance of the owners, master, or other custodian, or the consignees of which the same are committed, shall be liable to forfeiture, and may be proceeded against as in cases of frauds against the revenue laws, for which forfeiture is prescribed by existing law.

Approved, March 3, 1875.[1]

Document 2: Samples of a Chinese American Prostitute's Labor Contract

An agreement to assist the woman Ah Ho, because coming from China to San Francisco she became indebted to her mistress for passage. Ah Ho herself asks Mr. Yee-Kwan to advance for her $630, for which Ah Ho distinctly agrees to give her body to Mr. Yee for service as a prostitute for a term of four years.

There shall be no interest on the money. Ah Ho shall receive no wages. At the expiration of four years Ah Ho shall be her own master. Mr. Yee Kwan shall not hinder or trouble her. If Ah Ho runs away before her time is out her mistress shall find her and return her, and whatever expense is incurred in finding and returning her Ah Ho shall pay.

On this day of the agreement Ah Ho with her own hands has received from Mr. Yee-Kwan $630.

If Ah Ho shall be sick at any time for more than ten days she shall make up by an extra month of service for any ten days' sickness.

Now this agreement has proof. This paper received by Ah Ho is witness.

Twelfth year, ninth month, fourteenth day [1873]. TUNG CHEE.[2]

An agreement to assist a young girl named Loi Yau. Because she became indebted to her mistress for passage, food, &c., and has nothing to pay, she makes her body over to the woman Sep Sam to serve as a prostitute to make out the sum of $503. The money shall draw no interest and Loi Yau shall receive no wages. Loi Yau shall serve four and a half years. On this day of agreement Loi Yau receives the sum of $503 in her own hands. When the time is out Loi Yau may be her own master, and no man shall trouble her. If she runs away before the time is out and any expense is incurred in catching, then Loi Yau must pay that expense. If she is sick fifteen days or more, she shall make up one month for every fifteen days. If Sep Sam should go back to China, then Loi Yau shall serve another party till her time is out; If in such service she should be sick one hundred days or more, and cannot be cured, she may return to Sep Sam's place. For a proof of this agreement this paper.

Dated second day sixth month of the present year [1873]. LOI YAU.[3]

Table A1. Excerpt from the 1870 San Francisco Census Schedule, Ward 4, William Martin, Enumerator

Page No.	Dwelling No.	Family No.	Name	Sex	Age	Occupation	Place of Birth
251	1701	2335	Ah Gang	F	50	Prostitute	China
			Ah Chee	F	20	Prostitute	China
			Ah Will	F	19	Prostitute	China
			Ah Dee	F	26	Prostitute	China
			Ah Fou	F	21	Prostitute	China
			Ah Long	F	20	Prostitute	China
			Ah Jim	F	18	Prostitute	China
		2336	Ah Tai	M	32	Laborer	China
			Ah Yan	M	30	Laborer	China
			Ah Lik	M	36	Laborer	China
			Ah Ming	M	34	Laborer	China
			Ah Roi	M	30	Laborer	China
			Ah Poo	M	23	Laborer	China

Table A2. Excerpt from the 1870 San Francisco Census Schedule, Ward 4, William Martin, Enumerator

Page No.	Dwelling No.	Family No.	Name	Sex	Age	Occupation	Place of Birth
296	1744	2471	Ah Ching	F	21	Prostitute	China
			Ah Lin	F	25	Prostitute	China
			Ah Me	F	36	Prostitute	China
			Ah Fan	F	32	Prostitute	China
			Ah Wan	F	19	Prostitute	China
			Ah Yan	F	18	Prostitute	China
			Ah Chee	F	20	Prostitute	China
			Ah Man	F	20	Prostitute	China
			Ah Toy	F	21	Prostitute	China
		2472	Ah Hing	M	41	Laborer	China
			Ah Yet	M	40	Laborer	China
			Ah Sam	M	39	Laborer	China
			Ah Jim	M	37	Laborer	China
			Ah John	M	37	Laborer	China
			Ah Wing	M	36	Laborer	China
			Ah Chan	M	4	At Home	California

Table A3. Excerpt from the 1870 San Francisco Census Schedule, Ward 6, Henry C. Bennett, Enumerator

Page No.	Dwelling No.	Family No.	Name	Sex	Age	Occupation	Place of Birth
033	161	273	Moin Ah	M	27	Clerk in Store	China
			Kum Ah	M	45	Gen. Storekeeper	China
			Yung Ah	M	32	Laborer	China
			Hank Ah	M	32	Cook	China
			Tin Hoo	M	20	Laborer	China
		274	Chuck Ah	M	30	Cigar Maker	China
			Hee Hi	F	24	Keeping House	China
			Put Ah	M	10	At Home	California
			Pee Ah	M	8	At Home	California
			Noi Ah	M	4	At Home	California
			Nip Ah	M	8/12	At Home	California
			Kew Ah	F	10	Domestic Servant	China
		275	Mow Ah	M	29	Carpenter	China
			Me Ah	F	25	Keeping House	China
			Quom Ah	M	37	Cook	China
			Leen He	F	30	Shoebinder	China
		276	Lup Toi	M	40	Storekeeper	China
			Heen Ah	F	27	Keeping House	China
			Hack Kee	M	34	Fisherman	China
			Yeet Ah	F	30	Keeping House	China
		277	Hop Shi	M	35	Butcher	China
			He Wee	F	27	Keeping House	China
			Low Kee	F	12	Domestic Servant	China

Table A4. Excerpt from the 1880 San Francisco Census Schedule, Ward 4, E.D. 27, Vincent Lincoln, Enumerator

Page No.	Dwelling No.	Family No.	Name	Sex	Age	Marital Status	Relationship to Head of Family	Occupation	Place of Birth[a]
017	067	150	Fong Tip	M	70	M		Prostitute	Kwantung/China/China
			Fong Tip	F	40	M	Wife	Keeping House	Kwantung/China/China
			Fong Moy	F	12	S	Daughter	Apprentice Bawd	S.F. Calif./China/China
			Fong Fung	F	5/12	S	Daughter		S.F. Calif./China/China
		151	Wah Sing	M	40	M	Wife	Pedler	Kwantung/China/China
		152	Lum Kan	M	44	M		Pedler	Kwantung/China/China
			Kum Hoey	M	34	M	Lodger	Pedler	Kwantung/China/China
			Hung Yow	M	32	M	Lodger	Pedler	Kwantung/China/China
		153	Chan Yung	M	25	S		Pedler	Kwantung/China/China
			Fook Mow	M	37	M	Lodger	Pedler	Kwantung/China/China
			Chang Chung	M	33	M	Lodger	Pedler	Kwantung/China/China
			Hoo Quong	M	24	S	Lodger	Works for Druggist	Kwantung/China/China
		154	Mow Sing	M	44	M		Huckster	Kwantung/China/China
			Mow Sing	F	32	M	Wife	Keeping House	Kwantung/China/China
		155	Chang Lok	M	24	S		Pedler	Kwantung/China/China
			Quock Tuk	M	21	S	Lodger	Pedler	Kwantung/China/China
			Lee Quong Foy	M	42	M	Lodger	Pedler	Kwantung/China/China
		156	Chu Sing	M	32	M		Barber	Kwantung/China/China
		157	Chu Sing	F	28	M	Wife	Keeping House	Kwantung/China/China

a. Place of birth is given for the individual named and for, in order, his or her father and mother.

Table A5. Chinese Female Immigration to the United States, 1852–1904

Period of Free Male Immigration		Period of General Exclusion		Period of Free Male Immigration		Period of General Exclusion	
Year	Number	Year	Number	Year	Number	Year	Number
1852	0	1883	47	1868	46	1899	2
1853	0	1884	100	1869	974	1900	12
1854	673	1885	123	1870	1,116	1901	42
1855	2	1886	92	1871	349	1902	123
1856	16	1887	89	1872	183	1903	40
1857	450	1888	80	1873	892	1904	118
1858	320	1889	68	1874	243		
1859	467	1890	318	1875	385		
1860	29	1891	233	1876	260		
1861	515	1892	241	1877	77		
1862	650	1893	179	1878	354		
1863	1	1894	247	1879	358		
1864	164	1895	116	1880	70		
1865	10	1896	59	1881	83		
1866	5	1897	29	1882	136		
1867	4	1898	10				

Source: Statistics taken from Mary Roberts Coolidge, *Chinese Immigration* (New York, 1909), 502.

Table A6. Estimated Chinese Arrivals and Departures for San Francisco, 1852–82

Year	Arrivals	Departures	Year	Arrivals	Departures
1852	20,026	1,768	1868	11,085	4,209
1853	4,270	4,421	1869	14,994	4,896
1854	16,084	2,339	1870	10,869	4,232
1855	3,329	3,473	1871	5,542	3,264
1856	4,807	3,028	1872	9,773	4,887
1857	5,924	1,932	1873	17,075	6,805
1858	5,427	2,542	1874	16,085	7,710
1859	3,175	2,450	1875	18,021	6,305
1860	7,343	2,088	1876[a]	22,781	8,525
1861	8,434	3,594	1877	10,594	8,161
1862	8,188	2,795	1878	8,992	8,186
1863	6,435	2,947	1879	9,604	9,220
1864	2,696	3,911	1880	5,802	7,496
1865	3,097	2,298	1881	11,890	8,926
1866	2,242	3,113	1882	39,579	10,366
1867	4,794	4,999			

Source: Statistics taken from Mary Roberts Coolidge, *Chinese Immigration* (New York, 1909), 498.

a. After 1875, Coolidge's record of arrivals included transients as well as immigrants, and her list of departures was not limited to Chinese. See Coolidge, *Chinese Immigrants*, 499.

Notes

Foreword

1. Barth, *City People*, pp. 15–16; for his earlier views, see Barth, *Bitter Strength.*

Preface

1. Takaki, *Strangers from a Different Shore*, pp. 7, 8. Gail Hershatter, in a study of the prostitution industry in twentieth-century Shanghai (*Dangerous Pleasures*), has lamented the same problem, that of trying to tell the stories of "voiceless" subjects (p. 4), which suggests that both racial and class prejudice have conspired to erase the contributions of female laborers to Chinese American history.

2. Salyer, *Laws Harsh as Tigers*, p. xiii.

3. Coolidge, *Chinese Immigration*, pp. 499, 500.

4. Chan, "Preface," in *Entry Denied*, ed. Chan, p. viii.

5. Chan, *Asian Americans*, pp. 104, 106.

6. Chan, "The Exclusion of Chinese Women," p. 109.

7. Espiritu has agreed with this assessment of the Page Law's negative impact on female immigration. See *Asian American Women and Men*, p. 18.

8. I have treated the post–1882 period as a single unit because the focus of my study stops with exclusion. I concur, however, with Chan's division of these years into three distinct segments. "Preface," in *Entry Denied*, ed. Chan, p. viii.

9. Pascoe, *Relations of Rescue.*

10. Yung, *Unbound Feet*, p. 13. Espiritu's work (*Asian American Women and Men*) might also be added to the category of social history of Chinese American women.

Chapter 1: Invisible Women and Untold Stories

1. Peffer, "Forbidden Families"; Peffer, "From Under the Sojourner's Shadow."

2. Takaki, *Strangers from a Different Shore*; Chan, "The Exclusion of Chinese Women"; Tong, *Unsubmissive Women*; Yung, *Unbound Feet.*

3. Coolidge, *Chinese Immigration*

4. Baker, *Chinese Kinship and Family,* pp. 3, 15, 16.

5. Ibid., p. 250.

6. Takaki, *Strangers from a Different Shore,* pp. 10, 11; Lydon, *Chinese Gold,* p. 488. For additional discussions of the relationship between Chinese and European sojourning, see Peffer, "Forbidden Families," pp. 3, 4.

7. Although probably fictitious, Arthur Smith's commentary on Chinese village life describes one way in which this economic partnership purportedly moved outside the home village in his description of a strategy he identifies as "'falconing with a woman.'" *Village Life in China,* p. 296.

8. After describing the process through which some sons established nuclear families away from their parents while at least one son and his wife stayed at home to care for them, Lang explains that "to let parents live alone seemed unthinkable." Thus, one daughter-in-law could emigrate without rejecting this familial responsibility, provided that another remained at home to fulfill it. *Chinese Family and Society,* p. 15.

9. Freedman, *Lineage Organization in Southeastern China,* pp. 28–29.

10. In "Socioeconomic Origins of Emigration," Mei, for example, has identified a major China-based factor as "the separation of the peasants from the land."

11. Freedman, *Lineage Organization in Southeastern China,* pp. 28, 134–35.

12. Yung, *Unbound Feet,* pp. 42, 43.

13. Thus far, no consensus has been reached on the actual Chinese female population and number of prostitutes in San Francisco for these census years. Chan reports the 1870 female and prostitute populations as 2,022 and 1,452, respectively, with the 1880 numbers being 2,052 and 444. Hirata lists the total number of females at 2,018 in 1870 and 2,058 in 1880 and the number of prostitutes at 1,426 and 435. Tong's calculations are 1,565 prostitutes out of a total female population of 2,499 in 1870 and 305 out of 1,742 in the following decade. Chan, "The Exclusion of Chinese Women," p. 107; Hirata, "Free, Indentured, Enslaved," p. 421; Tong, *Unsubmissive Women,* p. 98.

My calculations, in conjunction with census reports contained in San Francisco newspapers, yield an aggregate of 2,040 in 1870, with 1,452 prostitutes and 408 prostitutes in a total female population of 2,052 in 1880. The calculations of Chan, Hirata, and myself are not substantially different, however, and together suggest that Tong's may be the least reliable. "San Francisco as Viewed through the Census"; "Census Returns of San Francisco for 1870"; U.S. Bureau of the Census, Tenth Census of the United States (1880), Population Schedules, San Francisco, RG 29, reels 76, 77.

14. For example, see Hirata, "Free, Indentured, Enslaved," p. 421.

15. Ibid., pp. 414, 428.

16. U.S. Bureau of the Census, "Chinese Population by Counties, 1870–1890," *Report of the Population of the United States at the Eleventh Census, 1890,* p. 437.

17. Hirata, "Free, Indentured, Enslaved," p. 412; Yung, *Unbound Feet,* p. 30.

18. Hirata, "Free, Indentured, Enslaved," p. 410.

19. Coolidge, *Chinese Immigration,* pp. 488, 502.

20. Hirata, "Free, Indentured, Enslaved," p. 421.

21. Recognizing this reality, Tong has attempted to account for misidentified women in the 1870 and 1880 censuses, acknowledging that the total number of prostitutes was likely overstated. *Unsubmissive Women,* pp. 97, 99, 100.

22. Sandmeyer, *The Anti-Chinese Movement in California,* p. 52.

23. Ibid., p. 53.

24. Gibson, *The Chinese in America,* pp. 146–55.

25. "An Act Supplementary to the Acts in Relation to Immigration (Page Law)" (document 1 in the appendix of this volume). While the Page Law expressly prohibited the immigration of Chinese laborers coming to America under a service contract, it failed to address the problem of examining large numbers of Chinese men seeking to emigrate to the United States.

26. Persons suspected of involvement in the immigration of Chinese prostitutes could be charged with a felony and, if found guilty, fined up to $5,000 and sentenced to a maximum of five years in prison. Ibid.

27. Bonacich and Cheng, "Introduction," p. 32; see also Espiritu, *Asian American Women and Men,* p. 17.

28. From 1869 to 1875, an average of 592 Chinese females immigrated to the United States each year, nearly three times the annual average from 1852 to 1868. For the data used to calculate these averages, see Coolidge, *Chinese Immigration,* p. 502.

29. Chan, "The Exclusion of Chinese Women," p. 108.

30. Tang, "Chinese Women and the Two-Edged Sword of Habeas Corpus," p. 51.

31. Ibid., pp. 48–56.

32. Chan, "The Exclusion of Chinese Women," p. 95. Other works have also recognized the Page Law's importance in limiting the number of Chinese female immigrants who came during the preexclusion period. See, for example, Takaki, *Strangers from a Different Shore,* p. 40; and Yung, *Unbound Feet,* pp. 32, 33.

33. McClain, *In Search of Equality,* p. 149. Happily, Lucy Slayer's examination of the same anti-Chinese legislation has corrected this mistake, noting (*Laws Harsh as Tigers,* p. 6) that "the act of 1882 and, even more, that of 1875, represented significant departures for United States immigration policy."

34. Mei, "Socioeconomic Origins of Emigration," p. 498. For a discussion of the role Mei's article has played in shaping the historiography of Chinese female immigration in the preexclusion period, see Peffer, "From Under the Sojourner's Shadow," pp. 47, 48.

35. Tong, *Unsubmissive Women,* p. 98.

36. Yung, *Unbound Feet,* p. 41. Individuals such as physicians, interpreters, and teachers should be included in the list of occupation groups that could afford to support a second family in the United States, but Yung is correct in focusing on the merchant class. Only eighteen Chinese physicians and druggists were recorded in the 1870 San Francisco census, for example, a number that had grown to only thirty-nine in 1880. U.S. Bureau of the Census, Ninth Census of the United States (1870), Population Schedules, San Francisco, RG 29,

reels 73, 74; and Tenth Census of the United States (1880), Population Schedules, San Francisco, RG 29, reels 76, 77.

37. Chan, *Asian Americans*, p. 104.

38. Yung, *Unbound Feet*, p. 46.

Chapter 2: A Comparison of Chinese Immigrant Communities

1. For a description of the labor contract system for Chinese males, see Saxton, *The Indispensable Enemy*, pp. 3–10. For a description of the labor contract system for Chinese females, focusing on its atrocities, see Hirata, "Free, Indentured, Enslaved." For a sample of the kind of contract used in the prostitution industry, see document 2 in the appendix of this volume.

2. By the time of the 1880 census, San Francisco's Chinese population had reached 21,745. U.S. Bureau of the Census, "Chinese Population by Counties, 1870–1890," *Report of the Population of the United States at the Eleventh Census, 1890*, p. 437.

3. Chan (*This Bittersweet Soil*, p. 28) has estimated the cost of steerage passage from Hong Kong to San Francisco at $50 to $55. Under cross-examination at her habeas corpus trial, one Chinese woman testified that her fare from Hong Kong to San Francisco was about $35. U.S. District Court, *In the Matter of Wah Ah Chin and Others*, pp. 86–88.

4. While middlemen used their positions in the lineage/clan hierarchy to keep wages low and prevent labor strife, they also assumed the responsibility of guaranteeing employment for members of their clan or lineage group. Saxton has noted the unusually low rate of Chinese unemployment in America, crediting lineage ties between laborers and middlemen for this phenomenon. He has also characterized the masses of white workers, pushed from their jobs by the 1876–77 depression, as major contributors to the growth of California's anti-Chinese movement during this period but makes no mention of a corresponding loss of jobs by Chinese laborers. *The Indispensable Enemy*, pp. 7–10, 105–9.

5. Bonacich and Cheng, "Introduction," p. 34.

6. Tsai has described the Hakka-Punti War as "dreadful internecine strife" in which both groups had "inflicted heavy casualties on each other." *The Chinese Experience in America*, p. 46. Chan (*This Bittersweet Soil*, pp. 20, 37) has pointed out that some of the prisoners taken during this conflict were allegedly "sold to coolie traders" and that female prisoners may have been sold as prostitutes. Chan has also explained that the war "pushed Cantonese [the Puntis, or natives] out of their homeland." That displacement would have pressed both husbands and wives to contemplate emigration.

7. Freedman, *Lineage Organization in Southeastern China*, pp. 27–30; Hsu, *Under the Ancestors' Shadow*, p. 113.

8. Lang, *Chinese Family and Society*, p. 139. Hsu has concurred with this assessment, pointing out that "the big family system is an ideal aspired to, but not reached by the great majority of Chinese families." *Under the Ancestors' Shadow*, p. 113.

9. Barth, *Bitter Strength*, p. 5.

10. Yung, *Unbound Feet*, p. 45.

11. See, for example, Glick, *Sojourners and Settlers*, p. 213.

12. This report has been reproduced in *International Migrations,* ed. Willcox, vol. 1, p. 913.
13. Ibid.
14. Virtually all writers discussing Chinese immigration have emphasized the importance of contract immigration. For example, see Hirata, "Free, Indentured, Enslaved"; Kitano and Daniels, *Asian Americans,* pp. 22, 23; Purcell, *The Chinese in Southeast Asia;* Glick, *Sojourners and Settlers;* Choi, *Chinese Migration and Settlement in Australia;* and Wickberg et al., *From China to Canada,* p. 5.
15. Similar statistical information is also available for other immigrant destinations in Southeast Asia, such as the Philippines, and substantial documentary evidence also exists for the Chinese communities in Canada, Peru, and Cuba. The six communities presented in this chapter, however, have been selected because they effectively represent three distinct patterns of female immigration.
16. Purcell, *The Chinese in Southeast Asia,* p. 248.
17. Ibid., pp. 254–55.
18. Willcox, ed., *International Migrations,* vol. 1, p. 913.
19. British officials recorded 2,053 female immigrants in 1881 and 4,710 the following census year, with the 1901 and 1911 totals being 11,822 and 19,754, respectively. Male immigration averaged almost 124,000 per year between 1881 and 1915, producing an increase in the proportion of females from 3 percent in 1881, to 5 percent in 1901, to 8 percent in 1910, and then to 11 percent in 1915. Ibid.
20. Purcell, *The Chinese in Southeast Asia,* p. 250.
21. Ibid., pp. 250–88.
22. Ibid., pp. 287–88.
23. Willcox, ed., *International Migrations,* vol. 1, p. 913.
24. Great Britain Colonial Office, *Straits Settlements Government Gazette,* 1881, pp. 14–15. These percentage increases resulted from a consistent growth in the number of female immigrants. In 1881 British officials reported 1,068 female arrivals from China, a figure that grew from 2,416 in 1891, to 4,128 in 1901, and to 7,302 in 1911. Willcox, ed., *International Migrations,* vol. 1, p. 913.
25. Lydon, *The Anti-Chinese Movement in the Hawaiian Kingdom,* p. 18.
26. Lind, *Hawaii's People,* p. 54.
27. Lydon, *The Anti-Chinese Movement in the Hawaiian Kingdom,* p. 16. In contrast to the Hawaiian policies toward female immigrants, Wickberg et al. have noted that during the 1840s Spanish officials in the Philippines considered recruiting Chinese nuclear families to promote agricultural development but failed to carry out such plans (*The Chinese in Philippine Life,* p. 174). Perhaps that failure offers at least a partial explanation as to why, even in 1903, the Philippines' Chinese population still contained only thirteen females per one thousand males.
28. Takaki, *Strangers from a Different Shore,* p. 39.
29. Glick, *Sojourners and Settlers,* p. 209.
30. Ibid.
31. Tsai has noted (*The Chinese Experience,* p. 30) that in 1887, chiefly in response to pressure from white American businessmen, the Hawaiian legislature "completely excluded the

Chinese." For a discussion of the means the planters used to gain control of Hawaii's government and of the impact that takeover exerted on Chinese immigration, see Glick, *Sojourners and Settlers*, pp. 215–23.

32. Takaki, *Strangers from a Different Shore*, p. 40.

33. Glick, *Sojourners and Settlers*, p. 213.

34. Ibid., pp. 212–14.

35. Ibid., p. 212. Chan (*Asian Americans*, p. 66) has observed that this Hawaiian group was part of a large organizational movement that swept across the United States and its areas of influence during the 1880s.

36. Glick, *Sojourners and Settlers*, p. 214.

37. In their studies of Chinese resistance against legislative discrimination in the United States, both McClain and Salyer have noted that the historical record discredits this image of Chinese passivity. McClain, *In Search of Equality*, p. 3; Salyer, *Laws Harsh as Tigers*, p. xv.

38. Takaki, *Strangers from a Different Shore*, p. 41.

39. Purcell, *The Chinese in Southeast Asia*, p. 241.

40. Purcell has marked the 1820s as the decade in which significant Chinese immigration to Malacca began. Ibid., p. 243.

41. Purcell has reported that prostitution was an especially active industry in Malacca's Chinese sector. Ibid., p. 274.

42. Ibid., p. 241.

43. Victoria, for example, enacted its first restrictive immigration legislation in 1855 in response to a Chinese immigrant population that had increased from 2,341 in 1854 to more than seventeen thousand at the time of enactment. Choi, *Chinese Migration and Settlement*, pp. 19–21.

44. Ibid., pp. 22–27 (for a discussion of this process of enactment and repeal). Choi has also stated that "the pattern of Chinese migration and settlement has been vitally influenced by Australian immigration restrictions" (xi).

45. Ibid., p. 46.

46. Choi has pointed out that "the original 1901 Act expressly permitted the entry of wives and children of migrants who were not prohibited (clause 3m), and also any person who satisfied an officer that he had formerly been domiciled in Australia (clause 3n)." Ibid., p. 39.

47. Ibid.

48. Ibid., p. 40.

49. While pointing out the small numbers of Chinese females who actually came to Australia under the grounds permitted by clause 3m of the 1901 immigration law, Choi has asserted that the government repealed this clause in an effort to "'maintain the scarcity of females amongst the resident Asian population as a permanent obstacle to the increasing of their numbers.'" Ibid., pp. 39–40.

50. Coolidge, *Chinese Immigration*, p. 498. New arrivals pushed the number of Chinese in America to nearly thirty-five thousand by 1860 and beyond sixty-three thousand by 1870. U.S. Department of Commerce, Special Report, *Chinese and Japanese in the United States, 1910*, p. 8.

51. Whereas female immigration had averaged 626 per year since 1869 and totaled 3,757

from 1869 to 1875, it fell to an average of only 215 per year (a total of 1,723) between 1875 and 1882. Coolidge, *Chinese Immigration*, p. 502.

52. U.S. Department of Commerce, Special Report, *Chinese and Japanese in the United States, 1910*, p. 8.

53. Coolidge, *Chinese Immigration*, p. 502.

54. Although the Page Law also prohibited male contract laborers from immigrating, the sheer volume of male applicants rendered that element of its restrictive efforts unenforceable. Thus, in reality at least, male immigration remained free of governmental interference until the implementation of exclusion.

55. Although the 1882 law did not specifically prohibit wives and children of Chinese laborers from entering the United States, subsequent court rulings extended exclusion to them as well. See Takaki, *Strangers from a Different Shore*, pp. 40, 41; Chan, "The Exclusion of Chinese Women," pp. 110–12; Yung, *Unbound Feet*, p. 23; and Espiritu, *Asian American Women and Men*, pp. 19, 20. For the Exclusion Act's full text, see "A Bill to Execute Certain Treaty Stipulations Relating to China (Exclusion Act)," ch. 126, 22 Stat. 58, May 6, 1882, *United States Statutes at Large*, pp. 58–61.

56. Mei ("Socioeconomic Developments among the Chinese in San Francisco") has identified the period from 1870 to 1882 as boom years for San Francisco's Chinatown, "when its population and businesses were at their peak" (p. 371). For statistical discussions regarding the impact of combining Page Law restrictions of female immigration with male perceptions of closing windows of opportunity during the interval between passage and implementation of exclusion, see Peffer, "Forbidden Families," p. 43; see also Takaki, *Strangers from a Different Shore*, p. 40; and Chan, *Asian Americans*, p. 105.

57. Singapore's Chinese population stood at 50,043 in 1860 and then grew to 54,572 in 1871, 86,766 in 1881, and 121,908 in 1891. Purcell, *The Chinese in Southeast Asia*, p. 263. The 1860 U.S. census recorded 34,933 Chinese residents, a number that increased to 63,199 by 1870, 105,465 by 1880, and 107,188 by 1890. U.S. Department of Commerce, Special Report, *Chinese and Japanese in the United States, 1910*, p. 8.

58. Sucheng Chan ("The Exclusion of Chinese Women," p. 95) has reached the same conclusion: "There is no question that patriarchal cultural values, a sojourning mentality, differentials in the cost of living, and hazardous conditions in the American West . . . all worked in tandem to limit the number of Chinese female immigrants during the early decades of the Chinese influx. But . . . from the early 1870s onward, efforts by various levels of American government to restrict the immigration of Chinese women became the more significant factor." Espiritu has echoed Chan's assessment, arguing (*Asian American Women and Men*, p. 17) that "labor recruiting patterns and immigration exclusion policies were the most significant factors in restricting the immigration of Asian women."

Chapter 3: A Stop on the Road to Exclusion

1. Coolidge, *Chinese Immigration*, p. 498.
2. Ibid.
3. Li, *Congressional Policy of Chinese Immigration*, p. 14.

4. For a complete digest of this and other California laws relating to Chinese immigration enacted between 1852 and 1882, see U.S. Congress, Senate, Immigration Commission, *State Immigration and Alien Laws,* vol. 21, pp. 533–55.

5. McClain, *In Search of Equality,* pp. 12, 13.

6. Coolidge, *Chinese Immigration,* p. 498.

7. Ibid.

8. U.S. Congress, Senate, Immigration Commission, *State Immigration and Alien Laws,* vol. 21, p. 545.

9. McClain has explained that justices in *People v. Downer* ruled against the state because they viewed the law as "an impermissible interference with the national government's exclusive power to regulate foreign commerce." *In Search of Equality,* p. 18.

10. Coolidge, *Chinese Immigration,* p. 498.

11. U.S. Congress, Senate, Immigration Commission, *State Immigration and Alien Laws,* vol. 21, pp. 546–47.

12. Ibid., p. 548.

13. Ibid., pp. 548–49.

14. Coolidge, *Chinese Immigration,* p. 498.

15. Ibid.

16. In "The Census of San Francisco," its survey of statistics released from the 1870 census, the *Alta* offered the following lament regarding San Francisco's continued gender imbalance: "The two sexes are about equally divided among the children under 16 years of age, but over that age there are 52,102 males and 38,116 females, or three to one; and if a count were to be made of those over 21, we suppose that the disproportion would be considerably greater. In many of the cities on the Atlantic slope, the ladies have a majority." Perhaps the author's mathematical exaggeration of the city's general sex ratio resulted more from the concern created by this issue than from miscalculation.

17. Data tabulated as a byproduct of my research has revealed that the 1870 census for Wards 4 and 6 in San Francisco, which contained virtually all of the city's one thousand or so Chinese prostitutes, also recorded twelve African Americans, sixty-two Latin Americans (mostly from Mexico), 181 European immigrants, one American Indian, and 100 white natives of the United States. U.S. Bureau of the Census, Ninth Census of the United States (1870), Population Schedules, San Francisco, RG 29, reels 73, 74. Because non-Chinese brothels were not restricted to these wards, however, considerably more women were employed in such establishments throughout the whole city than those figures indicate. Thus the numbers are reflective rather than indicative of ethnic makeup.

18. For a more comprehensive treatment of Ah Toy's storied career, see Tong, *Unsubmissive Women,* pp. 6–12; see also Espiritu, *Asian American Women and Men,* p. 32.

19. Espiritu, *Asian American Women and Men,* p. 32.

20. U.S. Bureau of the Census, Ninth Census of the United States (1870), Population Schedules, San Francisco, RG 29, reel 74, p. 81.

21. Ibid., pp. 53–82.

22. Tong, *Unsubmissive Women,* p. 12.

23. For a thorough description of the methods used to procure women and girls, see

Jaschok, *Concubines and Bondservants,* pp. 89, 90; see also Hirata, "Free, Indentured, Enslaved," pp. 407–10; and Tong, *Unsubmissive Women,* pp. 43–45.

24. Hirata has noted ("Free, Indentured, Enslaved," p. 408) that contemporary observers estimated the profits of the Hip Yee Tong, which dominated the importation business, to have been about $200,000 between 1852 and 1873. Reflecting the reality of potential profits afforded by this enterprise, Sinn has also pointed out in "Chiese Patriarchy" (p. 143) that by the early 1870s the kidnapping of girls had become an increasing source of alarm for Hong Kong residents.

25. Hirata, "Free, Indentured, Enslaved," p. 412; see also Espiritu, *Asian American Women and Men,* pp. 31, 32.

26. In 1873, for example, more than 90 percent of Chinatown real estate was owned by non-Chinese, and Hirata has pointed out that "white landlords, many of whom were prominent citizens of San Francisco . . . extracted high rents from brothel owners, often double or treble the rent they received from whites." "Free, Indentured, Enslaved," p. 414.

27. Although this ordinance was directed at all the city's houses of prostitution, police raids focused only on those staffed by Chinese and Mexican women. The result was that other brothels continued to operate unabated while the targeted businesses merely decreased their visibility. Chan, "The Exclusion of Chinese Women," p. 97.

28. Ibid., pp. 97, 98 (for a thorough discussion of this law's character and impact).

29. U.S. Congress, Senate, *Treaties and Conventions since July 4, 1776,* pp. 165–68.

30. Coolidge, *Chinese Immigration,* p. 498.

31. U.S. Congress, Senate, Immigration Commission, *State Immigration and Alien Laws,* vol. 21, pp. 549–50.

32. Ibid., p. 551.

33. "Arrival of the 'Great Republic.'" Because no report of the subsequent granting of a writ of habeas corpus was ever made, one must assume that the women were forcibly returned to China.

34. *Congressional Globe,* 41st Cong., 2d sess., 1869–70, p. 323.

35. For a thorough discussion of both Stewart's possible motivation for sponsoring the legislation and the process through which it became part of the 1870 Civil Rights Act, see McClain, *In Search of Equality,* pp. 37–40.

36. For an examination of Sumner's proposal and the forces that ultimately defeated it, see Saxton, *The Indispensable Enemy,* pp. 36, 37.

37. The amendment was defeated by a vote of thirty to fourteen. Ibid., p. 37. In 1878 Chinese petitioners in San Francisco made an attempt to use the law's extension of naturalization rights to persons of African descent as a foundation for arguing that it had, in so doing, defined "white" as non-African. The ruling of Judge Lorenzo Sawyer in the U.S. Circuit Court, however, rejected that line of reasoning and reaffirmed the government's right to deny the right of naturalization to Chinese immigrants. McClain, *In Search of Equality,* pp. 72, 73; Salyer, *Laws Harsh as Tigers,* p. 13.

38. U.S. Congress, Senate, Immigration Commission, *State Immigration and Alien Laws,* vol. 21, p. 551.

39. *Chy Lung v. Freeman,* 92 United States Reports 275 (1876), a copy of the court's rul-

ing on this case; see also Gibson, *The Chinese in America,* pp. 146–55. For a thorough discussion of the process through which the case moved from the state through the federal judicial system, see Chan, "The Exclusion of Chinese Women," pp. 99–105; and McClain, *In Search of Equality,* pp. 56–63.

40. U.S. Congress, Senate, Immigration Commission, *State Immigration and Alien Laws,* vol. 21, p. 552.

41. Ibid., vol. 21, pp. 552–53.

42. Saxton, *The Indispensable Enemy,* p. 106.

43. Norton, *The Story of California,* pp. 288–91.

44. Page's exact position within the mining industry is unclear, but at least by the late 1850s he had acquired the financial resources necessary to establish himself as a major investor. It was such investors who wielded the political clout required to persuade the legislature to push the Chinese out of mining by levying the series of foreign miners' taxes. Although the record fails to reveal whether Page actively supported the establishment of such taxes, his subsequent record on behalf of the exclusionist cause suggests that he most likely favored their passage. Such a history of allegiance to the anti-Chinese movement would have been more typical than exceptional for a white Californian in the latter half of the nineteenth century. Yet it adds a degree of historical background to the emergence of Horace Page as perhaps the most vocal of his state's anti-Chinese members of Congress. For a concise description of Page's business career, see U.S. Congress, *Biographical Directory of the American Congress, 1774–1961,* p. 1420.

45. *Congressional Record,* 43d Cong., 1st sess., 1873, vol. 2, p. 207.

46. Ibid., 1874, vol. 2, p. 716.

47. In a speech before Congress on January 29, 1879, Albert Willis (D.-Ky), although he failed to recognize the role of his Republican colleague, presented a thorough explanation of the manner in which Page's resolution influenced the later committee action and appointment of the joint congressional investigation. *Congressional Record,* 45th Cong., 3d sess., 1879, vol. 4, p. 793.

48. *Congressional Record,* 43d Cong., 2d sess., 1874–75, vol. 3, p. 19.

49. On September 21 a panel consisting of federal judges Lorenzo Sawyer and Ogden Hoffman and Supreme Court justice Stephen Field overturned the ruling of the California supreme court and ordered the release of Ah Fong on the grounds that the state had exceeded its authority in attempting to control immigration. McClain, *In Search of Equality,* pp. 58–60; Chan, "The Exclusion of Chinese Women, pp. 101, 102.

50. U.S. Congress, Senate, *Treaties and Conventions since July 4, 1776,* pp. 165–68.

51. *Congressional Record,* 43d Cong., 2d sess., 1874–75, vol. 3, pp. 224, 434.

52. For a complete text of the speech with which Page introduced the Page Law, see *Appendix to the Congressional Record,* 43d Cong., 2d sess., 1875, pp. 40–45.

53. Ibid., pp. 44–45. This reference to exclusion should not be surprising, given Page's earlier exclusionary resolution. *Congressional Record,* 43d Cong., 1st sess., 1874, vol. 2, p. 716.

54. "An Act Supplementary to the Acts in Relation to Immigration (Page Law)" (document 1 in the appendix of this volume).

55. Salyer has noted, for example, that Page's cause coincided with an American Medical Association study that concluded (also in 1875) that Chinese prostitutes represented an especially serious threat to the nation's health. *Laws Harsh as Tigers*, pp. 11, 12; see also Miller, *The Unwelcome Immigrant*, p. 163.

56. Li, *Congressional Policy of Chinese Immigration*, p. 25.

57. For an excellent discussion of the conditions that led to the organization of the Workingmen's Party in California, the relationship of this group to the two major parties, and the role of the Workingmen's Party in the anti-Chinese movement, see Saxton, *The Indispensable Enemy*, pp. 110–56. For a more concise summary see Salyer, *Laws Harsh as Tigers*, pp. 12, 13.

58. Sucheng Chan has also recognized the moral focus that characterized exclusion efforts before 1877, pointing out that the report of California's special legislative committee on Chinese immigration, presented to Congress in 1876, "focused on the moral effects of a continued Chinese presence." *This Bittersweet Soil*, p. 40.

59. Li, *Congressional Policy of Chinese Immigration*, p. 25.

60. U.S. Congress, Senate, Immigration Commission, *State Immigration and Alien Laws*, vol. 21, p. 553.

61. Ibid.

62. After Willis reported the bill from the Democratic-controlled Committee on Education and Labor, complete with the committee's amendments, he immediately demanded the previous question in an effort to limit debate on the proposed amendments. He succeeded in that effort, and after his speech in support of the proposed legislation Page accused him of making the bill "a subject of party caucus . . . with a view of giving the other side a partisan advantage, but which will be understood by the people of the Pacific Coast, and will be regarded as a cheap method of bolstering up the waning fortunes of the democratic party in California." *Congressional Record*, 45th Cong., 3d sess., 1879, vol. 4, pp. 791–92, 798, 800.

63. Ibid., p. 799.

64. Article 5 of the Burlingame Treaty provided for mutual and unrestricted immigration between the United States and China, providing the immigration was free and voluntary. U.S. Congress, Senate, *Treaties and Conventions since July 4, 1776*, p. 167.

65. *Congressional Record*, 45th Cong., 3d sess., 1879, vol. 4, p. 798.

66. For example, Congressman Townsend of New York delivered a stirring speech denouncing the character of Dennis Kearney and opposing the bill as an affront to the principle of human brotherhood. Ibid., pp. 794–95.

67. Ibid., p. 800;

68. Li, *Congressional Policy of Chinese immigration*, p. 26.

69. For a complete text of this directive, see U.S. Congress, Senate, *Chinese Immigration*, Executive Document, 1882, vol. 6, pp. 4–5; see also Li, *Congressional Policy of Chinese Immigration*, pp. 27–28.

70. U.S. Congress, Senate, *Chinese Immigration*, Executive Document, 1882, vol. 6, pp. 10–11. Since its effort to protect emigrant laborers through the negotiation of the Peking Regu-

lations in 1866 the Chinese government had worked hard to protect the rights of its overseas citizens, as the Burlingame Treaty's "equal status" provisions attest. Yen, *Coolies and Mandarins*, pp. 104–20; Irick, *Ch'ing Policy,* pp. 167–98.

71. U.S. Congress, House, *Foreign Relations,* vol. 1, pt. 1, p. 177. For an excellent discussion of the negotiations conducted between the commission and the Chinese government, see also Li, *Congressional Policy of Chinese Immigration,* pp. 29–33.

72. U.S. Congress, House, *Foreign Relations,* vol. 1, pt. 1, p. 185.

73. For a partial text of the 1880 treaty, see Li, *Congressional Policy of Chinese Immigration,* p. 121. Yen has concluded that three factors combined to pressure the Chinese government into accepting such clearly discriminatory treatment of its citizens: "the desire to retain a good relationship with the United States, the lack of expert advice from the Chinese Minister in Washington, and the lack of understanding of the problems of American Chinese." *Coolies and Mandarins,* p. 218.

74. Citing the archival work of historians on the Chinese mainland, Tsai has challenged the legitimacy of the 1880 treaty's provision for a suspension of Chinese immigration to America, asserting that the word *suspend* was deliberately omitted from the Chinese version of the treaty in order to prevent the Chinese government from realizing that its approval would pave the way for exclusion ("Chinese Immigration through Communist Eyes," 405). If accurate, that claim underlines more deeply the exclusionary purposes behind the treaty's revision.

75. Li, *Congressional Policy of Chinese Immigration,* p. 34.

76. Ibid., pp. 35–36 (a brief description of this bill).

77. Ibid., pp. 36–38. For an excellent discussion of the debate that led to eventual passage of the 1882 law, see Salyer, *Laws Harsh as Tigers,* pp. 15–18.

78. *Senate Journal,* 47th Cong., 1st sess. and special sess., Oct. 10, 1881–82, pp. 526–31; see also Li, *Congressional Policy of Chinese Immigration,* p. 39. Tsai has noted that President Arthur's veto message "cited almost exactly the reasons suggested by Cheng." *China and the Overseas Chinese in the United States,* pp. 66–67.

79. Li, *Congressional Policy of Chinese Immigration,* p. 40.

80. Ibid., pp. 40–41.

81. Tsai has explained that after President Arthur vetoed the original exclusion bill, Minister Cheng assumed that the matter was settled. Because his assignment also included representing the Ch'ing government in Spain and Peru, he then left to fulfill other responsibilities in Europe. Thus, when Congress passed the new bill, the task of voicing China's objections passed to his chargé d'affaires, Hsu Shou-p'eng, who lodged a formal protest with the secretary of state on May 4. When Arthur signed the Exclusion Act into law two days later, Cheng and Hsu could do no more than begin working to lessen the hardships that the new legislation would create for Chinese immigrants. Tsai, *China and the Overseas Chinese in the United States,* pp. 67–70; Yen, *Coolies and Mandarins,* pp. 213–18.

82. U.S. Congress, *Biographical Directory of the American Congress, 1774–1961,* p. 1420. Because the Democrats gained sixty-two House seats in the 1882 election while the Republicans lost twenty-nine, this explanation of Page's defeat may be overly simplistic. With the Chinese issue bolstering his candidacy, however, he had weathered an even greater shift in

power during the election of 1874, thus suggesting that much of the responsibility for his failure to remain in office after the Exclusion Act's passage lay in his identification with a single issue. For a history of the party affiliations of American congressman during this period, see U.S. Congress, "Members of Congress since 1789," pp. 176–77. For an example of how reaction to passage of the Exclusion Act by San Francisco newspapers might have undermined Page's 1882 campaign, see McClain, *In Search of Equality*, pp. 149, 150.

Chapter 4: The Hong Kong Consuls

1. For example, when John Mosby, one of the Hong Kong consuls, accused a predecessor of acting illegally in the collection and retention of an application fee for prospective Chinese female immigrants, the State Department replied that "'the instructions under which Mister Bailey [the predecessor in question] acted authorized the fee to be retained.'" U.S. Department of State, Dispatches from the United States Consuls in Hong Kong, 1844–1906, reel 12, dispatch 18, July 15, 1879.

2. "An Act Supplementary to the Acts in Relation to Immigration (Page Law)" (document 1 in the appendix of this volume).

3. U.S. Department of State, Dispatches from the United States Consuls in Hong Kong, 1844–1906, reel 12, dispatch 29, Sept. 22, 1879.

4. For a discussion of the roles that these officials played in the restriction of Chinese female immigration, see chapter 5.

5. U.S. Department of State, Dispatches from the United States Consuls in Hong Kong, 1844–1906, reel 12, dispatch 21, July 25, 1879.

6. Coolidge, *Chinese Immigration*, p. 419.

7. Hirata, "Free, Indentured, Enslaved," 10–11.

8. Although apparently limiting the blame for Bailey's shortcomings to the alleged illiteracy of his assistants, Tong has still depicted the consular service in Hong Kong as "culpable for aiding the trafficking [in Chinese prostitutes]." *Unsubmissive Women*, pp. 46, 47.

9. Ibid., p. 49.

10. U.S. Department of State, Dispatches from the United States Consuls in Hong Kong, 1844–1906, reel 10, dispatch 301, Aug. 21, 1875.

11. Ibid., dispatch 307, Aug. 28, 1875.

12. Coolidge, *Chinese Immigration*, p. 50.

13. U.S. Department of State, Dispatches from the United States Consuls in Hong Kong, 1844–1906, reel 10, dispatch 301, Aug. 21, 1875.

14. Ibid.

15. Ibid.

16. Ibid.

17. Ibid.

18. Ibid.

19. Sinn, "Chinese Patriarchy," p. 144.

20. U.S. Department of State, Dispatches from the United States Consuls in Hong Kong, 1844–1906, reel 10, dispatch 307, Aug. 28, 1875. For a thorough discussion of the Tung Wah

Hospital Committee's role in both the suppression of prostitute emigration and the social life of Hong Kong, see Sinn, *Power and Charity*.

21. Sinn, "Chinese Patriarchy," pp. 143, 144.

22. Coolidge, *Chinese Immigration*, p. 418; U.S. Department of State, Dispatches from the United States Consuls in Hong Kong, 1844–1906, reel 10, dispatch 307, enclosure 1, Aug. 28, 1875.

23. U.S. Department of State, Dispatches from the United States Consuls in Hong Kong, 1844–1906, reel 10, dispatch 307, enclosure 9, Aug. 28, 1875.

24. Ibid., dispatch 307, Aug. 28, 1875.

25. Ibid.

26. U.S. Department of State, Dispatches and Miscellaneous Letters from the Hong Kong Consulate, 1873–86, vol. 1, dispatch 462, Aug. 29, 1876.

27. In his telegrams to the collector of customs, Bailey always referred to the investigations conducted by the Tung Wah Hospital Committee, either certifying the good character of prospective female emigrants or warning of attempts to smuggle prostitutes into the United States. Ibid., dispatch 386, Dec. 21, 1875; U.S. Department of State, Dispatches from the United States Consuls in Hong Kong, 1844–1906, reel 10, dispatch 307, Aug. 28, 1875.

28. See, for example, U.S. Department of State, Dispatches and Miscellaneous Letters from the Hong Kong Consulate, 1873–86, vol. 1, dispatch 461, Aug. 18, 1876.

29. Ibid., dispatch 463, Sept. 1, 1876.

30. In relating the bribe's existence to State Department officials, Mosby told of Chinese applicants who "sent their bribes along with their applications for certificates." After arresting one offender and forcing another to flee for Macao, he then called a meeting of "the leading Chinamen" and told them that bribes would no longer be accepted. This meeting suggests that the bribes were not submitted by tong leaders desiring to smuggle prostitutes but by "respectable Chinese" who regarded them as supplementary filing fees. U.S. Department of State, Dispatches from the United States Consuls in Hong Kong, 1844–1906, reel 12, dispatch 21, July 25, 1879.

31. Bailey and Loring never acknowledged the certification of any woman without prior approval from both the British harbor master and the Tung Wah Hospital Committee, and Mosby stated that he required a bond from the committee before clearing female applicants for emigration. Ibid., dispatch 18, July 5, 1879.

32. Although not drawing the same distinction between the fee's likely impact on legal as opposed to prohibited emigrants, Tong has endorsed this interpretation of its significance. *Unsubmissive Women*, p. 49.

33. U.S. Department of State, Dispatches from the United States Consuls in Hong Kong, 1844–1906, reel 11, dispatch 387, enclosure 1, Feb. 1, 1877.

34. Ibid.

35. Ibid., enclosure 2.

36. Although noting that the consul's efforts ultimately proved ineffective, Irick has nonetheless recognized both their forcefulness and sincerity. *Ch'ing Policy*, pp. 219–21.

37. For a thorough discussion of Hayes's reform efforts, with particular reference to their

impact on the consular service, see Hoogenboom, *The Presidency of Rutherford B. Hayes*, pp. 103–8, 127–51.

38. U.S. Department of State, Dispatches from the United States Consuls in Hong Kong, Aug. 1, 1873–Aug. 4, 1881, vol. 1, dispatch 202, Sept. 2, 1873.

39. Coolidge, *Chinese Immigration*, p. 308.

40. U.S. Department of State, Dispatches from the United States Consuls in Hong Kong, 1844–1906, reel 12, dispatch 18, July 5, 1879; Sandmeyer, *The Anti-Chinese Movement in California*, p. 13.

41. U.S. Department of State, Dispatches and Miscellaneous Letters from the Hong Kong Consulate, 1873–86, vol. 1, dispatch 75, Aug. 20, 1878.

42. Ibid., dispatch 513, Feb. 3, 1879.

43. U.S. Department of State, Dispatches from the United States Consuls in Hong Kong, 1844–1906, reel 13, dispatch 163, Dec. 13, 1881.

44. Ibid., reel 12, dispatch 455, enclosures 2–3, Feb. 12, 1878.

45. After the second quarter of 1877, Bailey received no letters from the Tung Wah Hospital Committee (letters in previous quarters had dealt with questions on procedure), although he wrote to the committee more extensively than Loring. Again, Loring's continued correspondence with them suggests that the committee as well as the British officials continued to investigate the character of female Chinese emigrants. Ibid., reel 10, dispatch 330, Feb. 15, 1876; dispatch 345, May 23, 1876; dispatch 362, Sept. 2, 1876; and reel 11, dispatch 371, Nov. 16, 1876; dispatch 388, Feb. 1, 1877; dispatch 410, May 17, 1877; dispatch 423, Aug. 22, 1877; and dispatch 430, Oct. 24, 1877.

46. See Sinn, "Chinese Patriarchy," pp. 144, 145.

47. Coolidge, *Chinese Immigration*, p. 502. Although Tong has attempted to revive Sandmeyer's explanation for the increase in female immigrants during the tenure of Acting Consul Loring, he has offered no new evidence to support his claims but has merely recast the same statistics presented here while failing to address the more favorable information. *Unsubmissive Women*, p. 49.

48. Sinn, "Chinese Patriarchy," p. 145.

49. U.S. Department of State, Dispatches from the United States Consuls in Hong Kong, 1844–1906, reel 12, dispatch 29, Sept. 22, 1879. In the report, Mosby characterized Smith as an illiterate criminal, and it is on the basis of that assessment that Tong has attempted to acknowledge Consul Bailey's efforts to restrict prostitute emigration while at the same time decrying the corruption of his administration. *Unsubmissive Women*, p. 47.

50. Tong, *Unsubmissive Women*, p. 47.

51. U.S. Department of State, Dispatches from the United States Consuls in Hong Kong, 1844–1906, reel 12, dispatch 18, July 15, 1879.

52. Ibid., reel 14, dispatch 200, May 23, 1882.

53. Ibid., reel 12, dispatch 18, July 15, 1879.

54. Coolidge, *Chinese Immigration*, pp. 418–19.

55. U.S. Department of State, Dispatches from the United States Consuls in Hong Kong, 1844–1906, reel 12, dispatch 37, Oct. 18, 1879.

56. Ibid., reel 13, dispatch 151, Aug. 21, 1881.

57. U.S. Department of State, Dispatches and Miscellaneous Letters from the Hong Kong Consulate, 1873–86, vol. 2, dispatch 154, June 21, 1882.

58. U.S. Department of State, Dispatches from the United States Consuls in Hong Kong, 1844–1906, reel 13, dispatch 161, Nov. 14, 1881.

59. Each of these complaints was lodged on several occasions. Ibid., reels 13–14, 1880–82.

60. Sinn has pointed out ("Chinese Patriarchy," pp. 149–51) that the Po Leung Kuk, founded in 1881 to consolidate the work on behalf of Chinese women that had been performed by the Tung Wah Hospital Committee and other organizations, gradually shifted its focus from "suppressing kidnapping to the care of victims." Thus local efforts to stop the emigration of prostitutes seems to have peaked around 1875 and begun to decline shortly after exclusion.

61. Both Takaki and Yung have concurred with this assessment of the Page Law's ability to discourage unrestricted women from attempting emigration. Takaki, *Strangers from a Different Shore*, p. 40; Yung, *Unbound Feet*, pp. 23, 24.

62. In 1882 customs officials reported 136 Chinese female arrivals in the United States, by far the largest number recorded during Mosby's administration of the Hong Kong consulate. Coolidge, *Chinese Immigration*, p. 502.

Chapter 5: The San Francisco Port Authorities and Judges

1. U.S. Department of State, Dispatches from the United States Consuls in Hong Kong, 1844–1906, reel 12, dispatch 39, Oct. 21, 1879.

2. U.S. Treasury Department, San Francisco, Letters Sent by the Port Surveyor, 1864–86, box 4, April 20, 1875.

3. U.S. Department of State, Dispatches from the United States Consuls in Hong Kong, 1844–1906, reel 14, dispatch 208, June 8, 1882.

4. U.S. Treasury Department, Letters Sent from the Bureau of Customs in San Francisco, 1856–79, box 6, Aug. 12, 1875.

5. California Legislature, Senate, Special Committee on Chinese Immigration, *Chinese Immigration*, pp. 153–54.

6. For a record of Bailey's interview, see U.S. Department of State, Dispatches from the United States Consuls in Hong Kong, 1844–1906, reel 10, dispatch 307, enclosure 1, Aug. 28, 1875.

7. Ibid. (for a full description of the examination process established by Consul Bailey).

8. Testimony of Loy How, in U.S. District Court, *In the Matter of Wah Ah Chin and Others*, pp. 49–50.

9. Ibid.

10. Ibid., pp. 49–50; see also Testimony of F. A. Bee, Recalled, pp. 105–6.

11. "Watery Waifs."

12. Testimony of Col. F. A. Bee, in U.S. District Court, *In the Matter of Wah Ah Chin and Others*, pp. 19, 24.

13. For an example of the process through which female petitioners were first removed

from the steamers to the county jail only to be returned later, see "Removal of Chinese Courtesans."

14. Testimony of Henry W. Browne, in U.S. District Court, *In the Matter of Wah Ah Chin and Others,* pp. 15–16.

15. "A Cargo of Infamy."

16. Testimony of Wah Ah Chin, in U.S. District Court, *In the Matter of Wah Ah Chin and Others,* p. 1.

17. Testimony of Ching Ping, in U.S. District Court, *In the Matter of Wah Ah Chin and Others,* pp. 28–30.

18. Testimony of Wah Ah Chin, p. 2.

19. Ibid., pp. 2–4; Testimony of Loy How, p. 50;

20. Testimony of Ching Ping, p. 29.

21. Testimony of Capt. Alfred Roper, in U.S. District Court, *In the Matter of Wah Ah Chin and Others,* p. 35; see also Testimony of Wang Ah Yeun, p. 85.

22. Testimony of Wang Ah Yeun, pp. 86–88.

23. Testimony of Wah Ah Chin, pp. 4–5.

24. U.S. Department of State, Dispatches and Miscellaneous Letters from the Hong Kong Consulate, 1873–86, National Archives, vol. 2, dispatch 134, Jan. 6, 1882.

25. Ibid., dispatch 154, June 21, 1882.

26. Ibid., pp. 2–4.

27. Ibid., p. 6.

28. Testimony of Ah Po, in U.S. District Court, *In the Matter of Wah Ah Chin and Others,* pp. 94–97.

29. Ibid., p. 94.

30. Testimony of Ah Tchut, in U.S. District Court, *In the Matter of Wah Ah Chin and Others,* p. 96.

31. "Wailing Women."

32. Testimony of Loy How, p. 52.

33. Christian Fritz has attributed Hoffman's appointment to Daniel Webster, his father's friend and President Fillmore's secretary of state, and to his own friendship with the son of William H. Aspinwall, president of the Pacific Mail Steamship Company. "Judge Ogden Hoffman and the Northern District Court of California," pp. 101–2.

34. Ibid., pp. 103, 108.

35. Fritz has argued that although Judge Hoffman espoused a wholly negative view of the Chinese in general: "In his court he did not face the 'Chinese,' but rather individual Chinese petitioners. The thousands of separate hearings [the habeas corpus petitions created by the enforcement of exclusion] individualized the Chinese and forced Hoffman to see and hear them as human beings with distinct explanations and histories that had to be dealt with on a case-by-case basis. For instance, Hoffman expressed his delight at being able to avoid separating Chinese children form their parents. Likewise, he repeatedly spoke of the admirable and respectable qualities of individual Chinese even as he decried their limitations as a race." Ibid., pp. 109–10. Given this later history of compassion, it is doubtful that the judge could have listened to Loy How's story without being moved.

36. "The Chinese Women Released."

37. "Chinese Female Chattels"; see also U.S. Circuit Court, Northern California District, *Order for Writ of* Habeas Corpus, *Chou See Ti You et al. v. R. J. C. Todd,* pp. 4–6.

38. "Death of Samuel H. Dwinelle"; "Death of Judge Dwinelle."

39. Ibid.

40. Przybyszewski, "Judge Lorenzo Sawyer and the Chinese," pp. 25, 26.

41. Sawyer ran for city attorney in 1854 and for judge of the Fourth District Court the following year. Przybyszewski has explained that Gov. Leland Stanford, a fellow Republican, "offered Sawyer the judgeship of the Twelfth Circuit Court of California in 1862. A year later the Republican state convention successfully nominated him for a supreme court justiceship." Ibid., pp. 26–27.

42. Ibid., p. 27.

43. Ibid., pp. 30–31.

44. Przybyszewski has listed several cases involving the Chinese in which Sawyer's advocacy of individual rights and opposition to states' rights led him to rule in their favor. Ibid., pp. 34–41.

45. Ibid., p. 25.

46. "Chinese Question," Lorenzo Sawyer to H. H. Bancroft, Sept. 22, 1886, H. H. Bancroft Collection, pp. 2, 4–5.

47. "Chinese Female Chattels."

48. "The Chinese Damsels."

49. Ibid.; see also "The Chinese Wives."

50. "The Chinese Wives."

51. U.S. Circuit Court, Northern California District, *Order for Writ of* Habeas Corpus, *Chou See Ti You et al. v. R. J. C. Todd,* pp. 4–6.

52. "The Chinese Damsels."

53. Apparently, Sawyer was not impressed with their success, because he continued the trial without comment. The only recorded response to the demonstration of the petitioners' integrity came from the *Morning Call,* which reported ("The Chinese Women") that after Chou See Ti You and her husband had correctly identified each other for the court, the prosecution "introduced numerous Chinese witnesses who swore the alleged husband of Chow See Ti You, whose name is claimed to be Wong Tuck is none other than one Quan Yee, a well known gambler, instead of a tailor." Although the *Chronicle* ("The Chinese Damsels") mistakenly called her "Tie Ah Zan" (likely taken from one of Mosby's substitute certificates), it is remarkable that neither the press nor Sawyer expressed any positive reaction to the ability of these couples to pass the judge's identity test.

54. "The Chinese Wives."

55. Chan, *This Bittersweet Soil,* p. 32.

56. Chung, "Their Changing World," p. 204.

57. Yung, *Unbound Feet,* p. 2.

58. "The *Glamis Castle* Women Freed."

59. "Roper's Female Wards"; see also Petition for Writ, U.S. District Court, Northern California District, *In the Matter of the Application of Wong Wing,* pp. 1–2.

60. "Roper's Female Wards."

61. "The Water Front."

62. "Roper's Female Wards"; see also "The English Captains."

63. "Roper's Female Wards."

64. "Another Chinese Cargo"; see also "Chinese Chattels," *San Francisco Chronicle,* March 18, 1882.

65. "The British Sea Tramp"; see also "The *Anjer Head* Troubles."

66. "The *Anjer Head* Troubles"; "The English Captains"; "A Sea of Troubles."

67. "Roper's Female Wards."

68. In its report of the Page Law's passage, dated August 12, 1875, the *Hong Kong Times* offered the following analysis: "The chief evil it [the Page Law] is intended to meet is Chinese prostitution. It should, however, be noticed that throughout the new act the word used is 'importation,' as 'the importation into the United States of women for the purposes of prostitution is hereby forbidden.' Nothing appears to be said against voluntary emigration for such purpose. In the interview which took place on Monday between Mister Bailey, the United States Consul in this Colony, and the deputation of Chinese, this difference seems, however, to have been lost sight of. It was assumed throughout, and indeed was more than once stated, that the Act was also directed against voluntary emigration for prostitution." The *China Mail* and the *Daily Press of Hong Kong* offered similar interpretations, which, although Judge Hoffman may never have read them, anticipated his new understanding of the law. U.S. Department of State, Dispatches from the United States Consuls in Hong Kong, 1844–1906, reel 10, dispatch 307, Aug. 28, 1875.

69. For a thorough explanation of the role female go-betweens played in these enterprises, see Jaschok, *Concubines and Bondservants,* pp. 10–12, 89, 90.

Chapter 6: The San Francisco Press

1. Augustus Ward Loomis to H. H. Bancroft, May 7, 1876, H. H. Bancroft Collection.

2. For a thorough presentation and analysis of reports on the Chinese published outside California, see Miller, *The Unwelcome Immigrant.*

3. "The Social Evil in San Francisco."

4. "Fourth Ward Democratic Club"; see also "Anti-Chinese Convention."

5. "Cornelius Cole."

6. Ibid.

7. "A Cargo of Infamy."

8. "Chinese Clippings," Hubert H. Bancroft Scrapbooks, vol. 7, p. 5. Bancroft's "Chinese Clippings" contain articles related to the Chinese in America from newspapers throughout the Pacific Coast, many being extracted from publications for which archival collections are nonexistent or incomplete. Although months, and perhaps years, of study would be required to verify the exhaustiveness of the collection, it appears that Bancroft attempted to collect every story, regardless of its attitude toward the Chinese. Limited examinations of the archival collections of such San Francisco newspapers as the *Chronicle* and *Alta,* scanning the daily editions published in selected three-month periods, failed to uncover a single article on the Chinese not contained in "Chinese Clippings."

9. Ibid., p. 18.

10. H. M. Lai and Philip Choy have concluded that the federal hearings, although anti-Chinese in tone, "did present to the nation a large body of information concerning the Chinese in California, in which the views of both sides were represented" (*Outlines*, p. 86), thus making it more balanced than the openly exclusionist state investigation.

11. "Chinese Clippings," Hubert H. Bancroft Scrapbooks, vol. 7, p. 34.

12. Ibid., p. 35.

13. Ibid.

14. Ibid., p. 57.

15. Ibid., p. 50.

16. Ibid., pp. 73–74.

17. Ibid., p. 57.

18. Ibid., p. 68; Gibson, *The Chinese in America.*

19. Gibson, *The Chinese in America,* pp. 72–73.

20. Ibid., p. 114.

21. Ibid., p. 149.

22. "Chinese Chattels," *San Francisco Chronicle,* March 18, 1882.

23. "The Chinese Houris."

24. Ibid.

25. "Wailing Women."

26. Ibid.

27. Ibid.

28. Ibid.

29. "The Chinese Women Released."

30. "Chinese Chattels," *San Francisco Chronicle,* March 27, 1882.

31. "Chinese Female Chattels."

32. "The Female Cargo of the *Glamis Castle.*"

33. U.S. Circuit Court, Northern California District, *Order for Writ of* Habeas Corpus, *Chou See Ti You* v. *R. J. C. Todd,* minutes, p. 228.

34. "Chinese Female Chattels."

35. "Chinese 'Wives.'"

36. "Release of the Chinese Women."

37. "The *Glamis Castle* Women Freed."

38. Untitled paragraph, *San Francisco Chronicle.*

39. "Another Chinese Cargo."

40. "Who Offered the Bribe?" For a complete account of the charges and countercharges that the captain and the interpreter presented in court, see "A Serious Charge." See also "An Assaulted Chinese"; "A Sea of Troubles"; and "Briton and Coolie." For an account of Judge Hoffman's ruling on these charges in favor of Captain Roper, see "Captain Roper Vindicated."

41. "The Little Feet Women."

42. "Chinese Chattels: Some Light."

43. Ibid.

44. Quint used precisely this argument in presenting his case for Chan Si's release; see "Roper's Female Wards."

45. For a report of Roper's testimony regarding the alleged dereliction of duty committed by customs detective E. L. McLean, see "The English Captains." For an account of McLean's testimony and his charges against the captain, see "The Balky Briton."

46. "Roper's Female Wards."

47. Tsai, *The Chinese Experience in America*, p. 67.

48. Przybyszewski, "Judge Lorenzo Sawyer and the Chinese," 45.

49. Ibid.

50. Ibid.

51. Przybyszewski has concluded, quite reasonably, that this criticism emanated more from Sawyer's "controversial expansion of federal judicial power" than from anti-Chinese sentiment. Yet such a negative commentary in what she has described as "perhaps the country's leading legal journal of the time" still reflects the social and political clout of California's exclusionists. Ibid.

52. U.S. Department of State, Dispatches from the United States Consuls in Hong Kong, 1844–1906, reel 14, dispatch 210, June 20, 1882.

53. Chan, *This Bittersweet Soil*, p. 369.

Chapter 7: The Census Enumerators

1. For a discussion of the experiences of *mui tsai* in the United States, see Yung, *Unbound Feet*, pp. 37–41. For a more broadly focused explanation of the *mui tsai* custom's role in Chinese culture, see Jaschok, *Concubines and Bondservants*, pp. 8–12.

2. See Yung, *Unbound Feet*, pp. 42–47, for a discussion of the experiences of laboring wives in the United States.

3. For the review article in which these statistics were cited, see "The Chinese in California, by Rev. Otis Gibson," *San Francisco Post*, Feb. 10, 1877, in Hubert H. Bancroft Scrapbooks, vol. 7, p. 68; for the original work, see Gibson, *The Chinese in America*. That the newspaper review chose to highlight such statistical allegations illustrates the pervasiveness of this assessment of San Francisco's Chinese female population.

4. As with his other calculations, Gibson had put forth a much higher estimate of the city's Chinese population—32,880—than the government's tabulations can support. Yet his equally excessive estimate regarding the number of prostitutes, according to the Cheng model (chapter 1), would have serviced more than 109,000 patrons. "The Chinese in California, by Rev. Otis Gibson," in Hubert H. Bancroft Scrapbooks, vol. 7, p. 68.

5. Tong, *Unsubmissive Women*, pp. 97, 99, 100.

6. Anderson, *The American Census*.

7. Ibid., pp. 76–78 (a thorough discussion of this political struggle).

8. Wright and Hunt, *History and Growth of the United States Census*, p. 52.

9. Ibid., p. 156.

10. Ibid., pp. 156, 157.

11. Anderson, *The American Census*, p. 84.

12. Wright and Hunt, *History and Growth of the United States Census,* p. 156.

13. Anderson, *The American Census,* p. 88.

14. U.S. Bureau of the Census, Eighth Census of the United States (1860), Population Schedules, San Francisco, RG 29, reel 63, p. 76.

15. Ibid.

16. "New Suits."

17. U.S. Bureau of the Census, Ninth Census of the United States (1870), Population Schedules, San Francisco, RG 29, reel 79, p. 292.

18. Ibid.

19. Wright and Hunt, *History and Growth of the United States Census,* pp. 41, 42.

20. Ibid., pp. 152, 159.

21. Among the 1,584 Chinese females recorded in my study of the ward's schedules, Martin used *Ah* for all but ten. U.S. Bureau of the Census, Ninth Census of the United States (1870), Population Schedules, San Francisco, RG 29, reel 73. For an example of this approach, see table A1 in the appendix.

22. The *Alta*'s report of final census returns for San Francisco ("Census Report") lists a Chinese population of 3,898 males and 1,593 females in the Fourth Ward. Using my tabulation, which counted only 1,584 females in the ward, 1,288 among this total shared dwellings with 1,765 males.

23. Martin (ibid.) identified 173 dwellings containing both Chinese females and Chinese males and divided their inhabitants into 394 families, thus creating an average of 2.28 families per dwelling. For an example of his tendency to separate families according to gender, see table A2 in the appendix.

24. Among the 1,584 Chinese female residents of the ward I have identified, 1,411 were recorded as being more than twelve, and Martin identified 1,249 individuals in this group as prostitutes. Ibid.

25. Chung, "Their Changing World," p. 208.

26. Explaining the importance of her numerical adjustments, Chung has pointed out that the resulting decrease in prostitutes "would be significant, because it would indicate that there was an attempt to establish a 'stable' rather than a transient community at an early date." Ibid., p. 209.

27. U.S. Bureau of the Census, Ninth Census of the United States (1870), Population Schedules, San Francisco, RG 29, reel 74, p. 182.

28. Ibid.

29. For acknowledgement of Bennett's role as compiler, see "San Francisco as Viewed through the Census."

30. "The Chinese Problem: Lecture by H. C. Bennett."

31. "The Lecture Room."

32. Ibid. Bennett attributed this assertion to William Kelley, a member of Congress from Pennsylvania and member of the House Ways and Means Committee. Kelley, "the foremost defender of protection of American labor," had recently visited San Francisco.

33. Ibid.

34. "Lecture by H. C. Bennett."

35. Ibid. Although rejecting Bennett's arguments, the *San Francisco Chronicle* joined its counterpart in condemning the audience's mistreatment of him ("Free Speech"), concluding with the following words: "Were we not satisfied of the utter fallacy of many of Mr. Bennett's views, we would think the argument convincing from the attempt made to intimidate him."

36. "The Chinese Protection Society."

37. "Local Items."

38. Coolidge, *Chinese Immigration,* p. 260.

39. "The Chinese in California: Their Numbers and Influence."

40. Ibid.

41. "Some Facts Relating to Chinese."

42. Among the 393 Chinese females recorded in my study of the ward's schedules, Bennett used *Ah* for 263. U.S. Bureau of the Census, Ninth Census of the United States (1870), Population Schedules, San Francisco, RG 29, reel 74.

43. The *Alta*'s report of final census returns for San Francisco ("Census Report") lists a Chinese population of 2,540 males and 394 females in the Sixth Ward. Using my tabulation, which counted only 393 females in the ward, 280 among this total shared dwellings with 663 males. Ibid.

44. Bennett identified sixty-eight dwellings containing both Chinese females and Chinese males and divided their inhabitants into 186 families, thus creating an average of 2.74 families per dwelling. Ibid.

45. For an example of Bennett's work in recording information on the census schedules themselves, see table A3 in the appendix.

46. For a record of government regulations regarding the consequences of such errors, see Wright and Hunt, *History and Growth of the United States Census,* pp. 149, 155.

47. Among the 393 Chinese female residents of the ward whom I have identified, 345 were recorded as being over the age of twelve, and Bennett identified 183 individuals in that group as prostitutes. U.S. Bureau of the Census, Ninth Census of the United States (1870), Population Schedules, San Francisco, RG 29, reel 74.

48. Wright and Hunt, *History and Growth of the United States Census,* p. 59.

49. Anderson, *The American Census,* p. 99.

50. U.S. Bureau of the Census, Ninth Census of the United States (1870), Population Schedules, San Francisco, RG 29, reels 73, 74.

51. Wright and Hunt, *History and Growth of the United States Census,* p. 167.

52. U.S. Bureau of the Census, Tenth Census of the United States (1880), Population Schedules, San Francisco, RG 29, reel 76.

53. Anderson, *The American Census,* p. 99.

54. Wright and Hunt, *History and Growth of the United States Census,* pp. 169, 170, 171.

55. Ibid., p. 169.

56. Among the 1,313 Chinese females recorded in my study of the Fourth Ward's schedules, enumerators used *Ah* for only 74, whereas those in Ward 6 employed the term for but

29 of 663. U.S. Bureau of the Census, Tenth Census of the Unites States (1880), Population Schedules, San Francisco, RG 29, reels 76, 77.

57. My tabulation of census returns for San Francisco lists a Chinese population of 5,170 males and 1,313 females in the Fourth Ward, numbers that change to 3,101 and 1,261, respectively, when restricted to mixed-gender dwellings. Ibid., reel 76.

58. My study of the Ward 6 schedules has yielded a male population of 2,975 and a female population of 663, changing to 2,185 and 640, respectively, in dwellings containing both sexes. Ibid., reel 77.

59. The Ward 4 enumerators identified 253 dwellings containing both Chinese females and Chinese males and divided the inhabitants into 854 families, whereas those in the Sixth Ward reported 597 families living in 138 mixed-gender dwellings. U.S. Bureau of the Census, Ninth Census of the United States (1870), Population Schedules, San Francisco, RG 29, reels 76, 77.

60. The families-per-dwelling averages for Wards 4 and 6 were 3.38 and 4.33, respectively. Ibid.

61. Ibid., reel 77, pp. 4, 5, 8, 9, 11, 13, 15–18.

62. For an example of this speculative designation, see table A4 in the appendix.

63. Wright and Hunt, *History and Growth of the United States Census,* p. 171.

64. U.S. Bureau of the Census, Tenth Census of the United States (1880), Population Schedules, San Francisco, RG 29, reel 76.

65. Ibid.

66. For purpose of this calculation, I have used Hirata's report of 435 Chinese prostitutes living in San Francisco at the time of the 1880 census. Because she made no attempt to compensate for the bias of enumerators in her calculations, her count most closely matches that of the final census report. "Free, Indentured, Enslaved," p. 421.

67. "Chinese Women in California," Augustus Ward Loomis to H. H. Bancroft, 1876, H. H. Bancroft Collection.

68. The number of women labeled with some form of the "Prostitute?" designation constitutes 31.6 percent of Hirata's total and 36 percent of my total of 408, which was compiled directly from the census schedules.

69. Irick, *Ch'ing Policy,* p. 413.

Chapter 8: The Task of Restoring Female Visibility

1. Miller, *The Unwelcome Immigrant,* p. 62. Miller appears to have blamed the missionaries almost exclusively for the development of negative stereotypes regarding Chinese sexuality. Ibid., pp. 59–62.

2. Ibid., p. 169. Apparently, Greeley based his conclusions on reports he had read in California newspapers. Miller has summarized the process by which newspapers in the East developed these negative predispositions toward Chinese immigrants by explaining that "reports from correspondents in California and China on the nature of the Chinese . . . continually undermined the confidence of these [eastern] editors in the wisdom of permitting the Chinese to make even a temporary home in the United States." Ibid., p. 171.

3. Hershatter, *Dangerous Pleasures*, pp. 42–56.

4. For example, Yen, although noting that other scholars have recognized the existence of only a merchant and a laborer class in these communities, has proposed using "a modified three-class paradigm" consisting of "merchants [who] occupied the top social stratum below which was a thin layer of educated elite with the workers at the lowest level." *Class Structure and Social Mobility*, p. 1. Although documentary evidence does not support categorizing San Francisco's Chinese prostitutes according to either Hershatter's construct or a modified version of that proposed by Yen, it appears certain that at least some elements of the traditional hierarchy of prostitution were transferred to the immigrant community, albeit in a condensed form. Yet such distinctions were probably irrelevant for a host society already convinced that virtually all Chinese female immigrants were engaged in prostitution.

5. Miller, *The Unwelcome Immigrant*, p. 184.

6. Ibid., p. 171.

7. "Chinese Chattels: Some Light" is representative of American accounts regarding the manner in which Chinese women were enslaved as prostitutes and clearly implies that the fictitious opportunity to earn $1,000 a year through such work appealed to the women as a great economic opportunity. Chinese female immigrants were thus presented as willing participants in the prostitution business, providing that employers offered them a sufficient promise of profit.

8. Miller reports that the AMA, after concluding its study, regarded Chinese syphilis as no greater threat to public health than the European variety. Although their reference to a European strain of the disease may have referred to the European immigrants who made up the majority of San Francisco's white prostitutes, Miller does not comment on the meaning of the reference. *The Unwelcome Immigrant*, p. 163.

9. Sims concluded his address by urging "the government to terminate the importation of people who represented such risk to the national health." Ibid.

10. "Population—San Francisco, 1870–1871," p. 11.

11. *Appendix to the Congressional Record*, 43d Cong., 2d sess., 1875, p. 44.

12. For example, Horace Page lodged this complaint in his speech before Congress on February 10, 1875. First, Page presented a California labor petition that cited the discouragement of white settlement as one reason for prohibiting Chinese immigration. He concluded by asserting that, upon the elimination of Chinese immigrants from California, "through the Golden Gate and across the continent, will come a race of people to settle among us who will plant the vine, cultivate the soil, and add something to the substantial wealth of the country." *Appendix to the Congressional Record*, 43d Cong., 2d sess., 1875, p. 44.

13. Espiritu, *Asian American Women and Men*, p. 20.

14. From 1875 to 1882 an average female immigration of 626 would have yielded 5,008 immigrants. When the actual figure for these years (1,723) is subtracted from that total, the remainder is 3,285. Although such a projection does not account for the possibility of additional female repatriation, it still represents a reasonable approximation. For the immigration data used in this calculation, see table A5 in the appendix.

15. For the population statistics used in these projections, see U.S. Department of Commerce, Special Report, *Chinese and Japanese in the United States, 1910,* p. 8. For the immigration statistics, see table A6 in the appendix.

16. The Chinese male population grew slightly between 1880 and 1890 and then fell dramatically during the next two decades, reaching a total of 66,856 in 1910. Conversely, the number of females declined by 19 percent between 1880 and 1890 and then recovered to 4,675 by 1910. Ibid., p. 8.

17. The pattern of departure that America's Chinese community followed between 1880 and 1910 appears similar to that of Malacca, with exclusion representing one of the Malay settlement's economic downturns. If, given that pattern, the female population had remained at about nine thousand, the sex ratio would have narrowed to 135 per thousand compared to the seventy per thousand actually experienced. Ibid.; see also table A6 in the appendix.

18. Bonacich and Cheng, "Introduction," p. 32. Espiritu has echoed this assessment; see *Asian American Women and Men,* p. 17.

19. Sawyer, "Chinese Question," pp. 2, 4.

20. Ibid., pp. 4, 5.

21. Bonacich has argued that "exclusion was mainly the product of class struggle in California and was fostered by the anticapitalist coalition of small producers and white labor." "Asian Labor in the Development of California and Hawaii," p. 174. For an excellent discussion of the exclusion movement, argued from the perspective of class conflict, see *Labor Immigration under Capitalism,* ed. Cheng and Bonacich, pp. 57–185.

22. Peffer, "Forbidden Families."

23. Lyman, *Chinese Americans,* p. 87.

24. Hirata, "Free, Indentured, Enslaved," p. 406.

25. Leong, "Gender, Race, and the 1875 Page Law," p. 61.

26. To appreciate the problem of inconsistent transliteration, one need only examine the census schedules' "Place of Birth" column, where I have identified as many as five alternative spellings of *Kwangtung.* The possible variants for family names will likely prove to be no less numerous.

27. Yung, *Unbound Feet,* p. 7; see also Espiritu, *Asian American Women and Men,* pp. 20, 115, 116.

28. Noting that the Chinese patriarchal system counted all females as property, Sinn ("Chinese Patriarchy," pp. 146, 147) observes that Chinese leadership in Hong Kong "blamed English law and the English judicial system for encouraging their women to believe they were free." Although the vast majority of women who were not prostitutes no doubt emigrated with at least a joint family blessing, Hong Kong—the exclusive port of departure for female immigrants to the United States—would have been the likely source of any whose leaving represented an act of rebellion against patriarchal control.

Appendix

1. "An Act Supplementary to the Acts in Relation to Immigration (Page Law)" (document 1 in the appendix of this volume).

2. U.S. Congress, Senate, Joint Special Committee to Investigate Chinese Immigration, *Chinese Immigration,* 1877, p. 145.

3. Ibid., p. 146.

Bibliography

Letters and Unpublished Sources

Bancroft, Hubert H. Scrapbooks. H. H. Bancroft Collection, University of California Library, Berkeley.

H. H. Bancroft Collection. Personal correspondence with Augustus Ward Loomis, 1876, and personal correspondence with Lorenzo Sawyer, 1886. University of California Library, Berkeley.

Peffer, George Anthony. "Forbidden Families." Master's thesis, San Francisco State University, 1981.

Government Documents

Appendix to the Congressional Record. 43d Cong., 2d sess. (1875).

California Legislature. Senate. Special Committee on Chinese Immigration, *Chinese Immigration: Its Social, Moral, and Political Effect.* Report, May 27, 1876. Sacramento, 1878.

Congressional Globe, 41st Cong., 2d sess. (1869–70).

Congressional Record. 43d Cong., 2d sess. (1875), vols. 2–4, and 45th Cong., 3d sess. (1879), vol. 4.

Great Britain Colonial Office. *Straits Settlements Government Gazette* (1881). Microfilm copy, reel 2. International Population Census Publication. University of Texas.

"Members of Congress since 1789." *Congressional Quarterly,* 2d ed. Washington, D.C., 1981.

Senate Journal. 47th Cong., 1st sess. and special sess., Oct. 10 (1881–82).

U.S. Bureau of the Census. Census Schedules for San Francisco, 1860. Record Group 29. National Archives.

———. Census Schedules for San Francisco, 1870. Record Group 29. National Archives.

———. Census Schedules for San Francisco, 1880. Record Group 29. National Archives.

———. *Report of the Population of the United States at the Ninth Census, 1870.* Washington, 1872.

———. *Report of the Population of the United States at the Eleventh Census, 1890.* Washington, 1895.

U.S. Circuit Court, Northern California Circuit. *Order for Writ of* Habeas Corpus, *Chou See Ti You et al. v. R. J. C. Todd,* no. 2763. May 1882.

U.S. Congress. *Biographical Directory of the American Congress, 1774–1961.* Washington, 1961.

U.S. Congress, House. *Foreign Relations.* Executive Document. 47th Cong., 1st sess. Washington, 1882.

U.S. Congress, Senate. *Chinese Immigration.* Executive Document. 47th Cong., 1st sess. Washington, 1882.

———. Immigration Commission. *State Immigration and Alien Laws.* Report. 61st Cong., 3d sess. Washington, 1911.

———. Joint Special Committee to Investigate Chinese Immigration. *Chinese Immigration.* Report. 44th Cong., 2d sess. Washington, 1877.

———. *Treaties and Conventions since July 4, 1776.* Digest. 41st Cong., 3d sess. Washington, 1872.

U.S. Department of Commerce. *Chinese and Japanese in the United States, 1910.* Special Report. Bulletin 127. Washington, 1914.

U.S. Department of State. Dispatches and Miscellaneous Letters from the Hong Kong Consulate, 1873–86. Vol. 1. National Archives.

———. Dispatches from the United States Consuls in Hong Kong, 1844–1906. Reels 10–14. National Archives.

U.S. Department of the Treasury. Letters Sent from the Bureau of Customs in San Francisco, 1856–79. Box 6. National Archives.

———. San Francisco, Letters Sent by the Port Surveyor, 1864–86. Box 4. National Archives.

U.S. District Court, Northern California District. *In the Matter of the Application of Wong Wing, on Behalf of Chan Si and Ng Si, for Writ of* Habeas Corpus, no. 2499, June-July 1882.

———. *In the Matter of Wah Ah Chin and Others for Their Discharge on Writ of* Habeas Corpus, no. 2495, March 1882.

U.S. *Statutes at Large.* December 1873–March 1875. Washington, 1875.

———. December 1881–March 1883. Washington, 1883.

Newspapers

Daily Alta California, 1870–82; *Evening Bulletin* [San Francisco], 1870–86; *Evening Post* [San Francisco], 1870–86; *Morning Call* [San Francisco], 1870–82; *Sacramento Daily Union,* 1869; *San Francisco Chronicle,* 1870–82

Books and Journal Articles

Anderson, Margo J. *The American Census: A Social History.* New Haven, 1988.

"The *Anjer Head* Troubles." *San Francisco Chronicle,* June 24, 1882, p. 2, col. 3.

"Another Chinese Cargo." *San Francisco Chronicle,* June 17, 1882, p. 2, col. 3.

"Anti-Chinese Convention." *San Francisco Chronicle,* Aug. 19, 1870, p. 3, col. 4.

"Arrival of the 'Great Republic.'" *Daily Alta California* [San Francisco], June 15, 1870, p. 1, col. 1.

"An Assaulted Chinese." *San Francisco Chronicle*, June 27, 1882, p. 2, col. 3.

Baker, Hugh D. R. *Chinese Kinship and Family.* New York, 1979.

"The Balky Briton." *San Francisco Chronicle*, July 3, 1882, p. 1, col. 3.

Bancroft, H. H. *History of California.* 4 vols. San Francisco, 1884–90.

Barth, Gunther. *Bitter Strength: A History of the Chinese in the United States, 1850–1870.* Cambridge, Mass., 1964.

———. *City People: The Rise of Modern City Culture in Nineteenth-Century America.* New York, 1980.

Bonacich, Edna. "Asian Labor in the Development of California and Hawaii," in *Labor Immigration under Capitalism: Asian Workers in the United States before World War II*, ed. Lucie Cheng and Edna Bonacich, pp. 130–85. Berkeley, 1984.

Bonacich, Edna, and Lucie Cheng. "Introduction: A Theoretical Orientation to International Labor Migration," in *Labor Immigration under Capitalism: Asian Workers in the United States before World War II*, ed. Lucie Cheng and Edna Bonacich, pp. 1–56. Berkeley, 1984.

"Britain and Coolie." *San Francisco Chronicle*, June 29, 1882, p. 1, col. 2.

"The British Sea Tramp." *San Francisco Chronicle*, June 28, 1882, p. 2, col. 2.

"Captain Roper Vindicated." *San Francisco Chronicle*, July 27, 1882, p. 2, col. 4.

"A Cargo of Infamy." *San Francisco Chronicle*, Aug. 28, 1874, p. 3, col. 5.

"Census Report." *Daily Alta California* [San Francisco], Oct. 26, 1870.

"Census Returns of San Francisco for 1870." *Evening Bulletin* [San Francisco], Oct. 25, 1870, p. 2, cols. 1–3.

"The Census of San Francisco." *Daily Alta California* [San Francisco], Oct. 26, 1870, p. 2, cols. 1, 2.

Chan, Sucheng. *Asian Americans: An Interpretive History.* Boston, 1991.

———. *This Bittersweet Soil: The Chinese in California Agriculture, 1860–1910.* Berkeley, 1986.

———. "The Exclusion of Chinese Women, 1870–1943," in *Entry Denied: Exclusion and the Chinese Community in America, 1882–1943*, ed. Sucheng Chan, pp. 94–146. Philadelphia, 1991.

Cheng, Lucie. "Free, Indentured, Enslaved: Chinese Prostitutes in Nineteenth-Century America," in *Labor Immigration under Capitalism: Asian Workers in the United States before World War II*, ed. Lucie Cheng and Edna Bonacich, pp. 402–34. Berkeley, 1984.

Cheng, Lucie, and Edna Bonacich, eds. *Labor Immigration under Capitalism: Asian Workers in the United States before World War II.* Berkeley, 1984.

"The Chinese in California, by Rev. Otis Gibson." *San Francisco Post*, Feb. 10, 1877.

"The Chinese in California: Their Numbers and Influence." *Sacramento Daily Union*, Nov. 27, 1869, p. 8, col. 1.

"Chinese Chattels." *San Francisco Chronicle*, March 18, 1882, p. 2, col. 4.

"Chinese Chattels." *San Francisco Chronicle*, March 27, 1882, p. 1, col. 1.

"Chinese Chattels: Some Light." *San Francisco Chronicle*, June 24, 1882, p. 2, col. 5.

"The Chinese Damsels." *San Francisco Chronicle*, May 18, 1882, p. 2, col. 3.

"Chinese Female Chattels." *San Francisco Chronicle*, May 13, 1882, p. 2, col. 4.

"The Chinese Houris." *San Francisco Chronicle,* March 19, 1882, p. 1, col. 9.

"The Chinese Problem: Lecture by H. C. Bennett at the Mechanics' Institute." *Evening Bulletin* [San Francisco], May 23, 1870, p. 3, col. 3.

"The Chinese Protection Society: Meritorious Conduct Rewarded." *Daily Alta California* [San Francisco], June 25, 1870, p. 1, col. 1.

"Chinese 'Wives.'" *Daily Alta California* [San Francisco], May 19, 1882, p. 1, col. 5.

"The Chinese Wives." *San Francisco Chronicle,* May 19, 1882, p. 2, col. 3.

"The Chinese Women." *Morning Call* [San Francisco], May 20, 1882.

"The Chinese Women Released." *San Francisco Chronicle,* March 24, 1882, p. 2, col. 3.

Ching-Hwang, Yen. *Class Structure and Social Mobility in the Chinese Community in Singapore and Malaya, 1800–1911.* Adelaide, 1983.

———. *Coolies and Mandarins: China's Protection of Overseas Chinese during the Late Ch'ing Period, 1851–1911.* Kent Ridge, Singapore, 1985.

Choi, C. Y. *Chinese Migration and Settlement in Australia.* Sydney, 1975.

Chung, Sue Fawn. "Their Changing World: Chinese Women on the Comstock, 1860–1910," in *Comstock Women: The Making of a Mining Community,* ed. Ronald M. James and C. Elizabeth Raymond, pp. 203–28. Reno, 1998.

Coolidge, Mary Roberts. *Chinese Immigration.* New York, 1909.

"Cornelius Cole: The Senator Interviewed by a 'Chronicle' Reporter." *San Francisco Chronicle,* Oct. 23, 1870, p. 1, col. 2.

"Death of Judge Dwinelle." *Evening Post* [San Francisco], Jan. 12, 1886, p. 1, col. 3.

"Death of Samuel H. Dwinelle." *Evening Bulletin* [San Francisco], Jan. 12, 1886, p. 2, col. 4.

"The English Captains." *San Francisco Chronicle,* July 1, 1882, p. 2, col. 3.

Espiritu, Yen Le. *Asian American Women and Men.* Thousand Oaks, Calif., 1997.

"The Female Cargo of the *Glamis Castle.*" *Morning Call* [San Francisco], May 13, 1882, p. 1, col. 7.

"Fourth Ward Democratic Club—Exciting Meeting—Formation of an Anti-Chinese Society—etc." *San Francisco Chronicle,* July 20, 1870, p. 3, col. 2.

Freedman, Maurice. *Lineage Organization in Southeastern China.* 1958. Reprint. London, 1965.

"Free Speech." *San Francisco Chronicle,* May 22, 1870, p. 2, col. 2.

Fritz, Christian G. "Judge Ogden Hoffman and the Northern District Court of California." *Western Legal History: The Journal of the Ninth Judicial Circuit Historical Society* 1 (Winter-Spring 1988): 99–110.

Fung, Robert, et al., eds. *The Repeal and Its Legacy: Proceedings of the Conference on the Fiftieth Anniversary of the Repeal of the Exclusion Acts.* San Francisco, 1994.

Gibson, Otis. *The Chinese in America.* Cincinnati, 1877.

"The *Glamis Castle* Women Freed." *Morning Call* [San Francisco], May 26, 1882, p. 1, col. 7.

Glick, Clarence E. *Sojourners and Settlers: Chinese Migrants in Hawaii.* Honolulu, 1980.

Hershatter, Gail. *Dangerous Pleasures: Prostitution and Modernity in Twentieth-Century Shanghai.* Berkeley, 1997.

Hirata, Lucie Cheng. "Free, Indentured, Enslaved: Chinese Prostitutes in Nineteenth Century America." *Signs* 5 (1979): 2–30.

Hoogenboom, Ari. *The Presidency of Rutherford B. Hayes.* Lawrence, Kan., 1988.

Hsu, Francis L. K. *Under the Ancestors' Shadow: Kinship, Personality and Social Mobility in China.* Stanford, 1971.

Irick, Robert L. *Ch'ing Policy toward the Coolie Trade, 1847–1878.* Republic of China, 1982.

James, Ronald M., and C. Elizabeth Raymond, eds. *Comstock Women: The Making of a Mining Community.* Reno, 1998.

Jaschok, Maria. *Concubines and Bondservants: The Social History of a Chinese Custom.* London, 1988.

Kitano, Harry H., and Roger Daniels. *Asian Americans: Emerging Minorities.* Englewood Cliffs, 1995.

Lai, H. Mark, and Philip P. Choy. *Outlines: History of the Chinese in America.* San Francisco, 1971.

Lang, Olga. *Chinese Family and Society.* 1946. Reprint. New Haven, 1968.

"Lecture by H. C. Bennett." *Evening Bulletin* [San Francisco], May 23, 1870.

"The Lecture Room: White Labor and the Chinese Question." *San Francisco Chronicle,* May 22, 1870, p. 2, col. 2.

Leong, Karen J. "Gender, Race, and the 1875 Page Law," in *The Repeal and Its Legacy: Proceedings of the Conference on the Fiftieth Anniversary of the Repeal of the Exclusion Acts,* ed. Robert Fung et al., pp. 58–65. San Francisco, 1994.

Li, Tien-Lu. *Congressional Policy of Chinese Immigration.* 1916. Reprint. New York, 1978.

Lim, Genny, ed. *The Chinese American Experience: Papers from the Second National Conference on Chinese American Studies (1980).* San Francisco, 1984.

Lind, Andrew. *Hawaii's People.* Honolulu, 1955.

"The Little Feet Women." *San Francisco Chronicle,* June 21, 1882, p. 2, col. 3.

"Local Items." *Evening Bulletin* [San Francisco], June 25, 1870, p. 1, col. 5.

Lydon, Edward C. *The Anti-Chinese Movement in the Hawaiian Kingdom, 1852–1886.* San Francisco, 1975.

Lydon, Sandy. *Chinese Gold: The Chinese in the Monterey Bay Region.* Capitola, Calif., 1985.

Lyman, Stanford M. *Chinese Americans.* New York, 1974.

McClain, Charles J. *In Search of Equality: The Chinese Struggle against Discrimination in Nineteenth-Century America.* Berkeley, 1994.

Mei, June. "Socioeconomic Developments among the Chinese in San Francisco, 1848–1906," in *Labor Immigration under Capitalism: Asian Workers in the United States before World War II,* ed. Lucie Cheng and Edna Bonacich, pp. 370–401. Berkeley, 1984.

———. "Socioeconomic Origins of Emigration: Guangdong to California, 1850–1882." *Modern China* 5 (Oct. 1979): 463–501.

Miller, Stuart C. *The Unwelcome Immigrant: The American Image of the Chinese, 1785–1882.* Berkeley, 1969.

"New Suits." *San Francisco Chronicle,* July 7, 1870, p. 3, col. 3.

Nordyke, Eleanor C. *The People of Hawai'i,* 2d. ed. Honolulu, 1989.

Norton, Henry K. *The Story of California.* Chicago, 1913.

Pascoe, Peggy. *Relations of Rescue: The Search for Female Moral Authority in the American West, 1874–1939.* New York, 1990.

Peffer, George Anthony. "Forbidden Families: Emigration Experiences of Chinese Women under the Page Law, 1875–1882." *Journal of American Ethnic History* 6 (Fall 1986): 28–46.

————. "From under the Sojourner's Shadow: A Historiographical Study of Chinese Female Immigration to America, 1852–1882." *Journal of American Ethnic History* 11 (Spring 1992): 41–67.

"Population—San Francisco, 1870–1871." *San Francisco Directory*. San Francisco, 1871.

Przybyszewski, Linda C. "Judge Lorenzo Sawyer and the Chinese: Civil Rights Decisions in the Ninth Circuit." *Western Legal History: The Journal of the Ninth Judicial Circuit Historical Society* 1 (Winter-Spring 1988): 23–56.

Purcell, Victor. *The Chinese in Southeast Asia*. London, 1965.

"Release of the Chinese Women." *Daily Alta California* [San Francisco], May 26, 1882, p. 2, col. 3.

"Removal of Chinese Courtesans." *San Francisco Chronicle*, May 14, 1882, p. 7, col. 1.

"Roper's Female Wards." *San Francisco Chronicle*, July 21, 1882, p. 2, col. 4.

Salyer, Lucy. *Laws Harsh as Tigers: Chinese Immigrants and the Shaping of Modern Immigration Law*. Chapel Hill, 1995.

Sandmeyer, Elmer C. *The Anti-Chinese Movement in California*. 1939. Reprint. Chicago, 1973.

"San Francisco as Viewed through the Census." *Evening Bulletin* [San Francisco], Oct. 25, 1870, p. 2, cols. 1–3.

Saxton, Alexander. *The Indispensable Enemy: Labor and the Anti-Chinese Movement in California*. Berkeley, 1971.

"A Sea of Troubles." *San Francisco Chronicle*, June 28, 1882, p. 1, col. 2.

"A Serious Charge." *San Francisco Chronicle*, June 20, 1882, p. 3, col. 6.

Sinn, Elizabeth. "Chinese Patriarchy and the Protection of Women in Nineteenth-Century Hong Kong," in *Women and Chinese Patriarchy: Submission, Servitude, and Escape*, ed. Maria Jaschok and Suzanne Miers, pp. 141–70. London, 1994.

————. *Power and Charity: The Early History of the Tung Wah Hospital Committee*. London, 1989.

Smith, Arthur. *Village Life in China: A Study in Sociology*. New York, 1899.

"The Social Evil in San Francisco." *Daily Alta California* [San Francisco], July 27, 1870, p. 2, col. 2.

"Some Facts Relating to Chinese." *Sacramento Daily Union*, Nov. 27, 1869, p. 4, col. 3.

Takaki, Ronald. *Strangers from a Different Shore: A History of Asian Americans*. New York, 1990.

Tang, Vincente. "Chinese Women and the Two-Edged Sword of Habeas Corpus," in *The Chinese Experience in America: Papers from the Second National Conference on Chinese American Studies*, ed. Genny Lim et al., pp. 48–56. San Francisco, 1984.

Tong, Benson. *Unsubmissive Women: Chinese Prostitutes in Nineteenth-Century San Francisco*. Norman, Okla., 1994.

Tsai, Shih-shan H. [Henry]. *China and the Overseas Chinese in the United States, 1868–1911*. Fayetteville, Ark., 1983.

————. *The Chinese Experience in America*. Bloomington, Ind., 1986.

———. "Chinese Immigration through Communist Eyes: An Introduction to the Historiography." *Pacific Historical Review* 18 (Aug. 1974): 395–408.

Untitled paragraph. *San Francisco Chronicle,* May 26, 1882, p. 2, col. 1.

"Wailing Women." *San Francisco Chronicle,* March 21, 1882, p. 1, col. 2.

"The Water Front." *San Francisco Chronicle,* June 22, 1882, p. 4, col. 2.

"Watery Waifs." *San Francisco Chronicle,* July 28, 1882, p. 1, col. 2.

"Who Offered the Bribe." *San Francisco Chronicle,* June 21, 1882, p. 4, col. 3.

Wickberg, Edgar, et al. *The Chinese in Philippine Life, 1850–1898.* New Haven, 1965.

———, ed. *From China to Canada: A History of the Chinese Communities in Canada.* Toronto, 1982.

Willcox, Walter F., ed. *International Migrations.* Vol. 1: *Demographic Monographs,* vol. 7. 1925. Reprint. Chicago, 1969.

Wright, Carroll, and William C. Hunt. *History and Growth of the United States Census.* Washington, D.C., 1900.

Yen, Ching-Hwang. *Class Structure and Social Mobility in the Chinese Community in Singapore and Malaya, 1800–1911.* Adelaide, Australia, 1983.

———. *Coolies and Mandarins: China's Protection of Overseas Chinese during the Late Ch'ing Period (1851–1911).* Kent Ridge, Singapore, 1985.

Yung, Judy. *Unbound Feet: A Social History of Chinese Women in San Francisco.* Berkeley, 1995.

Index

George Anthony Peffer is assistant professor of history at Lakeland College, Sheboygan, Wisconsin. In addition to the early development of Chinese American communities, his research focuses on the role of ethnicity and cultural dynamics in shaping American society. He holds a D.A. in history from Carnegie Mellon University.

The Asian American Experience